SECRETS
OF THE SPITFIRE

SECRETS
OF THE SPITFIRE

The Story of Beverley Shenstone the Man Who Perfected the Elliptical Wing

Lance Cole

Pen & Sword
AVIATION

Also by the Author

Dedication

To the memory of my grandfather, Thomas Robert Godden (RAF), flyer, member of West London Aero Club, Citroen DS owner, and pipe smoker. Not a day passes that he is not missed. See you up there old chap, get the kettle on… Also, to my children, Emily and Jack, in the hope that they are taught the lessons of history and that they have a passion for the truth – that, like all truth, awaits the great adventure of exploration, discovery and investigation.

And in memoriam to unsung heroes, notably the great genius, Air Chief Marshal Sir Wilfrid Freeman, the man who did so much to ensure victory in the air 1939–1945.

First published in Great Britain in 2012
and reprinted in this format in 2018 and 2021
Pen & Sword AVIATION
An imprint of Pen & Sword Books Ltd
Yorkshire – Philadelphia

Copyright © Lance Cole, 2012, 2018, 2021
ISBN: 978 1 52674 384 8

Printed and bound in the UK on FSC accredited paper by 4edge Ltd, Essex, SS5 4AD

Pen & Sword Books Limited incorporates the imprints of Atlas, Archaeology,
Aviation, Discovery, Family History, Fiction, History, Maritime, Military, Military
Classics, Politics, Select, Transport, True Crime, Air World, Frontline Publishing, Leo
Cooper, Remember When, Seaforth Publishing, The Praetorian Press, Wharncliffe
Local History, Wharncliffe Transport, Wharncliffe True Crime and White Owl.

For a complete list of Pen & Sword titles please contact
PEN & SWORD BOOKS LIMITED
47 Church Street, Barnsley, South Yorkshire, S70 2AS, England
E-mail: enquiries@pen-and-sword.co.ok • Website: www.pen-and-sword.co.uk
Or
PEN AND SWORD BOOKS
1950 Lawrence Rd, Havertown, PA 19083, USA
E-mail: Uspen-and-sword@casematepublishers.com
Website: www.penandswordbooks.com

Contents

Acknowledgements

This book has been many years in the making. Without the following people it would not have happened and I am indebted to them for access to private papers, diaries and photographs. Principal thanks go to all the Shenstone family, notably Blair Shenstone and his brothers Brian Shenstone, Derek Shenstone, and Saxon Shenstone, and to Beverley's grandson Taro Harvey Shenstone Tint, who travelled across continents with his Uncle Blair to secure lost documents unseen for decades, and to his mother Masae Shibusawa Tint and to her late husband, David Shenstone Tint. Also to Doris Shenstone who kindly supplied further photographs.

Thanks also go to: the late Peter Coles at Pen and Sword for having the vision to commission this book; Brian Riddle, Chief Librarian at the National Aerospace Library and RAeS stalwart – for his patience and help; Dr Alfred Price for support and information; Sir Kenneth Warren FRAeS for doing me the honour of writing the Foreword; Peter Hearne FRAeS and his wife Georgina for their kind help and insight; Dr John Ackroyd PhD CEng FRAeS for his aerodynamics advice; Ting Baker, the book's editor, for her skill and patience; staff at the: Royal Aeronautical Society, Solent Sky Museum, The Spitfire Society, The British Gliding Association and Peter Stratten; The Vintage Glider Club – its President the late Chris Wills, Justin Wills, and Martin Simons and Bruce Stephenson; the late Rear-Admiral Nicholas Goodhart CB FRAeS for inspiration and wise counsel; the charity Fly2Help; former colleagues at the Engineering and Physical Sciences Research Council; and Dr Klaus Heyn at the Deutsches Segelflugmuseum for his kind assistance.

A donation from the sales of this book will be made to the Royal Air Force Benevolent Fund (RAFBF). I thank my former colleagues at the RAFBF, Martin Henshaw and Stuart Turnbull, for their past support.

Foreword

Beverley Shenstone would have got on well with Lance Cole. Of this I am sure because in this remarkable book Cole reveals not just an intriguing tale of a splendid Canadian polymath, but Cole's skill as a forensic researcher has unearthed previously unknown gifts made to the advancement of aeronautics by Shenstone as he developed into one of the greatest aeronautical engineers of the twentieth century. Both author and subject emerge from these pages as two men in harmony, yet a generation apart; one dedicated to advancing knowledge and the other to securing the recording of that achievement. Cole also renders service to all aviation historians by proving that without Shenstone's creativity the Spitfire would not have achieved its dominance in the Second World War.

In this book Lance Cole displays and deploys his diligent research in a most readable form, revealing the aggregation of personal contributions made by Shenstone to enhance the progress of aviation in peace and in war. My generation of British aeronautical engineers applauded Beverley Shenstone both as the first airline chief engineer to be awarded a seat on the Board of a British nationalized airline and for how he spoke up resolutely for British aviation to governments who regarded nationalized airlines as theirs to rule and so dictated the frontiers of British civil aircraft manufacture.

Claiming, boldly, that some personal reminiscences are the right of an author of a Foreword it is in an exciting, previously untold story of the Spitfire Lance Cole recounts that my own memory dwells. For three quarters of a century our eyes have feasted on Spitfires soaring across the sky, glorious blends of beauty and power. My first sight was a small, silver gleam reflecting the sun, far off on a runway, suddenly speeding up into the sky, its wings spread out in that classical, captivating ellipse.

Three years later I saw Spitfires soar skywards into battle over London, weaving white trails across the sky, so high no sound of battle came down. Adolf Galland, the German fighter ace, asked by Herman Goering what he needed to win the Battle of Britain replied caustically 'A squadron of Spitfires!' And on the only occasion in war when Spitfires faced Spitfires, the Egyptian and Israeli pilots just circled each other, refusing to fire on

Spitfires. Lance Cole will cause many readers, as he has me, to dwell on their own memories of a stunning aircraft to which Shenstone contributed new ideas based on his work with Lippisch in Germany, which melded so well with the design genius of Reginald Mitchell and developing from the successful Schneider Trophy partnerships with Rolls-Royce.

But I must not use my privilege here to tell more of the career Shenstone wove in combination with other great names who forged success in war and in peace: George Edwards, Wilfrid Freeman, Sidney Camm, and even with Winston Churchill. And that last name I must leave to tempt eager readers.

Lance Cole has produced a book of which he has a right to be proud because it is not just about one man, Beverley Shenstone, it is a major contribution to the records of the development of aviation.

I am honoured to have been asked to offer this Foreword and commend Lance Cole's work to you.

Sir Kenneth Warren, FRAeS

Introduction

This is not a war story, but in one vital context, it is. Without the Spitfire the Second World War might have had a different outcome, but the Spitfire's war story has been told and this is *not* another book about the aircraft's war. Instead it is, uniquely, a book about the how and the why of the Spitfire's design, and the work of a man who played a major part in its shaping, yet whose name is hardly known. Utterly professional, modest, and known as the 'quiet Canadian', Beverley Shenstone had no interest in self-glory. Few know of his role in perfecting the Spitfire's ellipse, or his further works: his story, wrapped around that of the Spitfire's, is the essence of this tale.

This book is the first biographical account of the man, and through that, the first book to reveal the deepest secrets of the Spitfire's science in such detail. As such, it is a fresh perspective of established stories – those that are based in fact, opinion, and in myth. This may be a controversial re-telling, but it is also grounded in the fact of real events.

There have been many books about the Spitfire, but this one is different and in a text unlike that of any other Spitfire story, the details of the Spitfire's design and its designers are here charted in a depth that offers the enthusiast, the academic, and the historical record a different perspective and a new conversation. The names of forgotten Spitfire contributors are cited, and for the true aeronautical enthusiast, the core elements of the aircraft's design, are discussed in exhaustively researched technical detail – a touch of forensic pathology, is deliberate.

Iconic, is an over-used word when it comes to the Spitfire, yet its shape, notably its knife-edged, ellipsoidal wing, gave the aircraft its edge and, gave it the status of a national icon. Somehow, rightly or wrongly, the Spitfire has become a cultural motif. Yet the story of how the Spitfire got that shape, and what it was about that shape that gave the Spitfire its advantage, has been a lesser strand of the legend that has grown over the last seventy-five years, a legend it has to be said, that has not always been portrayed accurately.

In 1940, Beverley Shenstone wrote the following words in an article, and they seem remarkably accurate today:

> Fighters are all the rage now. Everybody has become an expert on the relative merits of Hurricanes, Spitfires, Curtisses, Brewsters, Messerschmitts and Heinkels, and glib untruths are told about them all. Of course, it is difficult to be truthful when one doesn't know all the truth, but there are certain fundamental things which if realised would enable fairly reasonable comparisons to be made.[1]

Those words, especially about the realization of certain fundamental things, were an inspiration for the framing of this book's story. For it seems that there is, remarkably, still a lot unrealized about the Spitfire's design and its designers. There have also been inaccuracies told.

People also associate the Spitfire, and that old Spitfire versus Hurricane debate, with the Battle of Britain, but important though that event was, it was not the whole story. The functions and efficiencies of the Spitfire and Hurricane as designs, are far better quantified across the totality of the Second World War. One of this pair, the redoubtable Hurricane lacked the ability to be developed beyond a certain point, whereas the other (the sculptural Spitfire), was developed and retained its scientific superiority, even against the rush of advanced designs that the war delivered. The Hurricane has been unfairly treated across the years, shaded by the shapely glamour girl that is the Spitfire, yet now, as the Hurricane is defended by commentators, it has become fashionable to 'knock' the Spitfire and its designers. Let's be clear, the Hurricane was a fine aircraft that played a vital role. It was strong, reliable and it is often stated that it was a better gun platform. Its old-fashioned construction was easier to repair and more resistant to damage; after all, it did not have a stressed skin.

But has the Spitfire versus Hurricane pendulum swung too far?

If the Spitfire had to have its main wing structure (not just its wing skin, but even its spars) redesigned after 500 aircraft had been produced, in order to improve its design and to add much-needed speed, the current critics would be shouting from the rooftops that it had been weak or a failure and that its designers had made errors. Yet this significant re-design was what happened to the Hurricane when it switched from canvas to alloy wing skins – after several years of debate and prevarication. But the silence about such an issue is obvious, and we are constantly told how much easier to build the Hurricane was than the Spitfire. Similarly, if the Spitfire had had to have its tail fin redesigned after prototype flight testing, due to the discovery that it could not easily recover from a spin using the standard technique, its designers and its aerodynamicist would, based on the record of some commentators, have been vilified. Yet, this is exactly what happened to the Hurricane, but we hear little about it. Instead we are told about the Hurricane's stability and ease of taxying.

Both the Spitfire and Hurricane had vulnerable fuel tanks in front of the cockpit, but the Hurricane fuel tank had to be modified to reduce the risk of fire in the cockpit after a series of horrific incidents. The Hurricane also had a non-monocoque construction that meant that any fire in a wing tank could be vented straight through its alloy 'basket weaved' type structure and into the floor area of the cockpit. There were few closed off internal shields to stop any fire, so it was vulnerable in this respect as well. The Hurricane was a masterpiece of its era, a true war horse that made a massive contribution and was built in great numbers, but perhaps it was not the icon of industrial design perfection some wish to portray. The Hurricane had issues – issues that needed modification at the cost of time, money and more. The Spitfire was not perfect either, but last-minute, pre-combat, major structural and aerodynamic re-design is not on its records. And as this book will detail, the Spitfire contained advanced science in its aerodynamics, science absent from the Hurricane, which was designed at the same time.

The Spitfire's enemy, the Messerschmitt Bf109, was a superb aircraft, of that there is no doubt. Yet stemming from the mind of a glider designer, it strangely relies on engine power and brute force to power its small, slotted wings and its curiously uneven skin surface. Despite its efficient small wings, it was fast and furious rather than sleek and lithe. The Spitfire and the Bf109 may have been closely matched, but there were merits and de-merits to each and, crucially, there was one area that gave the Spitfire its advantage: the science of smooth, clean, lift.

Sadly, for the British, despite being on the same side, there have developed two camps (each defending 'their' aircraft – be it Spitfire or Hurricane), each attacking the other. In writing a book about the Spitfire, it is important to try and retain objectivity, but the irrefutable facts are that the Spitfire was a piece of advanced thinking – a new design language that was neither derivative nor unproven. Neither was it a response to fashion. As such it was, and remains, utterly timeless, remaining undated by seventy-five years of advances in design. The reader is asked to reflect upon these often unmentioned design characteristics, for they are the essence of what Mitchell and his men crafted. To frame the context, consider the design of the Concorde, the VC10, the Caravelle, the Austin

Mini, the Citroen DS, the Jaguar E Type, the Queen Elizabeth II Cunard liner, the Saab Draken aircraft, and Saab 92 and 99 cars, or reflect upon the form of an Omega watch, a Burt Rutan aircraft design, or a Lippisch delta wing, or a Horten all-wing aircraft. These are all timeless, beyond fashion, beyond the perceived wisdoms of their eras, as was the Spitfire.

The ellipse too, remained in use by a variety of aircraft – the famous P-47 Thunderbolt fighter ranged across several Second World War theatres upon its own elliptical wings, and even Lockheed's L-133 jet prototype of 1941 was fully elliptical. Heinkel's 176/8 and 280 jets of the later war years also used a forward distorted ellipse effect – more in homage to the Spitfire's uniquely modified ellipse than the 1932 Heinkel 70 perhaps...

That the Spitfire was invented by Reginald J. Mitchell CBE, FRAeS, AMICE, is fact. But, contrary to conditioned and perceived public wisdom, he did not design it alone. Mitchell always credited his team, but the created myth, and the cinematography that characterized the legend, suggested that R.J. Mitchell gazed up at a seagull, drew the Spitfire and then died of overwork turning it into reality to save the nation. Save the nation the Spitfire may well have done, but, say those who knew him, R.J. Mitchell was far from like actor Leslie Howard's upper crust, sky-gazing boffin. It is unlikely, say those who were there, that Mitchell stared at seagulls from a dramatic cliff top. And sadly he died from cancer. He did, however, work very hard indeed. But Mitchell came from normal origins in the Midlands in England, at the time the industrial heart of the nation and the British Empire.

Film legend also has it that Mitchell went off to see the Germans in the late 1930s, but that was dramatic licence. He did not. But Supermarine men, Mutt Summers and Beverley Shenstone, did go to Germany in 1938, and Shenstone had previously worked in Germany and spoke good, technical German. The screenplay of the film in question *The First of the Few*, also ignored the fact that both Mitchell and Shenstone had working relationships with German aircraft designers and that some of those designers, including Lippisch, visited them. Claudius Dornier even flew to Mitchell's Supermarine works at Woolston, Southampton, and moored his flying boat on the River Itchen outside the factory. There may have been a 'Mr Mitchell I presume' moment when Dornier walked up the slipway to meet the world's greatest, Schneider Trophy winning, float plane designer. Perhaps the thought of the British being friendly or even working with the Germans, was too much for the myth makers of British society circa 1940–1960.

But beyond the hyperbole and propaganda, the Spitfire, really *was* different; it was highly advanced.

Mitchell and his men, including Shenstone, were internationalists; they grasped new ideas and concepts. They were innovators at a time when the normal British psyche was one of Empire conceit, arrogance and, above all, of tradition. Mitchell and his Schneider Trophy men looked forwards, whereas mainstream British aviation looked to the past. Therein lay the reasons the Spitfire was such a shock to an industry that evolved old designs into revised versions of old thinking. For example, in 1935, The Royal Aircraft Establishment told Mitchell the Spitfire's tail fin was too small and that they wanted to increase the rudder size by 40 per cent. They decided this based on 'past experience'.[2] Neither Mitchell nor Shenstone cared about that kind of past experience, *they* were prepared to embrace a new future, and new thinking.

During and after the war, the suggestion that the Germans had anything to do with the British and their Spitfire would have been an issue, and even today it raises the ire of some. Yet, paradoxically, some British (and other) people are quite happy to accuse Mitchell and his team of 'copying' the Spitfire's wing from the German Heinkel 70, which is a falsehood that has become a myth – not least an internet myth promulgated by those unqualified to comment. Chapter 11 deals with the Heinkel 70 issue in detail.

The suggestion that part of the Spitfire, a key part, came from someone other than Mitchell the Englishman, could have been less than ideal PR for a nation and a race whose Empire encircled the world. Yet even the Schneider Trophy race teams, where Mitchell made his name, were, like today's Formula One motor racing teams, a global and pan-European polyglot society where thoughts, designs, and ideas were shared – design inspiration was international. One of Mitchell's gifts was to conceive an idea and then guide his team into crafting it. The Spitfire was a team effort, a fact that often gets glossed over by those who have not focused properly, through the mirage of time.

When Beverley Shenstone joined Supermarine in the summer of 1931, he was a junior man, but he spent seven years working for Supermarine, six under R.J. Mitchell, and by late 1934 he was the Spitfire's chief aerodynamicist. He had been promoted as he worked on the early, then unofficial, Type 300 'Spitfire' designs in mid-1934 as result of the earlier Supermarine Type 224's, failure. The majority of the Spitfire team were young men aged from twenty-five to thirty-five, and with their elders framed a collection of talents that surely were the right people, in the right place at the right time.

Some observers claim that Shenstone was just a fresh young student junior – they have cast him as theoretician with no real, workshop experience, a man who had never built anything. In fact, he had, in engineers' parlance 'got his hands dirty' during his time at Junkers in 1929–1931. There, he wore greasy overalls, worked on the factory floor and did his fair share of riveting, fabricating and metal working. He had also spent two summer vacations working on the factory floor of the Massey-Harris (later to become Massey Ferguson) engineering works and had been building boat hulls since he was a boy. He was a qualified power pilot and glider pilot, the first Canadian to gain a C licence at the Wasserkuppe. So, contrary to some published opinions, he was not just an academic theoretician.

Shenstone's is not the only forgotten name of Mitchell's Spitfire team. There were others who contributed to the shaping and building of the Spitfire – notably Alfred Faddy who was the engineering section team leader and a forgotten star of the Spitfire's structural design and development. Faddy was an experienced engineer. Shenstone's notes also name others whose names are rarely seen in works on the Spitfire such as Mr Fenner, Mr Fear, Mr Shirvall, Mr Davis, and others whose names are credited herein – for the first time in book form. The mathematical contribution of Professor Raymond Howland of what was then, the University College Southampton, is also cited for the first time. The names of Alan Clifton and Joseph Smith do, of course, frame the design and production of the Spitfire.

Political propaganda, wartime PR hype and even some books, allied to a growing legend about the Spitfire, have all created a picture that has painted the aircraft as the product of one man's mind and created an emotional mirage that has only grown with time. Without decrying the genius of R.J. Mitchell, this is in the view of many, both wrong and unfair. Mitchell may have thought of the Spitfire, but his team made it reality – as *he* always stated.

Some authors, notably Mitchell's son, Dr Gordon Mitchell, credit Shenstone in words, and in print, with playing a significant role in the Spitfire's wing. And in his engaging and charming Spitfire book, *Spitfire: A Biography*, Jonathan Glancey goes some way to crediting Shenstone, as do certain others. In the 1980s, Dr Alfred Price certainly credited Shenstone in his own defining work on the Spitfire – to which Beverley Shenstone contributed prior to his death in 1979. Dr Price, that most respected of Spitfire historians also wrote: 'Few people can be better qualified about the design of the Spitfire as Beverley Shenstone.'[3]

The esteemed Spitfire work of authors Morgan and Shacklady, cites Shenstone and frames several contexts in correct manner, but the depth of Shenstone's aerodynamic research work is not its remit. Some authors partially credit Shenstone's work. For example, Leo McKinstry in *Spitfire: Portrait of Legend*, names Shenstone yet the wing remains Mitchell's – as it does for Stephen Bungay in his detailed, *The Most Dangerous Enemy*. Various writers dismiss Shenstone as a junior staff member, others ignore him completely. Incredibly, there are Spitfire books that never mention the name of the man who shaped the Spitfire's wing and aerodynamics. In Ivan Rendall's *Spitfire: Icon of a Nation*, Shenstone is invisible – as are others. In the pages of that icon of Englishness, *The Daily Telegraph*, the letters page in 2005 was the place where claims that the Spitfire was a copy of the Heinkel 70 were also published. More recently, the internet is the scene of pages of factual inaccuracies (or should we say, just plain, alleged rubbish) about the Spitfire, its design and its designers.

The major differences in design between the Heinkel 70's simple ellipse, and the Spitfire's modified ellipse, remain unexplained by many commentators. The old 'copied the Heinkel 70' myth is trotted out across the worldwide web and in some printed works – using inaccurate facts. Some commentators state that Rolls-Royce bought a Heinkel 70, shipped it to Britain, and that Mitchell and his men copied it for the Spitfire. The problem with that being that the Spitfire's ellipse was first drawn up in 1934, and was heading towards its final design stage by early 1935 – nearly a year *before* the Rolls-Royce powered Heinkel 70 was constructed in Germany and sent to Britain on 26 March 1936, three weeks *after* the Spitfire's first flight.

As the Heinkel 70 was *not* unveiled in November 1934 (as so many have claimed it was to support their unsupportable theories), the related claims using that so-called fact, about its effect on the claimed decisions of November and December 1934 about the Spitfire's shape, must, by obvious default, be in error. But even if the inaccurate statements of a November 1934 unveiling of the He 70 are dismissed, there remains the claim that the Heinkel was, in its ellipse, a new shape, which as this book explains, it was not. Elliptical wings go much further back than the Heinkel 70 or its direct elliptical ancestors – the Bäumer Sausewind of 1925 and the Heinkel 64 of 1931. The long history of the ellipse is also, uniquely, presented in this book (see Chapter 6), as a defining reference point for the reader to make an assessment of its existence and its influence. The advantages of the ellipse were not, as some have suggested, unproven.

The important point, for the historical record and for the reputation of the men concerned, is that corrections to such claims are made – solely for the purposes of referenced, factual and historical accuracy. If Shenstone or Mitchell were alive, faced with some of the errors, I cannot help but think they would be consulting their lawyers. Who knows, in the great emotional cloud that now surrounds the Spitfire, amid error claimed upon error in a structure of myth, perhaps this author will be vilified by others. As for the ellipse, and numerous claims that it was unnecessary, a design overkill, and that a tapered wing with twist would have done just as good a job, read on to find out why that theory is blown apart by the facts of science as they *were known at the time*…

R.J. Mitchell was the father of the Spitfire, but one thing is obvious, the Spitfire was not the product of one man's mind. The idea or concept may have been Mitchell's, but, as he always said, it was his team that framed and shaped his sketch into scientific, aerodynamic and structural reality. And Shenstone was indeed young, but as this book shows, he was unique. His subsequent achievements surely prove the point. On acceptance by Mitchell, it was men such as Shenstone, Clifton , Davis , Faddy, Fenner, Mansbridge, Smith, Shirvall, and the Supermarine team that made the wing and the whole package, work.

This book does not challenge R.J. Mitchell in any away; to this author and to this book's subject Beverley Shenstone, R.J. Mitchell was a genius. In his unpublished private notes, Shenstone wrote of Mitchell and the Spitfire thus:

> It needed the genius of Mitchell to visualise – without precise knowledge – what had to be done to reach out into the unknown for something nearer to perfection than any other man had been able to reach. And we, who were involved, were inspired and suitably grateful for the unique opportunity to reach out without over-reaching.[4]

It seems that Vickers Supermarine actually recruited Shenstone and specifically asked him to bring to the design process the rare and perhaps unique knowledge he had learned in Germany. Indeed, it is possible that Mitchell knew of Shenstone long before he turned up at Supermarine. Was Shenstone head hunted by Vickers Supermarine director, Air Commodore Sir John Adrian Chamier, and invited to tell Mitchell his thoughts? Read on to draw your own conclusions.

Shenstone, and how he perfected the ellipse, is the core of this story, but it is not all his story. There is much more to the man and his work and that record is also told herein. Shenstone achieved high office – as President of the Royal Aeronautical Society, technical director at the British Overseas Airways Corporation (latterly British Airways), chief engineer and Board member at British European Airways and a consultant to several aircraft makers. He also designed two gliders, contributed to a third with the inventor Rear Admiral Nicholas Goodhart CB FRAeS, and was a well known aviation figure. He made major contributions to the Organisation Scientifique et Technique Internationale du Vol à Voile (OSTIV) and other bodies, notably in Canada, including the National Research Councils and the gliding authorities.

During the war Shenstone worked in the USA at the top secret Wright-Patterson air force base (or Wright Field), and was involved with the Air Ministry and its procurement works – notably for the P-51 Mustang, working under the brilliance of Air Chief Marshal Sir Wilfrid Freeman amid the Beaverbrook PR machine. Shenstone was a member of the 2nd Brabazon Committee and a proponent of all-wing aircraft. Shenstone had intimate knowledge of advanced German design and was linked to its transfer to the Allies under Operation Paperclip.

Surely, such a record confirms that Shenstone's early role in the Spitfire was neither fluke nor as invisible as some would suggest. His list of published papers makes its own statement. There are many twists to Shenstone's story, and one question focuses upon his actual status. Did he have some form of covert or intelligence-gathering role? Shenstone was also intimately acquainted with the advanced German technology that lay behind the Allies rush to space and supersonics after 1945.

Whatever the facts, and without creating a theory too far, here was a man whose quiet nature belied a towering intellect, one that changed its preference from wartime military design to air transport – a new world where he foresaw many of the developments that have come to pass in international aviation. Shenstone went on to be one of the most influential figures in airliner design and engineering. At one stage, Vickers tried to recruit him as a senior designer. Here, also published for the first time, are his thoughts on the Viscount and the Trident debacle. He worked closely with leading manufacturers, airlines and others. His work on sailplane design and man-powered flight are also significant.

Shenstone, even as a young man entering Supermarine in the 1930s, was not just a green, young theoretician fresh out of university. He was a star pupil – as Toronto University's first, Master in aeronautical engineering design. He worked in advanced wind tunnel focus under the tutelage of Professor John Hamilton Parkin CBE, FRAeS, FIAeS, at Toronto University. For Shenstone, perhaps Professor Parkin's most important scientific move was when, in 1922, the original University of Toronto wind tunnel was dismantled and relocated from the Hydraulic Laboratory to the Thermodynamic Building. Parkin took immediate advantage of this move to make significant improvements in the tunnel's design and airflow behaviour. This gave Parkin and his students a major advantage over other wind tunnels, even those in Europe. Shenstone was also taken under the protective wing of Air Marshal Ernest W. Stedman RCAF – an important act of assistance from the RCAF – part of the RAF in 1929. With Parkin and Stedman's help, in 1929 Shenstone set sail for Germany's crucible of advanced aerodynamic design.

By 1931, Shenstone was the only person outside Germany who had trained in alloy monoplane design and construction at Junkers and studied the all-wing or flying wing concept and who had worked with the birth of delta wings and the lift distribution theories that went with them (with Alexander Lippisch and his D1 design team). In fact, there is no known German who had studied as Shenstone did. Shenstone was also a qualified RCAF pilot and a German-trained glider pilot. Contrary to those who dismiss Shenstone as a cocky young theoretician, he was unique. And I am convinced that was why, on Adrian Chamier's lead, R.J. Mitchell interviewed him for a job. To support that view, Mitchell's comments about what Shenstone had learned in Germany, are published herein, for the first time.

How far ahead were the Germans? The answer is a very long way, which is why the USA, the UK, and the Russians grabbed as many of them at the end of the war as they could – and got to supersonics and into space as a result.

This book may rock the boat of perceived wisdom that stemmed from an age when a very British world view, one of some conceit, was formed. But to me, perceived wisdom is a contradiction in terms, as it relies upon the perceptions of its time and place, contaminated as they are by the assumptions of that specific era – a mental provincialism. Facts are different, and if properly supported, cannot be denied. In the age of the internet, when myth morphs into 'fact', defamation or slander, and opinions are deemed as factually accurate record, where there is little right of reply, the Spitfire story and the Spitfire men have suffered. I hope this book helps reveal a fuller story and silences some of the wilder theories.

Based on Shenstone's notes, diaries and unpublished autobiography and further researched and substantiated across interviews and a diverse range of sources, this book tells the story of a man who really ought to be better known in Britain, and a national hero in Canada.

As a writer and as person of English, Scottish, Canadian, Australian lineage from a family with a history wrapped in the Empire of the English, from Africa to Asia, it is a privilege to be the author that tells, for the first time, the authorized story of this great Anglo-Canadian. I am indebted to his sons for their kind help and friendship. This book was, in the main, written at the joining of the Hampshire, Wiltshire, Berkshire borders under the shadow of Walbury Hill, and the idea for this story began life in paradise, on Sydney harbour beside the old flying boat base at Rose Bay; flying boats seemingly being very relevant to this tale.

Writing about the Spitfire's origins and its hidden design secrets has been the realization of a long affair with flight. While still in the womb, I went flying in an old Auster piloted by my grandfather. In later years, he sat me on his knee and told me tales of his time in war-torn Africa. He had stories of the pilot and author Ernest Gann and his book *Fate is the Hunter*, and of flight. In Grandpa's flying logbook there was an entry that made the spine tingle – he was flying the Auster along the ridge of White Horse Hill at Uffington in low cloud and rain, when a Spitfire zoomed from the cloud base and shot past him. The memory of the excitement was palpable.

As a boy of the late 1970s, classic airliners and classic fighters became my thing, I flew on VC10s, Caravelles and Viscounts before the gliding bug became an obsession. Douglas Bader was local and the neighbour of a relative, so I listened to Bader's tales of Hurricanes and Spitfires. He had a reputation with some, but all I saw and received was kindness and encouragement. Bader clearly loved 'the Spit' as he referred to her. One of Beverley Shenstone's friends, Rear Admiral Nicholas Goodhart, the inventor, glider, and man-powered flight designer, was also present in my teenage life, so I have been privileged and lucky with tutors and mentors – including the presence and teaching of Concorde and Vickers test pilot, Brian Trubshaw.

I have also been lucky enough to crew an old 'PBY' Catalina Flying boat across Africa, and to actually fly it from the left-hand seat. I was also privileged to ride in the cockpit of the MATS Lockheed Constellation as it flew into UK airspace for a Connie's first UK appearance in over forty years. Rides in fast jets have also come and gone, and controlling a VC10 was also the realization of a dream. There have been wonderful days gliding across the Australian outback being tutored by the likes of David Goldsmith, Humphrey Leach, Roger Vaile, and the late, great, record-breaking glider pilot Hilmer Geissler – who had the smoothest flying technique I ever saw. But the day I sat in a Spitfire, now that was even better than discovering women. In fact, there is something faintly sculpturally exotic about the Spitfire. For the aircraft is a 'she' and filmstar thin but curvy with it – an Audrey Hepburn of a 'plane perhaps? I often wondered how the Spitfire got that perfect shape…

I always look up when a Spitfire or a VC10 fly over my house – as they both still regularly do, seventy-five and forty-five years respectively, after their early flights. Then, I wonder if Bev Shenstone is watching from his island in the sky where I trust he is quaffing vintage champagne and eating smoked salmon and caviar, off first class china and being served by a lovely BOAC girl, as the blue and gold liveried, Vickers, Rolls-Royce, Super VC10 thrusts ever higher. If he is not, then he will be on a BEA or Air Canada flight, or soaring above the Wasserkuppe, in the far blue beyond.

Without doubt, this is a story of design, circumstance and of events that frame history and that raise questions about fate and the coincidence or certainty of chance. As Britain's greatest aeronautical engineer, Sir George Edwards often reminded us, the truth always comes out – only usually too late to help…

I call it the afterwards and the before, which is what this story is about.

Lance Cole
Kintbury Berkshire

Prologue

Winter 1943

A Moment Amid the Tumult

The charcoaled seas of the Atlantic lay far below the aircraft, but high up in the sky, buffeted by icy winds, the thin wings of the B-24 Liberator flapped and twisted as the four-engined aircraft rode the tide of the sky.

As the props slashed around and threw chunks of ice onto the thin metal skin, there lay deep within the belly of this machine, a handful of men who shivered and awaited release from their suspended animation above the conflict raging below. Uncomfortable as they were, the hours entombed aloft were far preferable to the risks of a slow death upon the sea below, a sea prowled by expert killers in U-boats awaiting the arrival of the herds of ships making the risky crossing between Britain and North America.

In the Liberator, lying across the cabin floor on mattresses, eleven men, swathed in thick flying suits, each wearing two pairs of clothes, fought off the searing cold of the jet stream. Oxygen masks became brittle in the freezer-like conditions. Among these men was a man of importance, a man whose work had already affected history and helped to alter the course of the free world. His name was Beverley Shenstone and he was not yet forty years old.

In the early war years, Shenstone had been working with the British Air Commission in Washington DC. He was part of a high level campaign to secure British military influence in America from early 1941 – work that was famously backed by Lord Beaverbrook (W.M. Aitken). Shenstone had already encountered Aitken in the late 1930s during the procurement of the Spitfire, an aircraft that Shenstone had, at a relatively young age, been closely associated with. In 1943 Shenstone had been recalled to London by the British Government's Ministry of Aviation to become Assistant Director, Research and Development for Air Transport within the newly named Ministry of Aircraft Production – the MAP. Before the war, in 1938, Shenstone had worked at the Directorate of Civil Research and Production at the Department of Civil Aviation, at the Air Ministry under Roderick Hill. In the early war years Shenstone transferred to the Ministry of Aircraft Production and then worked for Air Chief Marshal Sir Wilfrid Rhodes Freeman – the unknown genius behind the aircraft procurement that saved the British nation and the free world. Shenstone had joined the British Air Commission and worked on design and testing at Wright Field, Dayton, Ohio. As a VIP, he had been commuting across the wartime Atlantic on a regular basis, and Shenstone is seen in company with Wilfrid Freeman in the official photograph depicting the August 1941 meeting between Winston Churchill and President Roosevelt, on the deck of HMS *Prince of Wales* at Placentia Bay, Newfoundland.

In 1943, once again, Shenstone had needed to get back to Britain and quickly. Atlantic travel by air had become a military reality by 1943, but it was neither comfortable nor without risk, but if you were important, the means were laid on.

Shenstone had boarded the battered Liberator that would take him back to wartime London, at Dorval, Montreal, and ascended from the tarmac of his native Canada on an icy, late winter morning. After four hours in flight, they landed at Gander, Newfoundland, for a refuelling before setting off on the dangerous sea crossing to Prestwick in Scotland. Ahead lay more than ten hours suspended in temporary detachment from a world at war.

Recalling the journey decades later, Shenstone wrote:

Eleven of us trooped across the frozen tarmac to the black Liberator, looking rather silly. It was cold, terribly cold; we couldn't talk because of the noise, there was no soundproofing, so we sat and read magazines. I found a projecting hinge from a window on which to hang my overcoat. I was anxious about that coat. It had half a dozen eggs in one pocket.

So we lay there and the cold began to penetrate very slowly, but quite surely. My feet were cold and my back was cold where I touched some metallic part of the aeroplane. After a while someone discovered some lunch boxes piled in the back. There were shelled hard boiled eggs, the shell being replaced by a thin layer of ice which cracked as one ate. There were sandwiches – frozen stiff. There were apples and chocolate, apparently unaffected by the cold. There were also thermos bottles of coffee.

We climbed to 15,000 feet and put on our oxygen masks. We did not fall asleep as it is dangerous with a mask. It might slip off. Also if you lie back, the condensation from your breath in the mask dribbles down your chin instead of down your clothes as it ought to. I had to take my mask off every hour and wipe the moisture out of it. We breathed the stuff for eight hours, lying there like black-faced pigs. I shall never forget reading and re-reading the markings on the fuselage skin: '24 ST 0-025' which faced me hour after hour. I looked at the structure. I looked at the swinging tail and I looked at my fellow passengers, trying to remember their faces beneath the masks.

Then dawn came and we went down to 12,000 feet and it grew warmer. So we doffed our masks and got up and stretched and peered through the portholes. We were flying steadily over a bank of clouds into the rising sun, and could see no water below, just sky and clouds. We seemed stationary, stuck there all alone and away from the world.[1]

Hanging in the sky, so far untouched by the enemy's aircraft, Shenstone had time to think, time to ponder upon the future of aviation, of what type of aircraft the world's airlines would need after the war was over and military needs lessened.

As the Liberator churned relentlessly onwards, Shenstone discovered that the tail gunner's position had been faired over, with a seat and large windows added, but no guns. It was the lavatory. There, at the point of the tail, he sat down on the cabin's only seat and gazed out at the sea and the landscape of the Scottish coast. Away to his left he saw the isles of Scotland, scattered before him across a bruised, metallic, sea. How different they looked in winter, to their benign summer vision of white sandy beaches facing a turquoise sea and low green hills marked with ancient standing stones glinting in the last airs of the Gulf Stream, stones that told of a once great knowledge, forgotten now, beyond the centuries.

Down there, far below the Liberator, were the Na h Eileanan an Ian – (the Western Isles) and the largest, Eillean Leodhais – Isle of Lewis and its capital Stornoway – birthplace of his mother's ancestors, a place as far removed from the land he had taken off from a few hours before as it was from his status in London. Would his maternal forefathers, the Paterson family of the Outer Hebrides, ever have dreamed that a child of the isles would soar so high above them and have played such a part in the fate of history…

Stornoway slipped by and landfall on the Scottish mainland beckoned. There was much to do. The war had changed everything, especially in aviation. The pace of development had been frenetic.

Shenstone had not just ridden the wind of change; he had seen the zephyr that carried change to the world. He had seen the future before mainstream, conventional opinion had even dismissed it. For he had seen giant triangular shaped delta wings, he had seen strange flying craft that had no fuselage and no tails – they were just sharply swept flying wings. He had sketched knife-edged wings and designed an ellipse that would become immortal. He had dreamed of gliders and vast human-powered aircraft that would prove that man could power his own flight. Inside his head, under that domed skull, his engineer's brain had raced ahead. Time was what he needed; at least on this flight back to London, there had been time to close off and be alone for a few brief hours of respite. Recalling the journey, Beverley Shenstone wrote:

> So we landed at Prestwick and were welcomed with a pleasant 'Good morning, have a good trip?' as if it had been nothing at all. And then I realised that it is nothing fly the Atlantic. Just a glimpse of tomorrow.[2]

From Prestwick, Shenstone was flown down to London, there to resume his work. He knew not what was to come. But before that fate was played out, there was the matter of how a tall, thin, German speaking, young Canadian of Scottish lineage, a man who loved sailing and whose genealogy hailed from the remote, storm-lashed Hebrides, became part of a very British story.

1

Before Take-off – Early Days in Canada

From School to Sailing, and a Meccano set

Beverley Strahan Shenstone, 1906–1979, MASc, HonFRAes, FAIAA, AFIAS, FCASI, HonOSTIV, was fortunate enough to be born into a well-heeled and well-connected Canadian family. He was of ancient stock – stemming from a lineage of Scottish and British ancestry, like many of Canada's early families.

The family name did not originally end in 'e', but somewhere along the line it morphed into Shenstone. Linkage to the English poet William Shenstone has been both suggested and denied. Ancestors ranged from Scotland, Northamptonshire, Oxfordshire, Warwickshire, and London, but it was emigration to Canada by Benjamin Shenston (without the 'e') on Friday 9 March 1832 aboard the *Florida*, 550 tonnes, at St Katherine's dock, London, under the command of Samuel Sherborne, that created the Canadian arm of the family that begat Thomas Shenston, Joseph Shenstone and then Beverley's father, Saxon Shenstone (with the 'e') and then Beverley Shenstone in June 1906. Before that, Thomas Shenston, a luminary of the Baptist Church in Canada, had set up home on a farm near Guelph, later renamed St Catherine's Ontario. Soon he moved to Woodstock, Ontario, and later became the Registrar for the new County of Brant.

Like many who go on to lead in their fields, Beverley Shenstone lost one of his parents as a child. On Christmas Day 1915, his father, Saxon, was out searching for his tame ducks, which had escaped from their pen at the family's home in Wychwood Park, Toronto. Saxon Frederick Shenstone complained of feeling dizzy and dropped dead on the spot. He was thirty-six years old and left a young wife, Katherine (Kitty), who was left with three young sons to bring up – Beverley aged nine, and his brothers Douglas, seven, and Wynn, four.

Katherine had not just lost her husband, she had also lost her mother and brothers in the recent past. She was deeply affected by her loss. Beverley's grandfather, Joseph Newton Shenstone, then sixty years old, stepped into the breach and according to Beverley's recollections: 'Provided for the family from that day onwards.'[1] Grandfather Joseph, and his family, notably Thomas, were leading members of the Baptist church in Canada and the boys were brought up surrounded by such influences. In contrast to the Shenstone family's religiosity, Wychwood Park was well heeled and perhaps a touch liberal in that it was created and built as home to a colony of writers, artists and sculptors, many of them leading figures in Canadian art and design. The Shenstones may have been the first non-artistic family to move into the new garden suburb.

Joseph Newton, or 'JN' as Beverley called him, had as young man worked for the Donnelley printing family and their Lakeside Press in Chicago. Joseph's sister Naomi married into the Donnelley family. Joseph moved back to Canada in 1876 and by 1881 had entered into partnership with the agricultural firm of A. Harris & Son of Brantford. By 1891, the Harris firm had merged with the Massey family firm to produce Massey-Harris, a company better known today worldwide in its new Massey Ferguson incarnation. Part of the Shenstone family had married into the Massey family. In the 1890s Joseph Shenstone had become a board member of the firm and became the president of the firm from 1925 to 1930, which was how tractors and agricultural engineering were also a large part of Beverley Shenstone's story – along with boats.

This background gave the young Shenstone boys, and Beverley as the eldest, access to an engineering background, good connections in Canada's hierarchy of leading families and the financial resources he would later need. His father had left very little money, but his grandfather, Joseph, was fortunate enough to be financially secure. In Toronto, the foundations of the young Beverley's thinking and personality were being laid. Another significant influence was the family's love of sailing. They owned a cottage up on the Nova Scotia coast at Smith's cove near Digby and were regular summer visitors. There, Beverley, or 'Bev' to his friends and family, learned to sail and was surrounded by the wooden and metal structures of boats. Beverley was clearly affected by place, and was certain it laid the foundations of his habits. He later wrote:

> It was the world of the sea and tides that made the most lasting impression on me. More than half a century later, the smell of seaweed at low tide says 'Nova Scotia' to me.[2]

He later spoke of his regret at not seeing the dying era of the West Indies timber trade ships during these childhood days. The last of these wooden schooners used to load at Bear River inlet, but he did not know this. But Beverley was taught to sail by his uncles, Allen and Osborne, in their small skipjack yacht, and also sailed one of the dories in the local racing fleet. Recalling his childhood in later life, Beverley wrote that boats had lurked in his background throughout his life:

> Not ships, just boats, and small ones at that. I cannot remember when I was not thinking of boats.[3]

The little skipjack boat he loved had a 20ft mast and was 20ft long with a wooden centre board and was fast in the cold waters of the Annapolis Basin. When Beverley was fifteen, the family took another summer cottage – in Muskoka just below Bala, Ontario, on a small island in the Mushkosh River. Perhaps it was there that the love of canoes and small yachts really took hold of Beverley. From that time on he was always tinkering with boats, designing and making hulls, and studying the effects of his designs on handling qualities. He spent the following winter carving a 44-inch hull from solid wood and sailed it in the spring.

Having encountered Henry Secord, the Toronto architect and model boat builder, Beverley spent the summer of 1922 building four different hulls to race. In the winter of 1923, Beverley built a model four foot skipjack using ⅛-inch pine planking, over frames. He designed his own adjustable keel. Soon afterwards, Beverley joined the Toronto model yacht club, which included Emanuel Hahn, the German émigré sculptor from Stuttgart, amongst its members. From him, Beverley tried to master the art of thinking in three dimensions. These early mentors, with their tutorials in chord, tumblehome, aspect ratio, critical separation point, steerage and flow characteristics, allied to the form and shape of sculpture, must have gone deep into Beverley's thinking; they were an excellent precursor to designing boats, float planes, and aircraft.

From 1924 onwards, Beverley concentrated on canoe trips along various waterways – on rivers such as the Moon, the Muskosh, and lakes such as the Peninsula, the Sturgeon, the Kawaratha, and the Fairy. The river and lake steamers the *Ojibway* and *Iroquois*, were still in regular use.

These long canoe trips were often supervised by an ex-Royal Flying Corps pilot named Frank Wood who was studying at the University of Toronto, and Beverley soon got himself onto Wood's staff. Wood, it seems, became a mentor to the young Shenstone. By 1926, Beverley was leading long, canoe and overland porterage trips around the lakes area under Wood's tutelage.

In 1927, Beverley decided to ask his grandfather if he would fund a vacation period canoe trip in England following the canals and rivers of the home counties and west country, which he had read about in the *National Geographic* magazine. Grandfather Joseph Shenstone agreed, and funded a companion ticket as well. So it was that Beverley, with his friend Ken Hunter, sailed to England, and arrived well before their canoe – a sixteen-foot canvas covered native Indian type that was bought in Quebec and shipped to Messum's at Richmond, Surrey. The pair spent the summer navigating the waterways of southern England, camping, eating and drinking in pubs and journeying up the Oxford Canal, onwards to the Warwick and Napton Canal and down to the Avon. Where the Warwick Canal crossed the Stratford Canal by aqueduct, they simply slid the canoe down the embankment into the Avon. They joined the Severn and went down to Sharpness, oblivious to the dangers of the Severn. It seems the locals did not believe that the boys had navigated the Severn in a Canadian Indian canoe – not until the boys proved it with their records.

Via Bristol harbour and sections of the partially closed Kennet and Avon Canal, the pair got to Reading and London.

After Ken had left, Beverley remained in England and worked for few weeks in a basement of the Science Museum in Kensington with an aeronautical student group placed within an Air Ministry laboratory. Maybe it was here that Shenstone's talents were first noted by those who were later to employ him in wartime. Was this his first brush with the men from the Ministry? This placement was arranged by contacts of his tutor Professor John Parkin of Toronto University. A student, associate membership of the Royal Aeronautical Society (RAeS) was also secured by the young Shenstone at this time. He also made another canoe trip – solo to Cricklade and the upper reaches of the Thames. The canoe was sold to Salter's of Oxford.

So it was small wooden boats, not aeroplanes, that were written large in the young Shenstone's psyche, and his knowledge of hydrodynamics and boat hull design, was growing. Perhaps also evident was the confident and unconscious ability to just go off across the world, at a time (the 1920s) when few could, framing the personality of the young Shenstone. Having money helped, of course, but even so, here was someone who had vision allied to focus and tenacity. Sailing and boats were, of course, deep within his blood – the ancestors from the Outer Hebrides had seen to that. It was, as can be seen, a comfortable childhood, yet not a lifestyle of indulgence or excess. Family members came and went, some often moving in. Beverley's mother's family, the Patersons, hailed from the Isle of Lewis, and also from Kirculdy on the mainland and one of them, grandfather John Andrew Paterson, came to live with the family in 1908 after his wife was killed by a cyclist at the bottom of Avenue Hill in Toronto. Paterson, son of a Presbyterian Minister from Stornoway and born in 1846, had emigrated to Canada when he was twenty. Within six years he had graduated from the University of Toronto with a BA. He married a Christina Riddell and they produced four children, one of whom, Ernest, became one of the first Rhodes Scholars at Oxford.

Intelligence was also evident in Beverley's late father Saxon and also in his grandfather Joseph Newton Shenstone's other boys who all went to university. Beverley's uncle Osborne became a well known engineer and his uncle Allen Goodrich Shenstone FRS served in the Royal Engineers in France in the First World War, served in the Second World War, and went on to become one of the world's leading atomic physicists based in Princetown, USA. He built an international reputation in atomic spectra and was described in his obituary (written by W.R.S. Garton FRS), as 'one of the great spectroscopists of this century'. Allen won a Military Cross in the First World War and in the Second World War earned an OBE as a Scientific Intelligence Officer, and had regular contact with his nephew Beverley during the war. Allen was also a member of the National Research Council of Canada alongside Beverely's mentor, Professor Parkin. The phrase, 'keeping it in the family' seems apposite.

Norman Shenstone became one of Canada's leading surgeons, notably in the field of pulmonary research. He also invented the Shenstone pulmonary tourniquet in 1929 with Robert Janes. Clearly, a student of genealogy and intelligence quotients would be astounded by finding so many inventive scientists in one gene strain, and young Beverley Shenstone was soon to add to this unusual level of family achievement on an internationally important scale. Sport, sailing, fishing and rugby were major themes in the Shenstone family – alongside an obvious level of superior IQ handed down through the genes.

The influences on the fatherless Beverley were clear, and were further underlined by the role his uncle Osborne Shenstone played in his young life. Osborne was a graduate engineer who encouraged the young Beverley in all matters related to engineering, as Beverley wrote in his own unpublished diaries:

> It is surely due to him that I took to engineering, a very important and lasting influence.[4]

Like so many, Beverley Shenstone's childhood forays into designing, building and testing structures and vehicles, were fostered by Meccano. He recalled spending any money he had on buying more pieces of Meccano. He also built those carved or planked wooden hulls to test into-wind handling and rudder effectiveness.

In his own words, Beverley notes that his mother (no doubt through her sense of loss) became overprotective of her sons, and there were times when it seems the boys were cloistered into a narrow and soft environment by their mother. Aged nine, Bev's brother Douglas disgraced himself by helping himself to apple sauce without using a spoon! For this crime and for what Beverley recalled as being described as other 'revolting acts' Douglas was packed off to a school in Oakville, twenty-five miles from home. As the boys grew up, they broke out of the maternal environment. Douglas left home early, or as Beverley recorded:

> Douglas revolted early and pretty well permanently whereas Wynn did not. I did not actually revolt but when I left home for Europe at 23, I never regretted it.[5]

Douglas did not go to university but found his own course, at one stage studying the art of pewter smelting and design as an apprentice under Rudy Renzius. After a period odd-jobbing around Canada, which included being a Pinkerton detective, Douglas joined up in 1939 and saw action with the Royal Hamilton Light Infantry. He was on the Dieppe raid, where he was Mentioned in Despatches. He was injured at the battle of the Falaise Gap and repatriated. Douglas returned to Canada, joined a government department and in 1973 retired as Assistant Director for the public relations function at the Department of Energy, Mines and Resources. He also returned to working with pewter, to some critical acclaim.

Wynn grew up as the youngest boy and seems to have had a closer relationship with his mother – the pair toured Europe on a BSA motorbike and sidecar in 1934. Wynn attended the University of Toronto, but did not graduate, preferring, it seems, to travel. From as early as 1929, while still at university, he signed on for working passages at sea. Later he undertook numerous sea voyages as crew on a number of freighters. He also hitchhiked to Los Angeles for the Olympics in 1932. But motorbikes were his thing, and he owned several. By the mid-1930s, his wanderlust was served by his working for the Canadian National Railway (CNR) company where he remained until the outbreak of war. In 1940 he joined the Canadian Army cavalry, yet he never saw a horse. Instead he set up an army motorbike training course using twelve 'Indian' motorcycles. As he got to Europe, the war ended as he arrived in the Netherlands with the army. In 1946, he was demobbed and rejoined the railways at Canadian National Railways. Wynn's son Roger enjoyed a career on Canadian radio.

Beverley went to school at Brown School on Avenue Road near St Claire, Toronto, which meant a daily ride on the new Toronto street car railway. From there he attended the University of Toronto's preparatory school. Beverley then went on to study at the University of Toronto and, after graduating in Engineering during 1928, his life course had begun to take shape. At Toronto University, Beverley had also met J.T. 'Jack' Dyment, with whom he subsequently enjoyed a lifelong friendship. Dyment joined Trans Canada Airlines (latterly Air Canada) as chief engineer on its formation and stayed there until 1969. Dyment also Chaired the IATA Technical committee for a year, a remarkable achievement that provided an interesting parallel with Beverley's own high-flying career, notably at British European Airways (BEA).

Shenstone later wrote of Jack Dyment:

> His clear thinking and sound views forcibly expressed soon won him recognition far beyond the confines of TCA and Canada. This was far from appreciated by his employers who tended to think of international activities as a waste of time. They were staunch 'little Canadians' whereas Dyment was and is a 'Big Canadian'.[6]

Other university friendships made at this time included those with Campbell Macbee, Price Brown, Ronald Bertram and Darcy Dingle. Other friendships were with Morley John Campbell Lazier who Shenstone describes as 'by far the brightest man in my year in mechanical engineering', and with Donald Carlisle and W.R. McIntosh.

As was clear by 1928, Beverley also had wanderlust in his veins, but by a series of circumstances his travels became something out of the ordinary.

2

Canadian Wings – From Water to Air

In 1928, 1929 and 1930, a series of defining events took place in Beverley Shenstone's life. First, his passion for boats led him, upon graduation, to further his studies in the field of flying boats and aerodynamics and hydrodynamics. He also then joined the Royal Canadian Air Force via his university place and learned to fly. And there was also the small matter of him marrying a young Scots-Canadian girl, named Helen Home, in 1929.

Helen was interested in sailing, flying, and liked sculpture. She came from Scottish roots and the Home family was linked by marriage to the Peuchen family of Coburg, Ontario. The Peuchen family were keen sailors and had a boathouse at Ashbridges Bay.

Sailing was indeed a dominant passion for young Bev. For him, it all started with those boats – not aeroplanes. Thus it was the fascination with boats and hull design that led Shenstone to thinking about flying boats, at which point, not long before Beverley's graduation in 1928, Toronto University's Professor John H. Parkin offered him a post-graduate scholarship, which could lead to a Master's degree. Parkin had been asked to research flying boat stability and he needed an assistant. The University of Toronto possessed a four-foot wind tunnel and Shenstone leapt at the chance to work in one. He had also just seen his first working flying boat, a Curtiss HS2L at Temagami Forest Lake in northern Canada.

The Canadian-built Vickers Vedette single-engined pusher-type flying boat was the subject of the study. Firstly, Professor Parkin set Shenstone the task of digesting the established and latest works on flying boat design.

Professor Parkin had created Canada's first wind tunnel and Canada's early wind tunnel work at the University of Toronto. He later headed research at the National Research Council of Canada. The University wind tunnel was used in the Vickers Vedette studies that were undertaken for the Royal Canadian Air Force engineering branch, which was run by Wing

Commander E.W. Stedman (later Air Vice Marshal) – a man whom Shenstone was to encounter during his RCAF provisional cadet pilot officer days. Both Parkin and Stedman, beyond the recorded tutelage they gave Shenstone, may well be the unsung heroes of this story as there is strong factual and circumstantial evidence that both men played significant roles in furthering Shenstone's career and that they influenced the placements that led to his early major work.

By using deep forensic analysis, Shenstone – the top student chosen to work on the Vedette study by Parkin – created a complex thesis invoking calculus and actual flow analysis with early smoke and tuft tests. His launching point was the subject of the rotary deviation of flow. With his background in boat handling and boat hull design and building, Shenstone was uniquely placed to bring all the strands together to suggest improvements to the Vedette design in terms of its behaviour and handling. He did this in his thesis entitled 'Certain Aspects of the Stability of a Flying Boat'.

It was as if those early days carving different boat hull shapes and then comparing their handling characteristics had laid the foundations. The link between aerodynamics and hydrodynamics were obvious to Shenstone and this work (latterly enhanced through his work with Alexander Lippisch) bordered on predicting the art of virtual flow dynamics that we know today. It made for a stunning thesis about the aspects for flying boat design and stability – a thesis that may have been unique at that time. The flying boat books that Professor Parkin told Beverley to read, included Bryan's *Stability in Aviation*, Bairstow's *Applied Aerodynamics* and Glauert's *Aerofoil and Airscrew Theory*. Shenstone wrote of the books and the course:

> I dived into them, but never really liked Bairstow, but found Glauert's carefully phrased ideas and statements almost inspiring. Of course, such a wind tunnel in 1929 had no recording equipment, so readings took a long time and much had to be repeated because of basic imprecision which could only be dealt with by the statistical approach.
>
> One of the amusing sidelights was the use of a cream separator gearing to speed up the model propeller to near enough scale rpm. This was suggested by my Uncle Osborne Shenstone.
>
> During this year I also studied some additional mathematics and I attended a special lecture course on hydro- and aero-dynamics by a professor in the physics department. These lectures were unique for me as I was the only student and the professor stood at the normal distance and treated me as if I had been a hundred people. I began to wonder whether I was actually alone. Anyhow, he gave me a good introduction to such things

as conformal transformation and Joukowsky aerofoils. The concept of sources and sinks was quite outside our under-graduate engineering curricula.[1]

For his studies, Shenstone purchased a copy of *Differential Calculus* by H.B. Phillips. It was a book that he kept close at hand for the next twenty years.

In 1928 Shenstone had learned from a lecture by the then, Wing Commander E.W. Stedman RCAF, that the RCAF offered engineering students flying cadetships. He leapt at the chance and enrolled for three summers' worth of basic flying training at RCAF Camp Borden, near Barrie, Ontario. In June 1928, Beverley drove his old Model T Ford to his first RCAF flight school as a Provisional Pilot Officer – a PPO. The young students were taught by Flying Officers Ingram and Stafford. Upon learning that he needed a day off to attend his graduation ceremony, Shenstone was interviewed by Squadron Leader Shearer, second in command at Camp Borden, who offered him a permanent RCAF commission – providing Shenstone could fly solo within ten hours of training: Shenstone achieved this solo flight target in nine hours and four minutes of flying.

The aircraft used was the larger-engined Avro 504 model N variant. The instructor was Flight Lieutenant 'Mike' McEwen. Shortly after going solo, Shenstone had a lucky escape:

> At just after two hours solo, my engine cut out at a height of a few hundred feet on the climb after take-off. I obeyed the written and memorised words: nose down, land straight ahead. Trouble was, straight ahead was a field of tree stumps bordering the airfield. I had so little time to think and so little experience that I stuck to the book and didn't try a 180 degree turn and land down-wind, but landed among the stumps without striking a single one! I climbed out and soon somebody arrived with first aid stuff and shortly afterwards Mike himself. Never one to waste words: 'Don't think you're clever. You are just bloody lucky'.
>
> Why did the engine cut? A maintenance man had replaced the fuel cock so that the on position was actually off. There was just enough fuel in the system for, say 5 minutes operation.[2]

It took the ground crew two days to dismantle and extricate the aircraft.

The 1928 course ended in August and Shenstone returned to the University of Toronto for his postgraduate year under Professor J.H. Parkin and the Vedettte flying boat studies. In the summer of 1929 he returned for further flying under the tutelage of Flight lieutenant F.V. Beamish who was described by Shenstone as a 'perfect instructor'. Shenstone wrote of this time:

The Avro 504s had all gone, being replaced by the Gypsy Moths. About twenty of them. I had a pretty rough time with the Moth as it had arubber sprung undercarriage instead of the hydraulic type on the Avro which had a lot of damping. The result was that if you landed the Moth as you would an Avro 504N, the little devil would bounce 10ft or more into the air. I did 70 landings of which 36 were good, 23 fair, and 11 bad. By mid August, I had thirty five hours solo.[3]

Beverley tried to keep quiet about another incident at Camp Borden, but his notes tell us about his first crash. He wrote a letter to Professor Parkin on 22 June 1929:

Have learnt some interesting details about the famous Moth aeroplane, by being dumb enough to crack one up last Monday. The trouble is that when the stick is pulled back to land, the nose goes up instead of the tail going down. That is under the same conditions that would bring an Avro's tail down. Of course it is just a matter of holding off longer. This I did not do, and after a few extremely bouncy landings, solo, I made a super-bounce, dropping from about five feet. The undercarriage held, but the front cross wires in the centre section failed, or rather one of them did. It was enough. The rear centre section wires, which for some reason are only attached to the plywood fuselage cowling, ripped the said cowling out by the roots, and I had the pleasure of seeing the top of the fuselage suddenly rend in front of me and gape. Thereupon, the centre section being no longer triangulated, sagged to one side, and I landed from the bounce very cock-eyed and staggering, but fortunately on the wheels. Rapid visions of ground looping, but none happened. I switched off, and jumped out, being extremely disgusted. So was my instructor, who, it is told, took off his parachute and jumped upon it in rage. When I finally got near him, I was told a few plain truths, oh very plain indeed.

It took me two full days to learn to land after that. During those two days I was told many things, including the fact that of all the students that had come under the eye of my instructor in five years, I am the dumbest and slowest to learn. That is unique if nothing else.[4]

By this time, Shenstone had become Toronto University's first scholar with a Master's in the Applied Sciences of Aeronautical Engineering. Shenstone had also read Claudius Dornier's lecture in the December 1928 issue of the *Journal of the Royal Aeronautical Society*. It was a moment of significant importance, as Shenstone later wrote:

This lecture and the discussion hit me between the eyes. 'That's the place to go and learn about the flying boat future', I said to myself and also to Parkin who was always receptive to expressions of youthful exuberance. Parkin contacted Stedman, but in spite of his efforts, there were no openings in Dornier for me. But Stedman somehow discovered through his UK contacts that since the Junkers F-13 aeroplane had recently been accepted from the airworthiness standpoint by Britain, Junkers might well accept the presence of such as me in the main factory at Dessau.[5]

In this extract, Shenstone clearly credits Ernest Stedman (later Air Vice Marshal) with having the high level contacts in London to get Shenstone placed into the then cradle of advanced aerodynamics, Germany, via the British Air Attaché in Berlin. Clearly things like this did not just happen. Professor John Parkin was also instrumental in arranging and supporting the placement and it seems that the British Air Attaché in Berlin, Group Captain M.C. Christie, was known to Stedman. Once again, wheels within wheels, were at work…

As we shall see, subsequent events confirm that suggestion: Parkin and Stedman clearly are the unsung heroes of Shenstone's early advancement. Although he wanted to work for Dornier, Shenstone later revealed that finding a post at Junkers was key to his development. And once again, Parkin and Stedman played a role in Shenstone's life.

> The disappointment about Dornier was to some extent outweighed by the facts that Junkers was not only flat out for the monoplanes, but all-metal monoplanes. Although the monoplane was barely tolerated in UK or USA, many young people such as myself were convinced that they were the future. We weren't cleverer than our elders, but our brains were relatively uncluttered, and we could see through the clutter of struts, bracing wires and multiple wings and visualise, often not accurately, the clearly obvious and beautiful future monoplanes. The present-day equivalent of this is the SST airliner.[6]

Dr Hugo Junkers, one of the founders of German aviation, was also arguably then the world's leading resource on all-wing or flying wing aircraft – despite his famed corrugated aircraft designs, which were not state of the art in production terms.

Known in Germany as the 'nurflügel', this vee or arrow-head shaped concept was literally the wing only, and its design offered significant drag reduction by getting rid of the fuselage and tail. Junkers had, as early as the pre-1920 era, investigated and patented flying wing designs. As late as 1929, he was attempting to build the Junkers G-38, an all-wing bomber. Although Junkers was building corrugated skinned aircraft, he was all-out for the monoplane and its all-wing derivative. Young Shenstone, the monoplane enthusiast, was placed into this deep receptacle of aerodynamic and structural knowledge at an ideal moment in aviation history.

Hugo Junkers was neither a Nazi nor a warmonger. In fact, he refused to hand over his factories to the Nazis in 1933 and was soon arrested by the hated secret police known as the *Geheim Stadts Polizei* – the Gestapo. After hours of interrogation and threats he signed over 51 per cent of his company. Days later the Gestapo were back and forced him to hand over his company, its research assets and rights, whilst he was under house arrest: Junkers was banished from his Dessau factories and left a broken man; he was dead within two years. Shenstone's 1929 placement at Junkers would, however, curtail the final year of the RCAF flying training. Shenstone went to the RCAF headquarters in Ottawa and asked if he cold defer his flying training until he returned from the Junkers placement. The RCAF said that he could not, but that as he was a provisional pilot, he could walk away from the RCAF without formality. Shenstone recalled:

> I wished him good day and vanished from the RCAF. It was one of my real turning points.[7]

As we know, Shenstone was now Canada's first-ever man with a Master's degree in Aeronautical Engineering. As such, he had the backing of many important and useful people, not least Messrs Parkin and Stedman who clearly had the clout to play an instrumental role in getting Canada's brightest aeronautical student dropped into the heart of the German aviation industry, a move that would have consequences that would manifest upon the future of a war and its outcome.

On completion of his time in Germany, Shenstone discovered that, in fact, Stedman and the RCAF would have had him back to recommence his pilot training. But by then, a different die had been cast.

Before then, some kind of PR machine seems to have been in action, as firstly the Toronto media ran a story noting that Shenstone was Canada's first Master in Aeronautics and then a further story about how Canada's brightest aerodynamics student, was off to Germany: 'Toronto Boy Climbs in Aviation Circles'.[8] Shenstone's mother was behind these bits of promotion for her serious-looking, tall, very thin boy – whose physique would remain so for his entire life.

3

To Southampton via Dessau, and the Wasserkuppe

On 26 September 1929, the recently graduated Beverley Shenstone, Professor John Parkin's star pupil of the famous 'year of 1928', and Canada's first Master in aeronautics, and somewhat cocky in his aeronautical opinions (by his own admission), yet shy and not arrogant, took a train from Toronto to Montreal. It was the first stage on his European adventure – one that would ultimately lead him to the office of Reginald J. Mitchell, 'R.J.'.

Bev hoped to find a cheap passage to Hamburg, yet he had 385lb of luggage – hardly a student backpacker it seems. He hoped to work his passage on a freighter, but the freight trade was dead. However, a steamship was soon to depart for Europe and offered Beverley a passage at $4 Canadian a day for a twenty-day passage. In the meantime, the young adventurer lodged in the YMCA for $1.75 a day. Wealthy the Shenstone family may have been, but here was someone out to be independent. But fate and connections intervened. Visiting the Canada Steamship Lines office, Beverley met the boss, a Mr Doherty, who said: 'My God since I know your father in the Massey-Harris. It is your father isn't it?

Shenstone told him it was his grandfather, not his father whom Doherty knew.

'Well, since I know your grandfather in the Massey-Harris, I will give you a rate of three dollars a day instead of four.'[1]

The 6000-ton vessel the *Storburg* was a Norwegian ship that was actually built in Japan in 1918 as the *Meichu Maru* would be leaving in few hours, with Captain Hamre at the controls. There turned out to be only one other passenger, a Kurt Wittern of Hamburg whose idea of annual holiday fun was a return trip on the ship. After a run down the St Lawrence and then out into the open sea, passing great liners such as the *Megantic, Duchess of Atholl, Letitia* and Canadian Pacific's *Empress of Canada*, the *Storburg* made good passage and reached Le Havre after eleven days. On 17 October near the Blohm and Voss yard in Hamburg where the giant liner *Europa* was being completed, Beverley Shenstone alighted onto the soil of a land that would give him learning and yet, through such learning, equip him to be part of its ultimate defeat.

Taking the train to Berlin, Shenstone stayed at the Christliches Hospiz near the Friedrichstrasse Bahnhof. Then, clutching a letter of introduction from Professor Parkin to Professor Dibelius at Berlin University, he entered its great halls and German lessons were quickly arranged. Then, it was off to the Massey-Harris German office, where the family connections had laid on a helping hand in the form of a Mr Scott who helped Beverley find lodging, provided his car, and made arrangements for onward travel and accommodation in Dessau – home of the Hugo Junkers factory. There was also the news that grandfather Shenstone had laid on a line of credit for Beverley to draw upon if needed. Having a grandfather who was a senior figure in a firm with offices in Europe was a piece of great fortune.

Beverley Shenstone moved into a flat on the Lutherstrasse for one month whilst he found his bearings and learned some basic German. On 24 October Shenstone called, by previous instruction, upon Group Captain M.C. Christie, the British Air Attaché at the British Embassy in Berlin. Shenstone's notes reveal an interesting issue:

> I called on Group Captain Christie. He said the Junkers people were good eggs and advised me not to stay for too short a time. He said if the German government heard of me working there, they would have a fit. To think of a Britisher learning anything about their sacred aeroplanes! He suggested that I say I am an American rather than Canadian (the first time I did say I came from America the retort was: North or South?).[2]

In this extract, we see a British diplomat, with a military background and remit, telling a twenty-three-year-old Canadian who was about to be placed into the heart of German aviation research, by arrangement, to pretend to be American, and to stay as long as possible. This makes an intriguing moment and cannot help but force the reader to wonder at just what level, via Parkin and Stedman and their London RAF, Air Ministry and academic contacts, had the placing of the young Shenstone into the crucible of advanced German research, been created? And if Shenstone, was just a recently graduated student and nothing else, what was he doing there, and why did he have an appointment with the British Air Attaché for Germany? Group Captain M.C. Christie was about to depart to see the giant new Junkers G-38 all-wing type design fly for the first time. Clearly the opportunity to place someone into the German industry, or make the most of such a placement, may have been too good a chance to miss for the powers in London. But perhaps that is a theory too far? Forty-three years later, looking back on this time, Shenstone wrote:

> I am astounded still at the luck I had in all this in being helped by so many people who had no real reason to help. It wasn't as if I had made some invention or was doing something off-beat. I just wanted to work in a modern aircraft factory.[3]

Was this naïve interpretation true, or was it a cover for something else? For a man at such a young age with little experience, it would be rash to suggest that Shenstone was some form of industrial spy, and yet his subsequent rapid rise and appointment to various Air Ministry and government level roles must indicate a relationship with power and influence.

It would not be long before the intrigue of espionage would surround Shenstone.

One month after that meeting with the Air Attaché in Berlin, as 1929 eased towards 1930, Massey-Harris supplied a driver and car to take Beverley Shenstone to the Junkers factory in Dessau. For Beverley, the highlight it seems was the trip in this car – a Hansa four-cylinder tourer with blown exhaust, a loose connecting rod and an objection to starting. On arrival in Dessau, with accommodation at Agnes Strasse 26, for the sum of RM 40 per month, and a bicycle purchased for $15 dollars, Beverley Shenstone presented himself (as expected) at the Junkers front office. Junkers was the father of German aviation, a high priest of aerodynamics and structural ingenuity. His factory was enormous and there on 11 November, Shenstone met Junkers propaganda director Dr Bohm who gave him a factory tour, which according to Shenstone's notes revealed:

> I had a good look around. I expected to see the well known F-13, W-33 and others. They were there, but what was unexpected were three obviously military aircraft, which I thought they were not allowed to build. These were two seaters (J-48) with Jupiter engines and were all-metal like all Junkers aircraft. One was covered with perfectly smooth duralumin and another was corrugated. Undercarriages like Siskins, which means complex and draggy. They had twin-fin tails, thus giving the observer-gunner a field of fire directly aft.[4]

Meanwhile, outside lay a shock for Shenstone – his first sight of the giant, 107ft span, all-wing theory Junkers Ju 38, or G-38, a massive short-bodied, small-tailed, bat-winged behemoth of an aircraft with a wing so thick (6ft thick at the root), that it could carry freight inside it and allow access to the engines in flight. There were even seats visible through the transparent leading edge. The aircraft had just made its first flight and could carry forty passengers over a vast range. It was a symbol of just how far advanced German aeronautical design was.

'She just seemed to float in,' said Shenstone of his first exposure to a flying wing. The G-38 was, he added, 'like a bat with oversize wings.'[5]

Shenstone latterly wrote that although he and others felt at the time that the G-38's pioneering all-wing shape would become a design trend of the future and that the all-wing would dominate design, it did not. He wrote that he and others had been wrong – as the skies of the world became full of small, high lift equipped wings, supporting massive fuselages. Little did he know that after his death, and soon after the millennium, the all-wing or blended-wing theory, of which he was so fond, would become the future of aviation. Back inside the Junkers works, Bohm sat Shenstone down for a chat with Junkers men, Messrs Auer and Kohler; these two spoke as few words of English as Shenstone then did of German. Wagner, a Junkers designer with an interest in tailless design, was also present. After a struggle, working hours and terms of employment were arranged. The day started at 0700 and finished at 1630, but there were numerous breaks. In the afternoon, Shenstone was back talking to Bohm, when Kohler telephoned. Shenstone recalled:

> Kohler rang up Bohm and asked him whether I intended to exert myself and work or not. I was furious. Bohm said 'Certainly' without asking me. As I wrote at the time: 'Did this sonofabitch think I would travel more than three thousand miles just to sit on my arse? He annoyed me and still does'.[6]

Shenstone's first day at work with Junkers was on 12 November under *Herr* Schollinger. Those first few weeks covered panel beating, riveting duralumin, working in the sheet metal department and making the discovery that there were several foreign students working as volunteers at Junkers: Japanese, two Egyptians and some Finns. After some weeks, Shenstone was moved to working on the cowling for Jupiter engines on the military J-48 aircraft, this proved problematical as the engines were licence-built Gnome-Rhone copies and differed in sparking plug locations.

Shenstone wore workshop clothes – a stained, greasy jacket and trousers – or overalls, and got his hands dirty doing manual metal work in the great halls of Junkers. He had done the same thing within the workshops of his grandfather's agricultural engineering business, Massey-Harris.

As the spring of 1930 dawned, the dark mornings of early rising in Dessau and the silent bicycle ride to the factory alongside hundreds of other workers cycling across the cold, wet cobbles of the town, eased, and new opportunities opened up. Despite Hugo Junkers' pioneering work on all-wing and swept wing aerodynamics, Junkers had become known for the structural integrity of its aircraft, and for the famous corrugated skin techniques that imparted monocoque type strength and allowed the traditional airframe chassis to be lighter at the expense of drag. Shenstone studied the wing designs and the internal structures and his notes recall:

I had enough time to pay a lot of attention to the production of the Junkers Junior J-50 light aeroplane. This was an all corrugated tandem open cockpit 2-seater with an Armstrong Siddeley Genet engine of about 60hp.

On a simple jig the frames were set up and a few longitudinal stringers were added. The corrugated skin was applied in two halves and was pre-cut to exactly the right size with corrugations beaten flat along the edges. As in all Junkers types of this date, the originally flat skins were corrugated by a special press, one corrugation after another – a slow job. They were then cut to shape using a wooden or metal pattern. After that, some or all of the edges were flattened by bashing them so that the requisite riveting could be done. I was rather concerned by this hammering out of corrugations as it must have made the dural somewhat brittle. In the case of the Junior, two sheets, one each side, covered the entire fuselage. In spite of the fact that it was not conical, but longitudinally curved, made possible by the 'give' due to the corrugations. I have never seen a simpler, metal fuselage.

The wings consisted of two spars with tubular flanges and leading and trailing edge members. The junior was the first Junkers production type that did not use the former linked triangular spars, well known as in the F-13 and W-33 and others. The Ju 52, which first flew before I left Junkers also had spars like those in the Junior.

The Junkers Junior had an interesting development problem. The prototype, which I saw, had a slab sided fuselage which was flat at the wing (to fuselage) junction. The performance and control were quite satisfactory. When it went into production the fuselage was oval in section, being easier to make and looking better. The performance and control were however not as good as the prototype. It was not until a large wing-root fillet was introduced that the troubles was cured, but the cure came rather late.[7]

Through such records, the essence of how the Junkers Flugzeugwerk worked and what it was like inside the factory, known as the 'Teil-Klempnerei', can perhaps be felt. It was here that Shenstone did his first real metal airframe working. He learned panel beating and metal cutting, and he learned how to relate drawings to actual metal work. It was also here at Junkers that he studied the all-wing theories and advanced art of its aerodynamics – for Hugo Junkers himself had patented his all-wing ideas as far back as 1912, and worked on elliptical and arrow-head shaped wing planforms in his own wind tunnel. As will be shown, Shenstone's study of the Junkers Junior wing root fillet was a lesson for the future.

There was interest from the local workers as to what Shenstone was doing at Junkers:

> I was rather pestered by my fellow employees asking me whether my government had sent me or whether I came privately. If I said the latter would they think I should not be taking money from a poor bleeding nation like Germany? If I said the former, would they object to a damned foreign nation reaping the benefits of the great Junkers know how? I finally asked Schollinger, the general manager. He said I should say I am a private worker, which was, of course, the truth.[8]

In February 1930, Shenstone was visited by his friend Jeff Supple, who had just been accepted into the RAF and, prior to going to his training, attempted to cycle from London to Dessau – until bad weather forced him to use the train. Other visiting friends included Bill Sheldon and Corky Burk from Canada. Close to Dessau, Shenstone found the origins of the Bahaus design movement in its first, built incarnation. He wrote that he found the architecture remarkable and the design work highly original. It seems that at the time he disapproved of the innovation, but subsequently changed his mind:

> It was as is well known, disapproved of by Hitler and the staff left Germany to enrich the rest of the world with the best Bahaus ideas.[9]

Shenstone was also noting the design of cars, gliders, Dornier flying boats and the aircraft of the Rohrbach company. In design terms, Shenstone was particularly taken with the Junkers Ju 50, the Junior, and it could be conjectured that its fuselage shape influenced his later thoughts. He wrote to Professor Parkin about its design:

> A perfect darling, clean as a whistle, and a delight to behold. Remove the undercarriage and there would only be a torpedo with wings, and not one excrescence, except the cylinders of the Genet engine.[10]

Shenstone was fascinated with the Junkers Junior and had himself photographed in front of one in Berlin in June 1930. Junkers was also using a new alloy – elektron – which had many advantages but was given to an all too easy self-combustion. The firm was also experimenting with other alloys and combinations thereof. Back in Britain, the fashion remained for canvas-clad, wire-braced biplanes ranging from the Handley Page 42 to the Gloster Gladiator. The idea of a monocoque, stressed skin monoplane was too much for the conceits of perceived wisdom…

A highlight of 1930 was the flight from Dessau to Tokyo in August, of a Junkers 50 Junior, piloted by a Japanese national named Yoshuhara Seiji. This adventurous pilot flew across Russia, landing on remote locations to refuel. His Junkers Junior needed meticulous preparation and Shenstone worked closely with the pilot in making the craft ready for its record-breaking journey. Junkers made much of the opportunity and many photographs were taken for media and PR use. Beverley Shenstone, clad in stained overalls, happens to have found his way into them as he fettled the little machine. Japan was quite a theme for Shenstone – he had sailed to Germany on a ship that was once Japanese, he assisted Seiji on his flight back to Tokyo, and, latterly, one of Shenstone's sons married a Japanese woman.

There were also numerous air rallies in Europe at this time, and Shenstone, along with Kurt Bruegman, as fellow pilot, attended several of them. Shenstone kept his flying hours up by piloting whatever aircraft was available. Bruegman and Shenstone flew a biplane to Magdeburg in 1930, and various Junkers craft to other locations.

After months deep within the function of the Junkers Flugzeugwerk, where he had seen much – notably internal wing and fuselage structures and aerodynamics effects – Shenstone found himself with another opportunity. He had heard of the revolution in German gliding or sailplane design and wanted to see for himself what was occurring. On 1 July Shenstone wrote:

> Today I venture forth into the unknown. That is, I left Dessau this morning for the Wasserkuppe. I know this much about it; it is supposed to be the best gliding school in the world and it is the birth place of sailing or soaring aeroplanes. There has been gliding here since 1919. Apart from that I knew nothing. I wrote, I applied and paid. That's all. And that's why I say, 'into the unknown.'[11]

So Shenstone took a leave of absence and travelled to the home of German gliding – the Wasserkuppe near Gersfeld in the Rhön mountains. There, after a five-hour, standing room-only train journey, he set foot on the hallowed turf of the centre of world gliding on 1 July 1930. He also found that several other non-Germans had turned up to join the summer gliding course that he had enrolled in. There was Si Cassady (an American), Cliff Jackson, Paul Adorian, and Shutte from Portsmouth. Germans on the course included a Dr Brand, Barthe, Siebbicke, and a Lieutenant Tamm (later shot down in the Second World War), and a young woman named Karin Mohr-Mannesman. The instructors were Günter Groenhoff and a man named Grube. The students all signed in with Fritz Stamer, who ran the school, and Shenstone decided to lodge in the lower of the two bunk blocks that nestled into the side of the hill.

As a qualified power pilot, Shenstone joined the advanced course and began his conversion from motored flight to motorless flight. The first flights, on 9 July, were in an open glider – the 'Zogling' – a concoction of skid, seat, wood, wires and wing with no cockpit, just a seat facing into the open. Of his first flight Shenstone wrote:

> I sat in the open in front of the wing, well strapped in place. The instructor told me where I must hold the stick and warned: 'Don't move the stick back'. The starting cable was attached to an open hook. Eight men, members of the course, grasped both ends of the starting bungee, forming a vee in front of the glider. The instructor stood at one wing tip, holding the glider upright. Two men were holding on to the tail, bracing themselves. The instructor shouted 'Ziehen' (Pull) and the launch crew stretched the bungee at a walking pace. After a few steps the command came 'Laufen' (Run) and the crew ran fast down the slope. While they stretched the cables as hard as they could, there came the final shout 'Los' (Let go) and the tail-holders let go. There was a sudden acceleration, a pressing back on the seat, and one was free in the air. I pulled the stick back without knowing it, because of the acceleration, and the glider rose too much and I had to push the stick forward or stall. A few seconds later I landed hard though not badly. One is instantly airborne and in no time down again: no time for real thinking. You must be automatically right.[12]

From these early experiments, Shenstone went on to master turns and even soared along the ridge. His longest flight in the training glider with a proper fuselage and body was over seven minutes. It seems that landings were the difficult part – not least because of the Wasserkuppe's terrain and the large number of rocks strewn about. After two weeks, a good strong southerly wind arrived, enabling take-off from the summit of the Wasserkuppe hill in the 'Prufling' a more advanced trainer type. On 21 July 1930, after the advanced trainers had been damaged by other pilots attempting their C badge (a five-minute flight) Shenstone took to the air in an old 'Schnecke' type glider. Wire braced and rickety it may have been, but in the strong wind it soared along the ridge and caught the updrafts. Shenstone wrote:

> Suddenly, 'Los', the noise of the wind in the wires, and the plane leaps up. I feel the starting cable fall away and I go up like a kite in the updraft… Then I get the nose down to the right position below the horizon, which is the only way to be sure one has enough speed and not too much. There were no instruments whatever. I turn left and slide crab-fashion towards the Messstand which is far below. All this in a few seconds….Then I'm shot

upward by the new up-current and have to keep an eye on the horizon to keep my speed right. The wind roars past like 60mph. I am not wearing goggles. The ground seems stationary, which oddly enough is true. Now I nose about 45 degrees into wind and slide across above the road. Now to turn and slide back to the Messstand. I give rudder and she is slow to answer. I give her bank and she comes back quick but I lose height. Back to the Messstand with still lots of height. All I remember seeing was the group below me all watching me intently and no doubt critically…. I am afraid to go out and away from the 'Kuppe for fear of losing the updraft. I'm afraid I am going in too far. I make my turns sharp and steep. I know the instructor is watching and criticising every movement I make.

I have no idea of the time I have been aloft. Does five minutes go fast or slow? I get a little bit too far out. I turn in with bank and rudder. I am far enough and try to go straight. I give opposite rudder too soon, while still banked. I side-slip toward the earth. I lose speed. The wind whips around me and I am tearing down out of the up-current toward the buildings below. But I get control again… I see the instructor Günter Groenhoff below me. He waves me to continue….

On my next turn I am a little below the Messstand and Groenhoff waves me to land. I straighten out and make a fair landing in the fields below.

So ended the most thrilling and exciting experience I have ever had. I was exhausted. I sat limply, my mind a blank…. Then Fritz Stamer comes up and gives me the insignia with the three white gulls on the blue background, the 'C-Schein'.[13]

This was an auspicious day, as not only did Shenstone soar above the Wasserkuppe and gain his C badge (one of the earliest issued at the Wasserkuppe to a non-German and the first to a Canadian) it was also the day he met Alexander Martin Lippisch (1894–1976). The introduction was made by Fritz Stamer, a relative of Lippisch by marriage.

Shenstone recalled:

Lippisch is youngish (he was then 36) with hair usually associated with artists. Speaks very sharply. When I was introduced, he asked me what I was interested in, in a manner that seemed to say: 'Well, are you just curious? Probably you don't know anything, but as Stamer has introduced you, I guess I must at least give you a chance.' He was relieved and a little surprised when he found I spoke German. When I showed interest in his tailless things, he opened up and showed me things he had written and talked about his wings, and other people's wings.[14]

On 2 August, Shenstone saw the first flight of the Delta glider model, noting in his diary:

This afternoon the new tailless machine was finished shortly after tea…. It is the cleanest thing imaginable… has a span of 42 feet with a small fuselage sticking out in front of the wing a little, but beautifully faired. Wing 18 inches thick at roots tapering out to nearly nothing, on which rudders are attached. Ailerons as usual but elevators are like ailerons but in two pieces taking up the remainder of the trailing edge left by the ailerons. We dragged her out to Pelznerhang. Groenhof climbed in through a trap door and sat perfectly enclosed by the leading edge. And then several smaller windows in the side of the fuselage. Five men held the tail and fourteen men pulled the starting cables. It made a tiny jump into the air but came right down again. Groenhoff said it was nose heavy and that he couldn't pull it off. Lippisch said he made it that way, as it was safer than tail-heavy. So they put weights in the tail and made several other attempts before getting the balance right.

But when she did fly, she flew wonderfully. She also looked astonishing because of the complete lack of a tail…. Lippisch was happy as a kid and jumped about with joy.[15]

So began a friendship that was to last forty years and so started Beverley Shenstone's first steps into the world of perhaps what was then the most advanced aerodynamics research office anywhere in the world – that of Alexander Martin Lippisch, the man who perfected the delta wing, beginning at the Ursinius House offices at the Wasserkuppe. Long conversations followed; Lippisch had little interest in the fashionable Schneider Trophy float plane races and less interest in Junkers' corrugated behemoths. Lippisch, it seems, was into smoothness and speed. Shenstone asked Alexander Lippisch if he could work for him in the coming winter – on an unpaid basis. Shenstone was accepted and before returning to Junkers for a few more months study, he got involved with Lippisch's work on the next delta-winged tailless aeroplane, the Delta that had been preceded by the Lippisch Storch. Also on hand was the Fafnir glider – Jacob's and Lippisch's attempt at creating the world's smoothest, most streamlined sailplane.

Shenstone was clearly very taken with the concept of the all-wing or tailless design. This was reinforced by the appearance of a delegation from the British Gliding Association at the Wasserkuppe – where Shenstone helped out with translation. Geoffrey 'G.T.R.' Hill, Britain's leading flying wing proponent, also turned up at the Wasserkuppe – making friendships with Shenstone and the pilot, Robert Kronfeld, who was to later meet his untimely end testing the British flying wing. Shenstone had long conversations with Hill, and assisted with translating when Hill and Lippisch met: Shenstone later recalled that he would have been 'happy working for either of them'.[16]

One of the keys to successful all-wing design was to achieve a stable centre of aerodynamic pressure – as the all-wing had no tail to balance any shift in pressure. Lippisch had just published his paper, 'Recent Tests of Tailless Aircraft', in the French publication *L'Aerophile* in February 1930. From this stepping stone, he was soon to move onto the delta wing, and Shenstone was to be part of it. This work was to be of benefit to Professor Parkin and it was to be very useful for Shenstone's future wing design work at Supermarine – where tail size was to prove a vital ingredient in design.

It was soon after the trip to the Wasserkuppe, upon return to Junkers, that the subject of espionage entered the young Shenstone's life.

His fascination with the all-wing or flying wing concept may well have begun at Junkers and then been later fed by Lippisch and his talk of flying triangles in the sky. At Junkers, Shenstone worked on advanced projects and aerodynamics. He was a junior assistant to a Junkers design team who were working on a large flying wing, tailless design named 'Empe'. This was, in fact, an advanced derivative of the Junkers J-38 all-wing bomber theory – but was a true tailless version. Before this design's first flight as a prototype airframe, a storm of controversy erupted when an identical prototype design was displayed in Italy.

The Germans were angry and recriminations were scattered about. Shenstone, as one of the few foreign students at the Junkers Dessau factory, was in the frame and questioned under suspicion, although why anyone would assume he was working for the Italians seems to have been missed. The Italians had built a version of the all-wing design – a copy of the Junkers aircraft had flown. How? The claimed answer was that an Italian student, also working at Junkers, had allegedly left and returned to Italy with stolen copies of the secret plans for the design. A high-level furore ensued and the German media got hold of the story – demanding that all foreign students working in the German aviation factories should be expelled immediately.

Shenstone was interviewed by the investigating body at Junkers and made to swear on oath before the authorities that he had not been involved in the stealing of the secret plans. He was allowed to remain at Junkers and this was largely through the backing of the all-wing team and its designer, who vouched for Shenstone's good character. It would be over a year before the details of the story got into the Canadian newspapers – after Shenstone had left Germany. On 9 July 1931, the headlines in the Toronto media ran with the lurid claims: 'All Germany in Uproar But Toronto Grad. Freed. Beverley Shenstone Vindicated After

Italy's Theft of State Secret Airplan Plan.'[17] The story then went onto relate that the spying affair resembled an Anthony Hope novel.

Needing to be 'freed' was probably a bit of media hype, but there *was* much at stake.

Wing Commander (later Air Vice Marshal) E.W. Stedman, so important to the young Shenstone's career, was in fact the chief engineering officer with Canada's Department of National Defence. In the act of his and Parkin's placing Shenstone into the heart of German design, and then asking Shenstone (in writing) to send back details of the advanced, canard, all-wing and delta designs he had seen or worked on in Germany, Stedman, along with his colleague, Professor J.H. Parkin, could have been using Shenstone for intelligence or information gathering. If not, why make such arrangements? The fact that Shenstone admits that he sent as much information as he could back to Parkin and Stedman, surely proves the point.

The fact that, just after the time of the 'spying' affair, Shenstone's mentor, Professor Parkin, happened to have arrived in Germany from Toronto on holiday and wanted to visit the Deutsche Versuchsanstalt für Luftfhart (DVL) – German Experimental Institute for Aviation, wind tunnels, with Beverley, was an interesting apparent coincidence. Yet now, we know from both Shenstone's and Professor Parkin's records,[18] that Shenstone had been writing to him on a regular basis – sometimes weekly, sometimes monthly. Although having sworn to the Germans that he had not divulged their secret to the Italians, Shenstone had been telling Parkin all that he could about the tailless and flying-wing theories. Parkin made use of such information – not least to pursue the subsequent setting up of a Tailless Research Council group in Canada. Thanks to his protégé Shenstone, Parkin knew more about German design and flying wing design than anyone in Canada. And Shenstone had proved his worth to people in high places…

Professor Parkin's arrival shortly afterwards, on 'holiday' in the crucible of advanced aerodynamics, was, however, unlikely to have been a coincidence. If it was, the number of appointments he and Shenstone had organized throughout German industry were an even stranger coincidence. On arrival, Shenstone gave Parkin a full tour of the Junkers factory and the Versuchsbau – the experimental department where advanced designs for wing radiators, pressurized cockpits and aerodynamics research were taking place.

Then, Parkin, on 'holiday', was taken to the Zeppelin works in Friedrichshafen. They were denied access to the wind tunnel, but they did get to examine the Graf Zeppelin. Next stop was the Dornier factory in Altenrhein on the shore of Lake Constance in Switzerland – Mrs Parkin and daughter accompanying the Professor and Shenstone on the train journey. Parkin and Shenstone were in luck as the giant Dornier DO.X flying boat (or flying ship?) was in for servicing and they made it on board.

The next stage was an overnight train trip to Berlin, where the following day the two men visited the *Versuchsanstalt für Wasserbau und Schiffbau*– the national hydraulic structures and shipbuilding research laboratory. They were met by the Director, Dr Weitbrecht. The next day, the pair went to Göttingen to the *Kaiser Wilhelm Institut für Stromungsforschung* to try and see its founder, famed aerodynamicist Dr Ing. Ludwig Prandtl, and his principal researcher, Dr A. Betz, who were absent – but later seen. All three wind tunnels and fluid motion labs were accessed, and a newer jet wind tunnel was also seen – Parkin noted how rough the tunnel's internal finish was, which could affect the results. The Canadian pair then went up to Hamburg to visit the *Schiffbau Versuchsanstalt* – ship testing laboratory where they met the Director Dr Ing. Kempf. By now, Professor Parkin had clearly got the flying wing bug, and managed to secure a flight in Holland on the bat-winged Junkers G-38; it even performed some mild aerobatics during the demonstration flight.

Parkin returned home to Canada via a conference in Sweden and Shenstone returned to Junkers at Dessau to spend some time in the engine workshop. There he saw an early diesel engine – the Jumo 205, 600hp – which was later built under licence by Napier in Britain and a derivation of which, became the 2500hp 'Deltic' type engine. Another advanced diesel engine in the Junkers works had a very unusual configuration of five (radial) cylinders. Again, many decades later, a German in-line five-cylinder design proved to be the basis of some of the best diesel engines manufactured in modern times.

Shenstone's further months at Junkers also included working in the *Technische Aussendienst* – a department focused on assessing airframe performance. After completing his time at Junkers, Shenstone was back on the train to the Wasserkuppe. There he began his time working in Alexander Lippisch's drawing and design office in the famed *Ursinus House* with Hans Jacobs, Willy Hubert, Fritz Kramer, Heinrich Voepel, as well as Wagner, Wegemeyer, and test pilot Günter Groenhoff, a team of young men under the lead of the thirty-six-year-old Alexander Lippisch, furthering the delta wing work that the rest of the world would finally accept and adapt as its own, over fifteen years later.

Lippisch had just flown his delta-winged Storch and was now moving quickly towards his futuristic Delta series. Lippisch's backer, Hermann Koehl, was also a frequent visitor and Shenstone met him.

Shenstone wrote of his winter of 1930–1931 working in Lippisch's drawing office:

This winter on the Wasserkuppe, working for Lippisch was enormously inspiring. His Delta 1, having successfully flown as a glider, was being engined by a Bristol Cherub engine and equipped with a tricycle undercarriage. He was working on the design of a Delta with two Pobjoy engines in tandem to compete in a future Europa Rundflug competition, and also extending his theoretical ideas on Delta aircraft to larger sizes.

Lippisch was nearly always buoyant and happy and talkative. He did not like to work alone, and had the gift of thinking aloud. So he would always have with him Hubert, Kramer, Voepel or myself, but always separately. To watch and listen to Lippisch working out his aerodynamic and stability problems turned out to be an education in itself. I learned how to attack such problems, and not be afraid of getting wrong answers or no answers at all. Indeed, I learned technical behaviour. He was naturally dramatic and in such a way as to underline what he was trying to do.

Quite apart from the immediate problems of his tandem-engined Delta project, he was interested in aerofoil development and problems of large Deltas. This sort of problem caused me to write two papers during the winter, one on aerofoils and another on drag/range problems, in German and English.

The winter was very snowy and I learned to ski rather badly. When good skiing weather turned up, Lippisch was likely to jump up and insist that we stop work and go skiing.[19]

In these dark winter days in the hills of the German landscape, long hours of calculus into wing shape aspect ratio, area, vortices, lift distribution and the special behaviour of airflow over the delta wing principal were all studied. The differing wing lift pattern and the very difficult stall behaviour of the basic flying triangle were to prove significant issues, but ones that taught Shenstone much. Also present was Peter Riedel, a name that was to echo around gliding and Shenstone, for years to come. Shenstone, his wife Helen, and the Germans got on well, and much partying and good humour was had by all – such tales being recorded in Peter Riedel's later writing.

Also of future relevance for Shenstone, the effects of smooth skinning, boundary layer work and the effects of forward sweep on the trailing edge, and the tuning of deltoid aerodynamic lift centres, were amid the areas of deep study throughout the time Shenstone was to spend with Lippisch. Later notes from Lippisch confirm that, despite his youth, Shenstone was closely involved with the design and calculus needed to perfect the delta wing shape on the first Lippisch Delta design, and made a contribution to the totality of the delta theory's development. In his own book on the delta wing Lippisch lists his design team and names Shenstone as part of it.[20] He also reveals the fact that it was Shenstone who introduced him and his team to the aerodynamic calculus theories of Glauert. Lippisch allied this to the theories of Birnbaum, and with Shenstone the team's main focus was on determining the centre of lift on the delta wing – and then using tuft testing and smoke (and snow) flow tests on the large scale models Lippisch built.

Creating a centre of pressure in a delta wing that was not subject to displacement was the key to its development. This was truly innovative work – right at the sharp point of the history of aeronautics, it was a unique opportunity for Beverley Shenstone. No other non-German student or assistant had this vital chance. Those who think that Shenstone was a green young student when he joined Supermarine, may care to reflect on the man's contribution to the success of the Lippisch delta wing designs at their genesis.

Lippisch also invented a method for vertical take-off, and pioneered the canard or fore-wing control surface – his early canard designs featuring elliptically shaped wings. Shenstone was also part of the work to cure the aerodynamic problems of wing to fuselage and cockpit canopy interference that the Fafnir I glider was to suffer from, the Fafnir II being the result. Shenstone's new wife, Helen, also a glider pilot, turned up to stay for the winter and enjoyed a close friendship with the team – snow ball fights with Lippisch being a speciality.

During the early weeks of 1931, the team built the 12ft wingspan model of a delta wing, which featured no tail fin but had winglets at each tip. The trailing edge was equipped with the combination of tabs and flaps that became known as the elevon. The model was launched on a launching track and was pulled aloft at speed through having the team haul on the cord. By the late spring, Günter Groenhoff was test flying the full-sized, powered delta wing prototype, the Delta 2. Alexander Lippisch and his work with triangular wings were making quite an impact on the world of aerodynamics by 1931, and by 1950 Lippisch's work had been seized upon by the victors of a war that had, by then, changed aeronautical design for ever. But in 1930 and early 1931, delegations of flyers and designers came to the Wasserkuppe to see the developments, and amongst them was an Englishman with connections high up in the portals of London society, and in the British aviation industry. His name was Adrian Chamier and his decision to go gliding at the Wasserkuppe, and to enlist Beverley Shenstone as his interpreter, was to be fateful.

Air Commodore Sir John Adrian Chamier CB, CMG, DSO, OBE was born in 1883 and after attending the Royal Military Academy at Sandhurst embarked upon a career with the Punjabi Regiment of the British Army via commissioning in 1902. He served in this capacity until 1915, then joining the Royal Flying Corps as a pilot in the First World War. After service in the Royal Air Force, he retired from it and in 1929 took a position with Vickers-Armstrongs Ltd – the company that bought Supermarine in 1928. In later years, Chamier made his mark as a founder of the Air Training Corps (ATC). He was, in the 1930s, Secretary of the Air League, an important body with Royal patronage, that remains to this day. Fortuitously, Adrian Chamier also happened to turn up at the Wasserkuppe. If he had been reading the correspondence pages of *Flight* magazine, he would have known that Beverley Shenstone was then resident at the Wasserkuppe – as Shenstone had just had his first aeronautical letter published in *Flight* with the Wasserkuppe as his address.[21]

Alternatively, Chamier may have gathered this information from his various contacts in the aviation industry, many of whom had met Shenstone on British visits to the Wasserkuppe in 1930 (see Chapter 9). Clearly, Toronto University's Professor Parkin, and the RCAF's Stedman with their strong connections with the Royal Air Force and aeronautics in London, knew how to make the most of having an Anglo-Canadian ensconced within the heart of advanced German swept wing and alloy monoplane design. Chamier was to become the next instrument of fate.

The German-speaking Shenstone became Chamier's interpreter and young accomplice at the Wasserkuppe gliding school. It was an important moment, for Chamier told Shenstone that he should come and work for the British – at Vickers, the company that owned Supermarine. So Chamier was the man responsible for Shenstone turning up at Supermarine in Southampton, where R.J. Mitchell gave Beverley the job of a lifetime.

Soon after this meeting, Shenstone travelled to the DVL research centre at Darmstadt and also attended the *Reichs-Schlepp und Kunstflugschule*, which was the main German national test pilots and aerobatics school, where his flying skills were improved. Later attendees at this elite school were Me262 rocket plane pilots and the cream of the *Luftwaffe*. After Shenstone's course ended, change manifested itself in his life.

4

Supermarine Days

By spring 1931, Shenstone's time in Germany was nearing its end, not least as by his own admission money was running short. Even with family backing, he had to pay his own way and with Canada and the United States in the depths of recession, there were no openings for him at home in Toronto. Ernest Stedman wrote to Shenstone in April 1931 from Ottawa warning him that:

> Things are likely to very quiet in Canada for some time to come, many of the Government Departments being cut down in order to save expense. I believe that this applies to the Research council as well as others, because I have heard Prof. Parkin say that they were not able to obtain any more staff. Under these circumstances it might be advisable for you to consider extending your stay in Europe.[1]

The evolving political situation in Germany was also becoming more obvious, Hitler was roaming the streets and a Nazi government was less than two years away.

Shenstone travelled to England in late May 1931 and, as previously requested, contacted Air Commodore Chamier. Shenstone also wrote to Sydney Camm asking for a job and the fact that Camm was prepared to see the young Canadian must have been encouraging, but when Camm interviewed Shenstone, it was not an easy interview, as Shenstone recalled:

> He looked very fierce and peered at me with considerable scorn, or so I thought. 'If you were told to work out a design to fit a fighter specification what would you do first.' I said that I would decide whether it should be a biplane or a monoplane. His answer was typically short:' 'No, you would not. It would be a biplane.'[2]

Camm had asked a revealing question. After Shenstone's Junkers monoplane experiences, and Lippisch delta work, Camm's biplane mind set (at that time) must have jolted Shenstone.

> I must say this shook me a bit or I would not remember it so clearly. Then he left the office. I didn't know whether I was to go or wait for his possible return. After some time I decided he had no use for me and departed.

Should I have waited longer? I wish I knew.

I don't damn Camm in any way, as I soon learnt that his roughness was superficial… Afterwards he was very friendly…[3]

If Shenstone had stayed, would Camm have given him a job? We will never know, but, subsequently during the war Camm and Shenstone had regular contact and Camm asked Shenstone to work on some ideas for him. What is certain is that in May 1931 the young Shenstone got fed up waiting for Camm to return and walked out! Others, with British deference, may well have sat there waiting with trepidation for ever for the great man to reappear, but straight-talking Shenstone, left in limbo, was off!

So Shenstone had been interviewed for a job by Sir Sydney Camm – the man who went on to make the Hurricane – the Spitfire's rival. But for the hand of fate, Shenstone might have been at Hawker's, not Supermarine's.

Geoffrey T.R. Hill, who post J.W. Dunne could be seen as the leader of British flying wing studies, and was an expert in lift distribution and boundary layer ideas, had met Shenstone at the Wasserkuppe and knew of his wing and delta work with Lippisch. Hill wrote to Shenstone and said that he had discussed Shenstone's case with R.A. Bruce at Westland, but no suitable vacancy was open at the time.[4] Shenstone says that the Fairey Company turned him down sight unseen, but that he had a letter from T.M. Barlow saying he was 'prepared' to offer him a role in the Technical Office. Shenstone thought that the offer of £5.10s.0d a week was not much, so that was that.

But Air Commodore Chamier proved as good as his word, for Shenstone, then aged twenty-four, soon found himself in front of R.J. Mitchell in his Woolston, Southampton, office. Mitchell was all-out for monoplanes – his Schneider Trophy machines had proven that. Shenstone recalled that he was interviewed in Mitchell's office, which was surrounded by factory noises and had a wash basin in the corner – all very utilitarian. At this time, Mitchell was focused on improving wing design and reducing the spectre of aileron flutter – a possible factor in the crash of one his Schneider trophy racers. Mitchell and his men were also working on a range of aircraft including a large flying boat and the company's first attempt at a fighter aircraft.

After various questions and answers, Mitchell asked Alfred Faddy, a senior draughtsman and designer, to bring in the plans for a six-engined monoplane flying boat that Supermarine had a contract to build. Shenstone tells us:

The wing was thick and only slightly tapered. 'What do you think of this wing,' asked Mitchell. I suggested that if he increased the taper and added a touch of washout, he would have a lighter wing and just as good aerodynamically. From the look on his face I could see he was taken aback by my comments. Mitchell asked me to leave a contact address and said he would advise me of his decision.[5]

Of note, at this moment in 1931, Shenstone had suggested an improvement by adding more taper and reducing the thickness of the wing as a change to the flying boat's design. Soon afterwards, on 10 June 1931, Shenstone's twenty-fifth birthday, he received a letter from R.J. Mitchell offering him two months' temporary employment at the sum of £45 per month. The contents of the letter make startling reading, as Mitchell seems to admit that Shenstone's knowledge gained in Germany was of considerable importance, yet at the same time, he suggests that he was hoping for more. Perhaps he was just setting some early boundaries for the quiet yet forthright young Canadian?

Mitchell wrote to Shenstone:

> We were hoping that you would have had rather more experience on the constructional side of monoplane wings, and would be able to supply us with information regarding the necessary degree of stiffness to avoid wing flutter and reversal of aileron control; also the stresses to be developed in corrugated coverings. However, we are of the opinion that your aeronautical knowledge may be of assistance to us.[6]

This important letter, publicly revealed for the first time herein, proves to the observer that R.J. Mitchell was quite happy to absorb whatever he could from wherever it came, in order to further his knowledge and output. Despite the apparent slap-down, Mitchell clearly admits that Shenstone had knowledge that Mitchell considered could assist him. Given that Vickers-Supermarine director Air Commodore Chamier had already paved the way for Shenstone with Mitchell, it is unlikely that Chamier would have backed Shenstone if he was not convinced of his brilliance. All Mitchell had to do was bring the young Shenstone on and test him out. This happened immediately on Shenstone's starting work at Supermarine. Shenstone worked under the head of the Technical Department, Alan Clifton, the office was up in the factory's roof reached by a flying staircase and uninsulated from factory noises and, according to Shenstone, 'metal bashing and swearing'.

Shenstone noted:

> As soon as I arrived, Mitchell said: 'You said our big wing could be improved. See if you can prove it.' I was free to try to improve the wing in any way, but obviously it must not take longer than two months.

So I dug into what I had said could be done. I decided two basic things about the new wing: The hull pick-up points were not to be changed, which meant that the root thickness would remain the same. I also left the span unchanged but considerably increased the taper. The root thickness / chord was less. I worked out the spanwise distribution of the lift coefficient at various angles of attack within the calculated performance, calculated the new spar weight and to shorten the story made a report to Mitchell indicating several hundred pounds weight saving. Mitchell accepted my report but did not change the wing. Indeed, my report was really my entrance examination.[7]

Shenstone reckoned he had shaved nearly half a ton off the wing's weight and improved its lift coefficient and he did it solo. Soon after this, Mitchell confirmed Shenstone's employment as permanent. The reason Mitchell did not change the wing was that the flying boat contract was cancelled, so it was never built. Shenstone, now a full-time Supermarine employee on a salary of £500 per annum, took a house just a few minutes' drive down the river at Netley, where he and his new wife Helen made their first home. Although quiet and maybe even shy, Shenstone was also assertive and forthright in his views – but only when he was absolutely sure that they were correct, had been double checked and could not be undermined. Mitchell, it seems, was made of similar stuff. If a man like R.J. Mitchell reckoned Shenstone was worth keeping – after the two-month trial, then it is obvious that despite his youth Shenstone must have had something special. If, as some have suggested, Shenstone was a young, inexperienced, theoretician with little proof of his conceptual ideas, why did Mitchell take him on?

The answer is that Shenstone, with his training under Parkin, and his work at Junkers and at the birth of the futuristic delta wing of Lippisch, was unique, however young he was.

Beverley Shenstone joined Supermarine in a relatively junior role, but over several years, he soon advanced to become chief aerodynamicist on the Spitfire project. He would spend most of the 1930s at Supermarine, and they were to prove to be happy times. Shenstone realized that he was the only person apart from one other at Supermarine who could speak and read German, notably technical German. This gave him the advantage of having first sight of any German published technical papers that came in. This factor was recorded by Shenstone in his notes of the time and reveals his combination of straight talking self-confidence and of a more humble self awareness:

In Germany a great deal of monoplane work was under way and being published. In spite of the words in Mitchell's letter accepting me for the job, I could contribute more than they or I thought.[8]

There now occurred one of those coincidences that affect life. Shenstone realized that although having experience in aerodynamics, he was in his own words, 'short', of mathematics experience in terms of theoretical problems with wing calculus. At Southampton's University College (now Southampton University) was to be found a Professor Raymond C. J. Howland – who was a mathematics man who lacked aerodynamics experience. The two seem to have had a fortuitous chance meeting – Shenstone called it 'by the greatest good fortune' – and they got together and exchanged knowledge at personal research meetings once a week for three years.[9] Shenstone improved his maths, and Howland improved his aerodynamics knowledge. This led to the publication of their important paper on the effects of inverse methods and modifications applied to tapered and twisted wings.[10]

Professor Raymond C.J. Howland of University College Southampton, died unexpectedly in 1936, but he knew that he had been a key part of the work that influenced the calculus of the design of the Spitfire – and also work that contributed to the development of wing design in general. Herein, is the first time his contribution has been cited in the Spitfire's published annals. His, is yet another forgotten name in the Spitfire's credits, happily now referenced.

Shenstone also enjoyed a good relationship with Major H.C. Payn, who was Mitchell's personal design assistant and de facto executive deputy designer. Payn was a retired test pilot. Shenstone also ran into Supermarine's works manager – Trevor Westbrook. Westbrook it seems, had a bit of reputation – numerous sources, including Shenstone, describe Westbrook's personality. He got things done though. Once, Westbrook refused to let Shenstone onto the factory floor until he took his hands out of his pockets, yet when Shenstone later asked if he could have some old, spare flying boat wing tip floats to turn into small sailboats, Westbrook reacted with: 'And I suppose you want me to b… well deliver them to your home? 'Not at all,' replied Shenstone, only to be surprised by Westbrook asking for his address with the promise that they would be sent. Shenstone duly converted them, and his wife, Helen, often sailed her converted wing tip float at Netley.[11]

Despite his developing cancer, it is very clear that Mitchell ran a happy ship and that there was a strong team ethic. Shenstone was clearly very happy and after just one year at Supermarine he was appointed as a deputy to Alan Clifton in the Technical Office. It was the beginning of a fast rise to prominence for a young man approaching his thirtieth year. He wrote:

> As the prototype Scapa and parts of the six-engined flying boat were both in the shop, we in the Technical Office were busy with the F.7 /30 single seat fighter. Gloster, Westland and Bristol were competing with us. We had just won the world's speed record of 408mph on the S.6B and the 250mph requirement for the fighter seemed easy. It wasn't easy.
>
> We worked on endless schemes for rather large flying boats to various specifications, but we lacked real information. There was so little collected aerodynamic data that could easily be applied directly to aircraft that I spent much time in preparing graphs for use in aerodynamic aspects of design, starting with an essay which I wrote at the Wasserkippe under Lippisch: 'A Study of the Inter-relation of Weight and Drag', which I had proudly written in both English and somewhat broken German.
>
> In 1932 I authored 'A Method of Determining the twist required on a tapered wing in order to attain any desired lateral stability at high angles of incidence'. What it amounted to, was to ensure that at these 'high incidences' the spanwise shape of the lift coefficient curve did not show an increase near the tip.[12]

In 1932–1933, Shenstone's main focus of work at Supermarine was aerodynamic study (Supermarine's Stranraer flying boat being the smoothest, cleanest flying boat of its day), and specialist technical issues such as heat dissipation from oil coolers. He also developed data on the drag of seaplane floats and worked on what he described as his most difficult task – the calculation of cantilever wing weights. This resulted in nine graphs covering the essential geometry of cantilever wings. Shenstone recorded that his colleague Reginald Schlotel took an interest in this work. This was Shenstone's first attempt at creating Data Sheets – and the Royal Aeronautical Society would later build upon his work for their own official Data Sheets.

At Supermarine, American reports and National Advisory Committee for Aeronautics (NACA) Technical Memorandum came to the Woolston offices, but Shenstone's notes clearly state:

> It was however, quite impossible for us to find, in the maze of language and reports, whether what we needed existed at all.[13]

These words, allied to other indicators, clearly demonstrate that Supermarine were going to have to work out, to create the data they would need for their most important aircraft – Type 300 – which became the Spitfire. Monoplane data had to be created, and first there came the Type 224, the Spitfire's ungainly predecessor.

Soon after joining Supermarine, Shenstone met William Munro who worked in the drawing office. Munro, older than Shenstone, had worked in flying boat design in the USA and UK, and was writing a book on marine aircraft design.[14] Munro asked Shenstone to contribute a chapter on wing design – for which Shenstone received a notable credit in the author's acknowledgements. Shenstone's early role was to work on the Walrus, Scapa and Stranrear flying boat designs. Shenstone just missed being part of the design team at Supermarine when the company won the Schneider Trophy for the third time and therefore retained it, in perpetuity.

It was during his time at Supermarine that Shenstone, with other Supermarine staff, became founding members of a local Southampton branch of the Royal Aeronautical Society (RAeS): By 1942, Shenstone was appointed a Fellow of the RAeS.

Air Commodore Chamier, the man who had recruited Shenstone, turned up regularly at Supermarine – he was after all a Vickers director. Shenstone recalled one visit:

> I shall never forget our problem with the installation of a gun in the Seagull V prototype. Chamier said there was no use starting off with sketches or drawings. He demanded a table and a gun, threw himself on the table, had the gun supported in some way to give the proper angle of fire, adjusted the gun himself and then said: 'All you have do to is measure me and the gun and our geometry and you have the answer.'[15]

To Shenstone, it soon became clear that the various factions of the British aeronautical industry did not share their findings and contact between them was rare. Supermarine's owners, Vickers, did, however, exchange team members and research between the respective companies. The visionary genius, Barnes Wallis, was at Vickers' main offices at Brooklands, Weybridge, yet it seems that an attempt to place Wallis at Supermarine failed. Shenstone was then to have a run-in with Wallis after Wallis had returned to his geodetic studies at Brooklands.

Mitchell told Shenstone to go to the Royal Aircraft Establishment (RAE) at Farnborough and find out the strength data on the Wellington bomber's wing – which had just been strength tested at the RAE Farnborough. At Farnborough, Shenstone asked if he could have the data from the RAE, who refused but suggested he went and asked Barnes Wallis, directly – on the grounds that Wallis was in the same firm as Shenstone. This Shenstone did, and Wallis's answer was a simple: 'No'.[16]

In 1932, Shenstone also wanted to know what other flying boat people were up to, so he applied as a Canadian to the Canadian Embassy in London asking if, as part of his studies, he could visit Short's flying boat base at Rochester. Without realizing who he was or that he worked for Supermarine, Short's welcomed the Canadian 'student' and showed him their wares. Shenstone offered his thanks and departed, Short's being none the wiser and Shenstone being considerably wiser...

Shenstone was on the staff during the design of Supermarine's first attempt at a military fighter – the Type 224 under Air Ministry contract F. 7/30. But as a newly joined junior, he had little to do with its design.

How a company that had produced such sleek machines as the Schneider Trophy aircraft as late as 1931 could then have produced such an ungainly cart horse as the Type 224, baffles many to this day. The Type 224 had a large, 46ft span, 295sq ft, kinked, gull wing, Junkers-style corrugations, a thick fuselage, a large tail fin and an open cockpit. Worse, it had massive 'trouser' fairings around its fixed undercarriage and a steam condenser cooling system for the engine that placed various constrictions upon the entire design. It was also designed to an Air Ministry specification that did not perhaps put ultimate speed as a main priority, but even so, it was an unwieldy beast with drag-inducing features. Despite much later attempts by some to claim that the specification was a limiting factor, Shenstone's records clearly show that Mitchell and his men did not blame the specification. They, blamed, for want of a better word, themselves – but they soon made up for it.

The explanation of the Type 224's design was that it grew from a realization by Mitchell and his men, that it could *not* work if it had been a re-worked Schneider Trophy type racing aircraft. A fresh approach was needed. Shenstone, perhaps, it has to be said, with the luxury or convenience of hindsight that came from his later knowledge, rather than his junior position of 1931, later said that the design of the Type 224 may have reflected a degree of over-confidence in design terms in that Supermarine had already got to very high speeds (400mph) with the S.6B float plane and that perhaps a 250mph specification fighter was thought of as easy to achieve.

Shenstone accurately suggested that the Type 224's simplicity of design may have been a reaction to the trials and tribulations of building the racing aircraft (which like a racing car, were intense, difficult, and labour intensive to design and keep racing; such a beast could hardly be suitable outside the confines of a small team of experts). The British attitude to monoplanes and fighter tactics also framed the official specification, but neither did that specification limit suggestions and thoughts – the field was as wide open as the mindset of the perceived wisdom of the time might allow...

Shenstone probably did not mean to sound harsh, and the fact was he was correct. The Type 224, otherwise known as F.7/30 as per its Air Ministry code, was a relative failure and its first flight in February 1934 revealed its flaws. From then on, Mitchell was itching to leap ahead into the future and to create something special. He had too – Supermarine could not afford another failed attempt as they needed an Air Ministry contract – even if they were busy with a whole family of flying boats. This was Mitchell's first military fighter, albeit in peacetime with thoughts of war years away. This may explain why ease of manufacture was not perhaps a primary consideration in 1934–35, the Spitfire being criticized for its complicated design and manufacturing process when war did come, although once the new workforces had been trained in the art of aeronautical fabrication, these production problems eased.

Mitchell's iron will and advanced vision, knew that the next attempt, the last chance, had to be not only a winner, but a leap ahead, to achieve its goal. Hawker's had years of military experience to build upon, whereas Supermarine did not. In one sense this lack of previous experience was a negative factor, but in another it was a positive – for Mitchell and his men were unencumbered by set ways of thinking, and the blinkers of perceived wisdom. They could reach out and innovate. Meanwhile, Camm at Hawker, the man who had interviewed Shenstone for a job in May 1931, continued doing what he had done best – in a new monoplane context.

Shenstone says that nobody could have foreseen the subsequent Spitfire's emergence – or the speed at which it happened. He was of the clear belief that:

> Mitchell's second thoughts based on the F.7 /30 produced the Spitfire, although we find more dissimilarity than similarity between the two. However, the one is actually developed from the other, not by extrapolation, but by a vivid appreciation by the designer of the things which had or might have gone wrong with the F.7 /30.[17]

The leap from the past to the future, as framed by the Spitfire, focused on structure and aerodynamics:

> The basic structure was simplified, the external shape made more complex from a manufacturing point of view although simpler from the aerodynamic viewpoint, that is, it was easier for the air to get past it. Straight lines were curved and corners were beaten out… It is probable that the Spitfire would never have come to life without the relative failure of the F.7 /30…[18]

Immersed in all this, Shenstone spent hours studying and advancing his knowledge base. Contrary to some published views, he had also served some time on a factory floor – getting dirty doing manual metalwork on Junkers aircraft. Prior to that he had worked in the metal and working shops of the family agricultural firm. He could also fly motor powered and motorless aircraft.

Above all, Shenstone could combine unique aerodynamic theory experience with some level of actual metal-bashing, structural knowledge. The combination of these elements with his academic mind were the key to his advancement.

Shenstone's notes of the period also reveal that as much testing had been done on the Type 224's design and components, and improving them meant that these items did not have to be re-tested from scratch – a significant time saving. Of interest in terms of how open Mitchell was to others' ideas, and how his staff felt able to advise him free of fear or hierarchical status, is an entry in Shenstone's diary for January 1934, just before the first flight of the Type 224, where he wrote:

> More work on the flaps. R.J.M. wants the ordinary tailplane adjustment. We try to convince him that his ideas are faulty.
>
> Hutter flap angles etc. Clifton and Mansbridge and others spent all the afternoon with RJ. All the controls were discussed. In my opinion it is far too late, as the design has gone so far.[19]

During his pre-Spitfire years at Supermarine, Shenstone was in early 1934, sent off to Germany to visit designers and notably, accompanied Ernest Hives and, James Ellor, of Rolls-Royce to Berlin. Then in May and June 1934, Shenstone accompanied the chief designer of Vickers, Rex Pierson, on a trip to the USA to visit American designers and view monoplane prototypes. Also on the trip was Mutt Summers, chief test pilot at Vickers-Supermarine, and Trevor Westbrook – Mitchell's works manager, latterly appointed as the Vickers, Brooklands, factory superintendent. For a man as young as Shenstone, albeit by now losing his hair and looking much older than his years, to move in such rarefied atmosphere was unusual, but if people of older years and greater experience were to include him in their circles, is it not fair to assume that they thought that he must have had something to offer. It was at this time that Shenstone also forged good relations with C.G. Grey at the *Aeroplane,* and after the untimely death of Jeff Supple, arranged for his paper on aspects of aircraft navigation design needs to be published in the publication. Shenstone was to become a lifelong friend of *The Aeroplane's* next editor, Thurstan James.

Shenstone made an extensive on-tour diary of the1934 trip. The team visited the National Advisory Committee for Aeronautics (NACA) laboratories, Sikorksy, Lockheed, Martin and the manufacturers of the

Los Angeles area. In California he also met the Hungarian émigré aerodynamicist Theodor Von Karman at the Douglas factory. The trip across the USA saw Beverley Shenstone and Rex Pierson crossing the country by train, and Mutt Summers and Trevor Westbrook flying across in a single-engined Lockheed piloted by Jimmy Dolittle. Shenstone did, however, get a ride in a Ford Trimotor, which he found deafeningly noisy.

Of particular note, Shenstone had the opportunity to investigate the new NACA 2220 series of aerofoils, which filled his mind with questions and answers about thin wing design, a subject close to R.J. Mitchell's heart.

Mitchell was one of the few aircraft designers in Britain whose mind was not hamstrung by convention and perceived wisdom. If he had been so conservative, would he have ever built monoplane Schneider racers? It should not be forgotten that other British Schneider Trophy entrants created biplane racers! Mitchell was prepared to try new ideas – even at some risk. Only by learning new theories and experimenting with them could advances in design be made, drag go down, and speed rise. This thinking contrasted sharply with the British aeronautical mindset of the time, which encouraged engineers to make alterations to known themes and to proceed with great caution by refining existing techniques.

The same resistance to change, the same attitude, also prevailed for some time in America, yet that was soon to shatter very rapidly. But in the world of the Schneider Trophy racers, rapid advancement and the need for speed drove design culture at a pace far greater than conventional minds could handle. The Italians and French, raced ahead, and of the British establishment only Mitchell kept up with, or outpaced them. Of course, when he won, he was suddenly no longer the maverick, but the respected genius.

How did the German aeronautical industry advance so far and so fast? Because it too was also open to new thinking and ready to throw off the constraints of the conventional mindset so epitomized in Britain. The German aeronautical design theorists proof tested their new ideas with models and full-size prototypes; they did not reinvent old ideas through slow methodical acceptance across decades. Theory, new theory, then the testing of theory, became the design research culture – as opposed to the general stagnation of known wisdom that prevailed in Britain until war forced change. British proponents of monoplanes and tailless design, did exist, but they faced an uphill battle. This is how or why the Germans – people such as Hugo Junkers, Ernst Heinkel, Alexander Lippisch, Wolfram, Reimar and Walter Horten, Hans Multhopp, Willy

Messerschmitt, Waldemar Voigt, and many others raced ahead and, for those like Mitchell and Shenstone, who had in their own ways, been part of a wider, new thinking, be it from racing float planes, to all-wing tailless triangles, and gliders, the opportunity to touch the future was possible. Fresh thinking could leave the lethargy of industrial weight, long behind.

To confirm the above standpoint, it is interesting to note that Shenstone wrote up his views of the new, open-minded world of American aviation and design in a paper – 'More Impressions of Aviation in the USA 1934', which was circulated at Supermarine. A key point was Shenstone's view that:

> The Americans are more daring than we are, or is it that their officialdom is more broad-minded than ours? Whatever it is, we should do something about it.[20]

Was such a broader mind set – one that extended to Mitchell and Shenstone – the new internationalists, partly to explain the fundamental issues of psychology and behaviour that framed the difference between the advanced design of the all-alloy skinned, monocoque construction, thin-winged Spitfire, and the conservative British establishment thinking of the partly canvas-clad, thick-sectioned, chassis-based, Hurricane?

5

Perfecting the Spitfire

The key to the Type 300 (the Spitfire), the essential factor in its performance, was its aerodynamics – its wing and body design. The Rolls-Royce Merlin engine was also vital to the recipe, but the same engine powered the Hurricane. Beyond sheer horsepower, the Spitfire had a special ingredient – the science of its wing design allied to an overall aerodynamics package that gave the Spitfire much lower drag than the Hurricane, or the Messerschmitt Bayerische Flugzeugwerke 109, or anything else in 1936.

The Hurricane, designed by Sydney Camm and his team (whose names also often go unmentioned), was a sound, partly-canvas clad, strong airframe that was eclipsed by the glamour of the ellipse of the Spitfire's shape. Sydney Camm's main team players on the Hurricane's design and development, as cited by *Flight* magazine on 31 October 1940, were: R.H. Chaplin, S.D. Davies, R. McIntyre and R. Lickley.

The Hurricane might be said to be an evolved monoplane version of the Hawker Fury biplane, because it followed the then traditional British behaviour of developing existing designs with a new slant, rather than creating a totally new concept, the Hurricane being built on biplane construction principles of girders, frames, bracing, and canvas cladding. Further proof of the Hurricane's roots, comes from the fact that its canvas wings had to be completely redesigned to more modern stressed skin and rib techniques, even as the first 500 canvas-winged Hurricanes were delivered.

But quite rightly, the Hurricane has a dedicated band of admirers – it was easy to build, and was an excellent and sturdy gun platform that resisted damage very well. Based around a girder chassis, the Hurricane had few vices and, with its broad undercarriage and good nose visibility, was certainly easier to taxi, take-off and land. Clearly, the Hurricane was a fine aeroplane and representative of its time – it was large, thick sectioned and had a huge tail. It was as simple, yet as strong, as it could be. However, given the need for major wing design changes and consequent production effects, and a last-minute design change to the tail fin to cure a spin-recovery handling problem, it is debatable whether it was the absolute paragon of design and of construction ease as portrayed by so many observers. Its handling was also less direct in comparison with the Spitfire's lightning responses.

The Hawker Hurricane, much maligned in the post-war years of the growing Spitfire 'icon' movement, was available in large numbers and was easier to fly for young raw recruits – its stability being noteworthy, if not as quick reacting as something less stable and more 'edgy'. Some praised this stability, but others knew that such stability hampered its reactions. As modern fighter aircraft design shows, the *less* stable airframe is much more responsive and is a sought after condition (with computers to juggle the instability). The Spitfire was criticized for being less stable – but therein was the clue – it was much quicker to react to pilot input than the Hurricane. The stressed skin, one-piece monocoque, made the Spitfire an integrated whole, and an aerodynamically optimized, singular structural item. As such it was more agile – if not as battle damage tolerant – as the collection of easily repaired, canvas-covered, alloy-girder chassis parts, that was the Hurricane.

The excellent but solid Hurricane, whose canvas could literally be sewn up if damaged, could not be developed beyond a certain point and its design was superseded by more efficient Hawker aircraft by 1943 – notably employing ellipsoid thin wings. The Spitfire's design was developed throughout the war and remained competitive in the face of rapid and massive aerodynamic advances. Surely this difference between the two mid-1930s designs underlines the scientific advantage of the Spitfire as a design? The never-ending debate often cites the Spitfire versus the Hurricane as designs framed by the Battle of Britain, yet the totality of the war years, perhaps even the entirety of the respective design lives of the pair, are a better arbiter of the success of their design function than just that of one period of combat in the summer of 1940. Make no mistake, the Hurricane and its pilots were good and key to the effort, and no slur upon them is intended, but the Hurricane was slower and less agile than the Spitfire. A Hurricane (especially flown by an experienced man), was a lethal threat to bomber or fighter (although it was often tasked with attacking the easier prey of bombers – easier to shoot down in large numbers – hence the Hurricane's high statistical 'kill' rate.) But the old argument about which was best has many contexts rather than a single answer for a single battle, and may best be answered by looking at the science of the two designs.

The reason the Hurricane did not instil the kind of fear that the Spitfire instilled into the minds of German pilots was, say many, down to 'Spitfire' propaganda and hype. In the reality of science, it was more likely down to the fundamentals of aerodynamics.

The Spitfire became an instant icon, and that status has been reinforced across the subsequent decades. The Spitfire is worshipped now, but it was also worshipped then. It is fair to say that, together, the Spitfire and Hurricane won the Battle of Britain, but it is also fair to ask that had only the Hurricane existed, if the outcome may have been different? The Hurricane was very good, and initially it was easier to build, but the Spitfire's aerodynamic advantage was decisive. The Hurricane was slower in top speed and slower in climb speed; crucially, although it turned tightly, it also retained less wing energy in a tight turn. The Hurricane relied on its turn *radius* at an optimum speed, whereas the Spitfire's ellipse retained speed and wing energy to allow it to better utilize its *rate* of turn, allowing its pilot to retain offensive rather than defensive ability – a Spitfire could be controlled right up to the edge of its wing's performance. No amount of Hurricane worship could get around these facts of science.

But was the Spitfire worship fair? Was the Spitfire *that* much more manoeuvrable, than the Hurricane, and of more relevance, the Bf109, at the time? Was the Spitfire *really* different from other monoplane aircraft? The answer was, yes, the Spitfire *did* fly like no other fighter, and it did have advanced technology in its design; the Spitfire's advantage had its basis in scientific fact.

The magic lies in the Spitfire's ultra smooth low-drag shape, its amazing rate of turn with lower wing drag in the turn, its quicker reactions to the controls, and its behaviour at high bank angles near the onset of the in-turn stall. Lift distribution, wing loading, boundary layer control and drag tuning were the key ingredients. The Spitfire had the handling qualities of a racer, even at high altitude, yet it was docile at slow speed and on the approach to landing – even if its on the ground, over-the-nose visibility was poor and the narrow wheel track made it twitchy to steer on the ground: in the air, it was a revelation. Because of the ellipsoid wingtips better aerodynamic behaviour with lower drag, the Spitfire had a superior in-turn performance retaining more wing energy, and had a docile stall where the wing tips remained 'flying' and the ailerons efficient. The Hurricane's stall was less benign and wing-drop was more likely from its traditional wing shape and outboard-wing, stall pattern. The Bf109 wing had to rely on leading edge devices to remain 'flying' and stalled before the Spitfire.

Crucially, the Spitfire wing *retained* more airflow energy, deeper into the in-turn stall regime – this was not despite, but actually *because* the Spitfire wing design deliberately traded levels of high-speed straight line, lift, for better aerodynamic behaviour at high angles of attack and turn angle. The Bf109's smaller, slotted wing actually offered a high lift efficiency factor in terms of wing area, but this advantage was sacrificed through its adverse wing loading and wing drag components.

The Spitfire's use of a large curved wing to body fillet was a major drag reduction factor, as was its slim fuselage with carefully shaped side walls and parallel shape. Even the location and shaping of the canopy were fundamental aspects of equalising pressures, reducing drag and adding lift and speed – techniques now widely known to monoplane aerodynamicists, but in 1934–1935 they were highly advanced knowledge.

In September 1942, as a result of flight tests in the USA, the Spitfire's specially tuned stalling behaviour was the subject of a top-secret, confidential NACA Advance Technical Report (later declassified) by Vensel and Phillips[1] at the NACA Langley laboratory and was originally issued to the US Army Air Force material testing department. The tests were conducted more thoroughly than usual, says the report, because, as it stated, the Spitfire's 'stalling characteristics were considered to be more desirable in some respects than any of the pursuit type aeroplanes formerly tested in similar manner'.

For the tests, the Spitfire VA was fitted with wool tufts to indicate airflow, and sensors/probes (with the aerodynamic effects of the sensors calibrated and assessed), which revealed that the Spitfire had a beneficially unique stall warning behaviour and that the stick could be pulled well back into the stall yet the ailerons continued to work and provide control/roll authority. The aircraft developed a natural nose down pitch – an automatic recovery effect at the full stall. Even beyond its maximum lift levels, no violent behaviour occurred. Any extreme, attitude-related rolling effect at high bank angle only took place after the warning signal of pre-stall buffet took place. The stall was benign and symmetrical.

Of great note, the report stated the Spitfire's stall warning characteristics were 'especially beneficial in allowing the pilot to reach maximum lift coefficient in accelerated manoeuvres'. In other words, the Spitfire wing's advantage was usable and not just theoretical; the aircraft could be safely flown right up to its limits without becoming dangerous – without risk of flick stall or sudden, violent spin. The flight test report highlighted that the Spitfire retained an unusual amount of lateral control, which was available and remained so across all flight conditions – even with full up elevator applied. This allowed the aircraft to be pulled rapidly into manoeuvres – that trademark Spitfire instantaneous reactive effect. This capability stemmed directly from Shenstone's work on the wing's behaviour and the effects of wing twist 'washout' and the lifting benefits of the wing root fillet that were unique to the Spitfire in 1935. Although the maximum lift coefficient was lower than the wing area would have suggested, this was deliberate – ultimate, raw lift was detuned to provide the safe stall and turning capability, which were the Spitfire's specific advantage. Neither did the open or closed nature of the gun ports create airflow affected opposing handling traits. The pilot was also able to pull rapidly to maximum lift coefficient in a turn without the danger of sudden stalling.

For the American tests, in-flight wool tuft testing using long strands of wool fixed across the wing surface that moved with the airflow's own movements showed that (as designed) the Spitfire wing stalled at the inboard wing root – leaving the wing tips still un-stalled up to a certain value, and the ailerons functioning, which was just what the pilot needed to out-turn a competitor. Of remarkable note, the flow ahead of the ailerons did not separate and lateral and longitudinal control was still available even *after* a full stall. The report also cited lift coefficients of above C_L 1.0, for the Spitfire, which are better than those subsequently cited or assumed by later authors in calculations.

This range of American findings about the Spitfire's wing behaviours confirmed Shenstone's remarkable achievement. In fact, the combined sensor and physical wool tuft test results confirmed the success of his mathematical calculus used to achieve the characteristics – yet no actual tuft testing was used by Shenstone when designing the wing. The fact that subsequent wing test results – physically seen and recorded as they demonstrated the actual airflow over the wing, matched the aerodynamicists theoretically calculated intended effects, is a significant testament to his work. The in-flight sight, of a neat circle of stalled tufts, inboard on the wing centre section and also an area extending to the wing root, provide great testimony to the theories deployed by the Spitfire's wing designer.

These independent, non-British tests of 1942, referenced in the NACA archive with a copy registered to Professor John Parkin at the Canadian National Research Council, which he received in November 1942 indicated as via Shenstone, are now revealed to a wider audience and categorically prove, once and for all, from calibrated, multiple sensor flight testing, the factual advantages of the Spitfire's wing design. Critics of the design and use of the modified ellipse by R.J. Mitchell and Beverley Shenstone can surely have little left to lean on.

* * *

The Drag Coefficients

The Spitfire also boasted very low, aerofoil-lift, and airframe, drag coefficients. Shenstone's figure for the pre-production Spitfire with early canopy, tailskid and ejector exhausts was C_D 0.01702. Drag figures for any aircraft's coefficient of drag, known as the C_D, depend on numerous factors, notably, efficiency, speed, lift induced component, skin smoothness, shaping, exhaust and propeller effects, and can be expressed based in various definitions. Drag measured under power, yet with a zero rated lift component is known as the C_{D0}. Working out the coefficient of lift-induced drag – the C_{Di}, which is the drag created by the wing as it makes lift – and adding it to the C_{D0} can allow extrapolations and interpretations of an overall coefficient of drag figure – the C_D – to be arrived at. Other coefficients taken into account must include a range of factors relating to the coefficient of lift – the C_L, the sectional drag and 'wetted area' and the aerodynamic, engine, and propeller efficiencies. The key aerodynamic expressions discussed here are:

C_D = Coefficient of drag. This is calculated by adding the C_{D0} (coefficient of drag at zero lift) to the C_{Di} (coefficient of lift-induced drag).

In the 1930s for the prototype Spitfire a coefficient of drag of around C_D 0.18 was calculated, [2] which was an astounding advance on the figures of around C_D 0.45– 0.60 for early 1930s fixed undercarriage monoplanes and some biplanes. Later production versions of the Spitfire, with cannons, blisters and extra skin addenda were cited at around C_D 0.21. The Spitfire Mk XIV saw an increase in drag to C_D 0.22.[3]

However, no singular drag coefficient across all the variants of one aircraft type can be considered reliable – alterations to propeller type, sealing, shape, armament, canopy, exhaust, and paint grain, can all affect the drag coefficient. These variations are evident in the C_D figures cited for the Spitfire and Hurricane, and especially so for the Bf109 due to is many design and skin alterations. A most notable assessment of these parameters was published in February 2000 by J.A.D. Ackroyd and P.J. Lamont of Manchester University's School of Engineering Aerospace Division, in the RAeS publication, *The Aeronautical Journal*.[4] This paper was principally concerned with investigating the turning radii for the Battle of Britain fighters – not least because of the findings of Mason,[5]

SECRETS OF THE SPITFIRE

repeated by author Len Deighton, [6] which contained the curious claim that the Bf109 could out turn the Spitfire in terms of turn radius!

Investigation showed that such earlier claims of Mason were reputedly in error and cited flight profiles of some concern. The separate issues of rate of turn and radii of turn are resultant from aerodynamic tuning and, in carrying out their investigation, Ackroyd and Lamont also published a list of drag coefficients (expressed to four figures) from several sources, and these are of relevance to any claim about the superior science of the Spitfire's aerodynamics. Ackroyd and Lamont's findings, confirmed with revised calculations that the Spitfire did have a tighter turning circle than the Bf109, yet one that was not as great as some had claimed.

A range of drag coefficient figures for the Spitfire, Hurricane and Bf109 aircraft have been presented across the years,[7, 8, 9] but the variances and factors within the figures, once seen in the context of their settings, can provide the reader with a basis for assessing one aspect of the aerodynamic merits of each design. The drag coefficients used by Ackroyd and Lamont, as expressed to wider numerical accuracy, provide the reader with some basis for aerodynamic parameters – noting that the higher the number the greater or worse the drag:

Spitfire prototype
C_D 0.0197 $\qquad$ C_{D0} 0.0187 $\qquad$ C_{Di} 0.0010

Spitfire Mk1 A (late model)
C_D 0.0192 $\qquad$ C_{D0} 0.0180 $\qquad$ C_{Di} 0.0012

Hawker Hurricane Prototype
C_D 0.0237 $\qquad$ C_{D0} 0.0225 $\qquad$ C_{Di} 0.0012

Hawker Hurricane 1 (late model)
C_D 0.0230 $\qquad$ C_{D0} 0.0213 $\qquad$ C_{Di} 0.0017

These figures show that the Spitfire prototype's C_D 0.0197 had less drag than the prototype Hurricane's C_D 0.0237, and that the Hurricane always had more lift-induced drag from its conventional wing design's thick, Clark YH aerofoil, and that the Spitfire had significantly lower drag figures as both a prototype and as a production item.

It may also be significant that the issues of the Hurricane's canvas fuselage and wing skinning have not been addressed by commentators or subsequent calculations. Such canvas skinning is likely to have suffered degradation in surface quality, and in combat repair related quality as well as in attachment tension, and these factors could have led to even higher drag coefficients for actual in-service Hurricanes. The switch to alloy-skinned wings for the Hurricane after 500 canvas-winged aircraft were produced can only underscore these aerodynamic concerns. However, the vagaries of a combat degraded, canvas-clad fuselage, should not be dismissed in terms of drag calculations for the Hurricane. However, the Hurricane's significant speed losses in comparison with the speeds attained by the similarly powered Spitfire must lie in the Hurricane's inferior aerodynamic performance as a whole. Improper combat repairs to the Spitfire's skin, with resultant likely drag effects were not unknown, but less likely to occur due to the very strict alloy skinning repair criteria.

Both the Hurricane and the Spitfire, as prototypes, suffered the effects of the early two bladed fixed pitch propellers fitted to them – which may represent significant factors in propeller efficiency figures in the prototype – related drag calculations. The reader should also note, that assumed figures for both prototype and production airframes, do not quantify the differing lift characteristics between the Spitfire's ellipse and the Hurricane's longer, tapered wing design (although the ellipse's lower induced drag is evident), or between the Spitfire and the Bf109. And that of the speed related effects of the Spitfire's smoother skin and wing fillet – advantages that manifested in the Spitfire's more responsive handling, quicker rate of turn, and higher speeds.

Because these coefficients all relied on a similar percentage figure for aerodynamic efficiency and wing lift figures to achieve their calculations, it may be possible that some of the aerodynamic benefits of the Spitfire's modified ellipse and smooth overall finish, are 'lost' to the calculations and therefore missing from the lift and other coefficients reached. Certainly, the Hurricane and the Bf109 with their drag creating tapered wing designs would have suffered a loss of wing lift efficiency and a de facto reduction of their aspect ratio due to tip drag, in comparison to the lower drag found at the Spitfire's elliptical wing tips. So using the same wing lift efficiency numbers (C_L) for the Spitfire, Hurricane and Bf109, as part of drag calculations, is worthy of discussion for future authors. Of interest, the carefully considered Ackroyd and Lamont paper postulated a maximum lift coefficient in the turn of C_L 1.35 for the Spitfire. This theoretical value is underlined in its efficacy by the maximum, in-turn, lift coefficient cited for the Spitfire V by the wartime tests reported by Vensel and Phillips, with a C_L of 1.22. Although lower than C_L 1.35 (probably due to the canon fittings of the Spitfire V wing), the two figures confirm the theory that the Spitfire's lift coefficients may not have been adequately credited by some critics.

The question clearly is, while the lower induced drag figures of the ellipse are obvious in the calculations, what of the Spitfire's smoother lift pattern, wing fillet, and boundary layer work tied into to the varying thin aerofoil sections of the Spitfire's wing? What of the higher coefficient of wing lift figures cited by that 1942 NACA report by Vensel and Phillips? Could these factors be further accounted for in the mathematics? And if so, would the Spitfire's drag coefficients and lift efficiencies be even better than the currently accepted basis of calculus?

To reinforce the point, it is worth noting that the seemingly unreferenced 1942 American NACA stall tests on a Spitfire VA, cited previously, show that these tests on a calibrated, sensor equipped Spitfire, produced a maximum lift coefficient in a 180 degree turn from level flight with the flaps up at 174mph, of C_Lmax 1.22 and that the test pilot noted that the aeroplane could be flown beyond the stall even at lower lift coefficients. And in the cruise, there was a lift coefficient of C_Lmax 1.68, and a C_Lmax of 1.15 in throttle-closed gliding flight with the gun ports open, cited in the American 1942 test results. These lift figures are better than those assumed by later authors where an identical lift coefficient is assumed as a basis of assessment for the Spitfire, Hurricane and Bf109.

Given the actual inflight findings as opposed to later assumed figures derived from theoretical frameworks, it could be argued that the Spitfire's very obvious far higher level of handling performance over the Hurricane and Bf109 far outweighs the numerically quantified difference in the mathematical drag coefficient, lift and efficiency numbers cited between the aircraft by post-war authors – *possibly* reinforcing the point that history may not fully have credited the aerodynamic efficiency factor of the Spitfire's modified ellipse. Putting the Spitfire's wing lift efficiency figures in with a 'mean' figure also applied equally to the Hurricane and Bf109, to reach a coefficient result, *may* have not fully revealed the true science of the modified ellipse in all its contexts.

In comparing the Spitfire's aerodynamics with its competitor, the fast and furious Bf109, the range of figures for the Messerschmitt have always been controversial, and long argued over, as so many differing fuselage shapes, engine profiles, and body skin criteria apply across the various Bf109 variants. The Bf109 also had a much higher wing loading – a relevant issue in terms of performance and its smaller wings had higher wing tip drag which reduced its effective aspect ratio and therefore its lifting efficiency. The Bf109 underwent numerous changes and in BF109K model, was subjected to an aerodynamic 'clean up' that is at least reflected in quoted figures.[10]

Selected drag coefficients for various Bf109

Bf109B

C_D 0.0277 C_{D0} 0.0258 C_{Di} 0.0019

Bf109E

C_D 0.0265 C_{D0} 0.0246 C_{Di} 0.0019

Bf109G/6

C_D 0.0310 C_{D0} 0.0292 C_{Di} 0.0018

Bf109K/4

C_D 0.0255 C_{D0} 0.0242 C_{Di} 0.0013

These figures for selected examples of the Bf109 family show a consistently higher level of drag compared with the Spitfire or Hurricane, and higher levels of wing lift-induced drag. One early model, test of a Bf109[11] indicated C_D 0.0199 – a figure so different from the Bf109's normal C_D range, that it may be considered to reflect anomalous criteria or airframe effects. Conversely, a cited C_D 0.0036 by some commentators[12, 13] for one variant of the Bf109G must also be seen as likely to reflect a differing criteria or condition – such as including exhaust thrust calculations, or adverse camouflage paint application for other fuselage fitment factors. With its small wings, the Bf109 is unlikely to have had a drag coefficient in excess of C_D 0.0036, whatever the excrescences of its lumpy fuselage and fittings. Assessing an average drag coefficient or the Bf109 is a risky and contentious issue, but perhaps theoretically assuming an average drag coefficient of around C_D 0.28–0.31 for the Bf109 circa 1939–1942, *may* arguably be a sound basis for consideration amid the vagaries of combat-related airframe degradation, modified air scoops and engine cowling shapes.

The prototype of the 1936 Bf109 was fitted with a Rolls-Royce Kestrel engine with a much smaller frontal and cross-sectional area.[14] The production version with the inverted Daimler-Benz engine received a new and larger front fuselage lobe shape, giving differing frontal area. But it was the standard model Bf109's square rigged canopy, tail plane bracing, fuselage scoops, rough surface plating and leading edge slots, that were its major drag triggers. The later, Bf109K model saw much work undertaken to clean it up. At one stage the Bf109 V48 (Works Number: 14003) was fitted with a V-shaped tail as an aerodynamic refinement and as a test bed for the Me 163. Stability issues resulted and the V-tailed 109 was abandoned. Yet despite its 'clean up' the Bf109's shape was still encumbered by wing slots and numerous bumps, openings and protrusions, notably the engine panel cladding, air scoops and wing skin addenda. In aerodynamic terms, the Bf109 had a fully turbulent boundary layer, whereas the Spitfire possessed a unique-at-the-time, smoother, natural boundary layer control of far less turbulence and drag – a boundary layer estimated at less than one inch in depth.[15]

To illustrate the Spitfire's low drag coefficient achievement, its drag is less than even the slipperiest of today's supercars, and was less than half the drag coefficient of previous biplane fighters with similar wing areas. It was also the lowest drag figure of any mid-1930s monoplane fighter. The (near-decade) later, late model variant, thin fuselage type P-51 Mustang just bettered the Spitfire's drag coefficient by small amount at C_D 0.0178 and a C_{D0} of 0.0163[16] – but that was with the benefit of wartime's subsequent aeronautical development, a laminar wing, and radiator design advances not available in 1935. Of note, the Merlin-powered Mustang's standard long-range specification for the job it was designed for and assigned to, meant that it flew with large, fuel drop tanks, which seriously affected its drag coefficient whilst they remained attached.

The Mustang's better range is often credited to its laminar-flow wing (whose degree of laminar efficiency beyond its prototype's wind tunnel claims was subject to numerous combat and operationally related adverse effects) but the fact that its standard internal fuel tank was twice the size of the Spitfire's may well be relevant. However, perhaps of more importance, the Mustang did boast a far more aerodynamically efficient 'Meredith' effect radiator inlet and outlet design, which also bled off localised boundary layer airflow to great effect. Yet the Mustang had a large tail fin – one that was implicated in a series of structural failures due to aerodynamic side loadings and modifications were required. The Mustang was also 1000lb heavier than the identically engined and similar sized later variant Spitfire IX.

The Mustang's designers at the North American company obtained three Spitfire IXs – one for wind tunnel testing, one for structural analysis and one to cut up into small pieces for strength testing. Even when discounting the engine's weight, the Mustang was still over 500lb heavier than the Spitfire. The reason why, lay in a range of fittings and pressing across the airframe design. The answer as to why these items were so much heavier is likely to have been based in making them easy to produce quickly, rather than for ultimate low design weight.

Prior to the Mustang's arrival, nearly seven years after the Spitfire's birth, the aerodynamic difference in the type and nature of the lift produced by the two differing sizes and shapes of the Spitfire and Bf109 wings – ellipse versus square taper – underpinned the Spitfire's aerodynamic advantage and explained that its bigger wing area was not a flaw, despite the Bf109's lesser surface area, which was far *less* efficient in terms of both induced and parasitic drag than its smaller size would seem to indicate if basic wing area theory is followed. And just as with the Hurricane, the Bf109's traditional wing tips caused more drag in a tight turn than those of the ellipse, with consequent adverse stall, energy and speed characteristics.

The fact was that the ellipse's, smooth, stable, lift with its more even distribution, made it much more efficient than the coarser lift gradient provided by the smaller square/tapered wing Messerschmitt, which also needed movable leading edge slots to provide lift below certain speeds and these sat in drag inducing housings on the wings. These slots were an invention that although labelled by many authors as a British, Handley Page company device, actually originated from the mind of Handley Page's, German émigré aerodynamicist, Dr Gustav Lachmann, who patented the idea only after overcoming the many barriers that had been put forward.

Bombers of the war era had coefficient of drag figures ranging between approximately C_D 0.39 and 0.55. The aerodynamic success of the Lancaster was due to its very smooth shape and finish and a C_D of 0.39 – an astoundingly low figure for a large machine circa 1942.

The Spitfire's minimal drag was achieved through low levels of lift-induced drag, and an ultra-smooth finish giving low levels of parasitic drag. With its smooth, clean panels, small frontal area and also its very small tail fin, which significantly reduced further drag losses, the Spitfire was aerodynamically cleaner than any of its contemporaries – and suffered less cumulative drag penalty when encumbered with under body armament or tropical radiators. Even with its large wing, and those underwing radiators, the Spitfire's advantage stems from its low drag design and the drag-reducing benefits of the ellipse – no matter how much bigger it was than the Bf109's conventional, square/tapered wing. The thick-winged Hurricane with its longer wingspan, very large tail fin, thick fuselage boom and ribbed canvas skin, suffered at the hands of its drag characteristics – speed being particularly affected. It was nearly 40mph slower than the Spitfire in top speed and much slower in climb speed.

Of the Hurricane, Shenstone wrote:

Hawker's Hurricane flew before our future Spitfire. The prototype Hurricane had fabric-covered wings and ours were entirely metal-covered. We had an opportunity to learn from our failure, but Hawker had only their biplanes from which to extrapolate. The Hurricane fuselage looked like a copy of any old Hawker biplane fuselage and the fabric-covered wing might have been a thick biplane wing. Naturally Camm shifted to an all-metal wing later, but the developing Spitfire kept pretty well on top.[17]

Sydney Camm later admitted that the Hurricane had been dated, but that this allowed quick entry into service and ease of construction; those were two things that not even the most ardent of Spitfire fan could claim. Yet the Hurricane was to undergo a complete redesign of its wing structure and wing skinning soon after actual production began – a complication often overlooked today.

The Spitfire's precise drag figures represent a spectacular advance on any aircraft then produced, and in light of the near ten-fold increase in power between a Spitfire and a First World War biplane type such as the SE.5A – with all the attendant needs of improved cooling, the reduction in drag, even beyond the benefits that could be expected from a monoplane, are significant. The Spitfire offered, with similar wing surface area, over 55 per cent less overall drag, a massive speed improvement, more armament, greater anti-twist strength and, uniquely due to the ellipse, much lower induced drag, not just of a benchmark biplane fighter but also (minus the armament) of a racing float plane, and crucially less drag than any contemporary fighter.

Like a modern computer-designed, ultimate efficiency jet fighter, the Spitfire truly was at the leading edge of knowledge. Compared with Sydney Camm's excellent but conservative design for the Hurricane, with its fully turbulent boundary layered thick wing, the Spitfire's aerodynamic performance was years ahead. Hawker's tried to catch up of course, but not until the later days of the war did their Tempest and Fury fighters have a thinner wing.

According to figures published in the 1930s,[18] assuming drag at 100ft/sec, the Spitfire's reputed overall drag measured in lb/force, is 62lb, whereas the biplane type SE.5 has 110lb of drag. Even accepting the obvious reductions that stem from removing bracing, this halving of drag was ground breaking. Specific details of Spitfire drag show that, measured in pounds, the profile drag caused by the shape of the airframe is a total of only 33.7lb, with the wings creating 20.3lb and the small tail only generating 7.3lb. The induced drag, that is drag as a by-product of lift creation, is only 2.4lb., with 0.6lb resulting from the 'washout' wing twist, giving a wing induced drag penalty of a mere 3.0lb. Taking every aspect of the Spitfire's drag characteristics into account, the aircraft has a total calculated drag figure in weight, of less than 60lb – an incredibly low figure. Allied to a very low wing loading, and its special surface and filleting features, the Spitfire's aerodynamics package, was unique.

But the crucial drag figure was not the whole story – for the nature and behaviour of that drag was also uniquely altered on the Spitfire by an early attempt at boundary layer control – the tuning of the layer of air close to the surface of an aeroplane skin which due to friction, is moving at a slower speed than the mass of air which is flowing over the aeroplane. This layer of air close to the wing and fuselage is slowed down by friction and interference. Above it, the air translates itself into faster flowing currents. It is within this region close to the aeroplane skin that the so-called boundary layer exists. Its behaviour is crucial to performance – especially upon the wings. The Spitfire deployed some early boundary layer thinking – at Shenstone's behest (see chapter 8).

The Spitfire's *combination* of such design elements – wing, fuselage and tail – were the key to its superior performance and handling. Shenstone's work on the Spitfire's lift distribution, boundary layer and suction control was the key factor, yet one that has remained ignored for decades. These were the factors that made flying the Spitfire feel so different to its pilots.

The Spitfire responded to the merest touch – it was if it knew what you were *thinking* it to do. To fly a Spitfire, the pilot held the control stick with his thumb and forefinger, and made small, almost imperceptible movements of the finger or hand – rarely of the arm. Many pilots flew in thin, soft-soled shoes as opposed to thick flying boots; this was so that they could feel the rudder pedals through their feet. This was how sensitive the Spitfire's controls were; the aircraft responded to the smallest input – very much in the way that a glider responds to minimal stick and pedal input. The Hurricane and the Messerschmitt had to be hauled around the sky. For the Spitfire, this exquisite sensitivity and instantaneous response, stemmed from its aerodynamic design, yet it is a factor, a difference, often unappreciated because so few modern commentators have actually flown a Spitfire, Hurricane or Messerschmitt in comparative analysis.

Most Spitfire observers focus on the curved, knife edged wing tips of the ellipse as the defining, iconic factor, however, the aerodynamic secret of the Spitfire's phenomenal rate of turn – a rate that meant it could turn *faster*, not just tighter in radius, which meant that it could out-turn any other fighter of the day – lay slightly less in those rounded wing tips and more in the factor of wing loading and lift distribution patterns stemming from shape and thinness. The control of lift induced, and other types of drag, was its unique achievement. Many commentators have written about one or other aspects of the Spitfire's elliptical wing shape. Few have tied all the elements together. Shenstone's contribution goes far beyond that which is generally realized, for he did not just suggest that R.J. Mitchell should choose the ellipse, he provided Mitchell with a unique shape that overcame many problems and gave the Spitfire its 'edge'.

Mitchell and Shenstone (a decade younger than his boss), got on well. They were both essentially shy men, yet also men who, once sure of their facts, would stick to their opinions. Both enjoyed sailing on the Itchen and the Solent estuary. Shenstone told others that he found Mitchell, 'Very gregarious – when out of the office'.[19]

Shenstone also had a constructive working relationship with Trevor Westbrook, the factory manager, a man whom Shenstone would later work with again at the Ministry of Aviation Production (MAP). In his early days at Supermarine, working on flying boats, Shenstone had also worked with Jim Weedy – the wing shop foreman, and with Arthur Shirvall. It was Shirvall who as Mitchell's in-house hydrodynamics specialist had contributed so much to the firm's hull and float profiles – learning his trade from the work of Oliver Simmons (who left at the end of 1929) and Ernest Mansbridge in the Schneider Trophy years. Mansbridge became the lead aerodynamicist after Simmons departed, and it would be several years before Shenstone rose to prominence.

Shenstone recorded in his notes that Shirvall contributed to the sculpting of the Spitfire's sculptural detailing and we should note that the Spitfire's tailplane shape closely matches the elliptical tailplane shapes of Supermarine's earlier Schneider Trophy series racers. Shirvall also designed the float hulls for the later 1940s Spitfire float plane – a poignant touch of Schneider Trophy reverse engineering. The team effort honed the shape under Alfred Faddy, the ex-Royal Navy man who lived in nearby Bitterne. Faddy was older than Shenstone. Originally from Newcastle-on-Tyne, he was the drawing office team leader under Joseph Smith and the force behind making the ellipse's engineering, function; his work has also often been overlooked.

It is clear that Mitchell, Smith, Clifton, Faddy, Shenstone, and the team evolved their respective aspects of wing design through hours of close work, principally in 1934–36. Mitchell, and Shenstone made many pencil sketches of curved winged shapes.

A. Faddy, R. Fenner, and W. Fear drew up the early revised Type 224 wing shapes chosen by Shenstone for the ellipse in autumn 1934 – drawing 300000/11[20] suggested as of dating from around the end of October/first week of November 1934, being very relevant as it showed an early ellipse suggestion – soon altered. Faddy was the structures man – suggesting or refining the internal details of the wing's shape and skinning.

There is no doubt that the conceiver, the inventor of the Spitfire, was R.J. Mitchell, and he had the overall decision about what wing shape to use. Mitchell had the Spitfire in his head, but his team made it reality and Shenstone's work, not just on the wing, but the aircraft's aerodynamics, was a significant part of the design process. Again, there were others who deserve to be remembered as the forgotten, associate designers of the Spitfire.

Therefore, however good Shenstone was, he was but a spoke in the greater wheel. Shenstone reported to Alan Clifton in the Technical Office, but from Shenstone's notes, it is clear that they worked closely with the drawing office. The two departments were co-contributors, not separate functions competing against each other – as can be the case. Mitchell's 'team' ethos was clear but he also commanded his team, for example, Mitchell was particularly keen on having a minimal frontal area for his racers and for the Spitfire – he insisted on it.

Shenstone names Alfred Faddy of the drawing office, as a lead player in what he calls the 'engineering department', but he also mentions, Mr R. Fenner, Mr W. Fear. Mr W. Munro, and Mr A. Shirvall, as co-contributors to the shaping of the Spitfire and its details. Ernest Mansbridge and Harold Smith are also cited. Shenstone specifically mentions Harold Smith as a 'very good structures man'[21] and it was Harold Smith who proposed the glider type D nose structural arrangement to R.J. Mitchell for Type 224 and Type 300. Shenstone also cites R.J Fenner as a lead name in the development of the revised Type 224 design that became the Type 300 Spitfire. R.J. Fenner worked with W. Fear, in the drawing office and Fenner said the three men received 'considerable advice'[22] from Shenstone – notably in mid-1934 just after his return from the tour in America with Rex Pierson – the Vickers chief designer.

Over the intervening years since 1934, it has proved difficult to name all the people who were working on the Type 224 and the Type 300 Spitfire. Shenstone's unpublished notes however, contain more name credits than any published book – names that closely match, and expand upon, those first revealed as late as the July 2008 issue of *Aeroplane* magazine in an article by Alfred Faddy's son, David.[23]

For the first time in a published book, the widest list of names so far for the period circa 1934–1936, is herein presented (in alphabetical order); any omissions are entirely accidental and apologies offered for any errors in what is intended as an attempt to more fully credit the Spitfire's people.

Supermarine Technical, Drawing Office, and Management Team Members Circa 1934:

H. Axtell
A. Black
C. Childer
A. Clifton
R. Conley
W. Cox
J. Davis
E. Davis
R.S. Dickson
T. Dixon
J. Eke
W. Elliot
A. Faddy
W. Fear
R. Fenner
H. Griffiths
J. Hammond
J. Harris
Hennesy
H. Holmes
R. Horrocks
Hughes

Houghton
C. Johns
J. Jupp
Kennedy
R. Kember
J. Kettlewell
G. Kimber
Knight
C. Labette
T. Lardman
E. Lovell-Cooper
MacFarlane
 E. Mansbridge
R. Mansfield
H. Miles
W. Munro
W. Musselwhite
H. Noble
J. Rasmussen
J. Rice
R. Rodgers
Pardoe

F. Parry
H. Payn (Major)
K. Scales
R. Schlotel
S. Scott-Hall (Resident
    Tech Officer Air
    Ministry)
B.S. Shenstone
A. Shirvall
Harold Smith
Joseph Smith.
H. Sommer.
T. Walker.
J. Weedy
W. J. Westbrook
M. White
Test pilots: 'Mutt'
    Summers, George
    Pickering, Jeffrey
    Quill.

* * *

R.J. Mitchell's son, Dr Gordon Mitchell, confirmed to the author that Shenstone's role in shaping the Spitfire was 'significant'. Dr Gordon Mitchell also said in his book *RJ Mitchell Schooldays to Spitfire*,[24] that in the designing of the Spitfire, Shenstone played a 'significant role'. Buried in the Appendices to that book we find a reference from Alan Clifton's recollections of working with R.J. Mitchell and these are the words that demonstrate the claim of fact that Shenstone chose the ellipse and suggested it to R.J. Mitchell and then designed its Spitfire application.

Alan Clifton said that the wing shape was proposed by Beverley Shenstone for climb advantages at high altitude. Clifton says that

Shenstone also advocated the thin wing that 'RJ' adopted against the advice of expert theorists of the day.[25] Such words by a leading Mitchell team member illustrate the choice of the Spitfire's ellipse and its Spitfire-specific, thin wing design, to Beverley Shenstone. In the early 1980s, and in subsequent editions, Alfred Price's excellent Spitfire works clearly cite Shenstone, and as late as 2006, the last of Mitchell's men, Harry Griffiths, also told a television documentary that the wing was designed by Beverley Shenstone – giving the first broadcast credit to Shenstone.

In 1941, *The Toronto Star*,[26] named Shenstone as 'associate designer of the Spitfire.' This may have been a touch of Canadian pride at work, but was certainly more accurate than other Canadian media citations[27] of Shenstone as the 'Spitfire co-designer'. To such claims, Shenstone retorted that he was not. However, American aeronautical sources at the time did underline Shenstone's major contribution to the wing design. Perhaps it is fair to say that just as R.J. Mitchell invented the Spitfire but did not design it alone, it could be fair to say that if Shenstone was to be perceived as some form of associate designer to the Spitfire – then so too were certain others deserving of 'associate' status.

However, for the Spitfire, the *wing* was the thing, and the young Canadian suggested it and shaped it. Shenstone worked out the unique aerofoil choices and wing shape, and through calculus, via working out cardinal points, finite sources, equipotential streamlines (analysis of flow behaviours), and stagnation points, he developed the non-standard ellipse. He calculated the deliberate forward swept distortion, solved the plots, cones, airflow pattern, lift distribution, centre of lift, vortices and washout. In blending the NACA 'thin' aerofoils he also had to address the airflow behaviour issues of 'sink' and 'source' within the aerofoils and their joining together. Shenstone worked out the very early boundary layer smooth surface effects and the preservation of the curvilinear lift distribution at the wing fillet and trailing edge. He also worked for a small tail empennage and tailplane – with full support from Mitchell and his men – who had also learned the benefits of such advances.

Evidence to support the claim of Shenstones 'significant' contribution is reinforced by the photograph of the last pages of Shenstone's copy of H. B. Phillips' book on differential mathematical calculus that he kept close at hand from 1927 to 1945. There, on the inside back cover, can be found Beverley Shenstone's, pre-drawing office sketch of a pencil-drawn, hand-created elliptical calculation stemming from a grid and with the necessary modified co-ordinates of cones and points evident and with supporting calculus. At the time, Shenstone's work was unseen and unknown beyond Supermarine. Subsequently, outside Britain, Shenstone's Spitfire work did not go unnoticed. On 2 April 1941, the *Toronto Globe and Mail*, said of Shenstone: 'Mr Shenstone is considered one of the leading airplane designers of the British Empire'.[28]

On 12 April 1941, the Toronto Times wrote:

A former Toronto aerodynamicist is prominent among plane designers smoothing out problems concerned with adding heavier armament to U.S. Combat planes for delivery to Britain. ...It has been ascertained from experts in the industry that Mr Shenstone was responsible for a part of the Spitfire's design that has made England's Spitfire fighter highly successful in its aerodynamic performance.[29]

Shenstone was always modest and cautious about his Spitfire wing design contribution – a claim supported by Dr Alfred Price who questioned Shenstone in 1976.[30] Yet, it is now obvious how advanced young Shenstone's design thinking was, and how brave Mitchell was in 1934 to accept his ideas – the ideas of man a decade younger than R.J. Mitchell himself, but one after several years at Supermarine, who was no longer a 'junior'. Going against the advice of known expert theorists and allowing a twenty-seven-year-old who had thrown out such old theories, to design the aerodynamics of the wing of arguably the most important military aircraft ever to be designed, was perhaps one of Mitchell's greatest acts of humility, self awareness and bravery. This act (and the resultant aircraft) cannot be under estimated. Again, we also have evidence that others were involved in supporting Shenstone's ellipse – one that also relied on Joseph Smith's structural input.

As discussed, it would be wrong to do as the Canadian media did in wartime and call Shenstone the Spitfire's 'co-designer' in the *singular* context. For the Spitfire was a team effort, Shenstone always said so, and we know from his own private notes that Shenstone disliked the erroneous 'co-designer' label. Shenstone credits Mitchell with the Spitfire and also credits the team with the Spitfire's design entity – a team he was an early member of. And a team in which his position became more significant over the course of several years. Mitchell was in his early forties when he died; several of his team, including Shenstone, were around thirty years old when the Spitfire was designed. These were not men aged in their fifties, with 'set' minds and narrow thinking, constrained by years of learning old ways of doing things in a post-Victorian psychology.

But what Shenstone *did* do, was to add precise knowledge gained through hours of analytical scientific research to Mitchell's idea. The detailed scientific facts presented herein, surely prove that, at a relatively young age, Shenstone's brilliance was a significant contribution to the winged icon of aerial combat that was the Spitfire.

Shenstone's diary recites the thoughts of an observer when he first saw the Spitfire prototype and its ultra-thin, elliptical wing:

'That wingtip! Just look at it, it's much too sharp and thin.'[31]

The brilliant mind that was Mitchell, son of a school master, and who came from working or middle-class roots, a man who had worked with railway engineers, was unconstrained by upper class establishment conceits, went with the young Canadian's ideas.

Alan Clifton's notes also undermine the claims made by some that Mitchell would not have been told what to do by Shenstone as the younger man. Shenstone did not tell Mitchell what to do, but he did persuade Mitchell to use the ellipse – modified into Shenstone's version of the ellipse – which contained an amalgamation of all that he had learned and seen. Added to that mix, complementing it, was all that Mitchell and his men had learned from flying boats and monoplane Schneider Trophy racers – notably the need for sculpted, smooth bodywork, and thinner wings. The lessons of the S.4, S.5, S.6/B and the failed Type 224 were part of the design process to which Shenstone contributed. Mitchell had first experimented with a true ellipse for the wing of his six-engined flying boat in late 1929, and although not an aerodynamicist, had discovered for himself the importance of smooth skinning, a small frontal area, a small tail, and the importance of tuned aileron design.

At this moment in history, all the coincidences and certainties of chance happenings, all the lessons and all the events, amalgamated, in a recipe that put these men and their respective learning, together, to produce perhaps what is the ultimate single-engined propeller aeroplane design of all time.

For the modification of the F.7/34 Type 224 and its emergence as the modified specification F.37/34 or Type 300 'Spitfire', Alfred Faddy was clearly of significance and his work with Joe Smith, on the Spitfire's main spar within the modified ellipse, rarely gets the praise it is due. By creating an internal wing structure that was forward chord biased, within the forward swept, modified ellipse planform, the drawing office men achieved maximum structural strength for the spar as it was mounted at right angles to the main centre structure and was optimised to reduce wing twisting under load. This process was assisted in the wing design in the drawing office by R.J. Fenner, H. Axtell, W. Fear, J. Harris, J. Jupp, and G. Kettlewell. Joseph Smith (later Supermarine chief designer) oversaw this internal wing structure design and Shenstone always recorded the contribution of Smith's work in such a confined aerofoil shape.

Type 224, with its steam cooling, had needed a D nose forward wing spar to accommodate this function, but carrying over the forward spar idea to the Type 300 Spitfire also reflected glider design techniques where a very strong forward spar imparted good strength and anti-twist characteristics – enhanced by the Spitfire's leaf – spring type, main spar contribution. Adding a load-bearing stressed skin to the Type 300 further improved its overall strength. In total, the Spitfire had everything the Supermarine team, could throw at it: as such it was not a copy of anything.

In his private notes, Shenstone makes his admiration for Mitchell, his character and his work, very clear. Shenstone wrote of Mitchell and the Spitfire:

> It needed the genius of Mitchell to visualise – without precise knowledge – what had to be done to reach out into the unknown for something nearer to perfection than any other man had been able to reach. And we, who were involved, were inspired and suitably grateful for the unique opportunity to reach out without over-reaching.[32]

So Mitchell had the vision, but there was a small team of men at Supermarine who helped Mitchell take his legendary aircraft from sketch to physical reality. Over the years 1934–1936 the Spitfire, was perfected. Over 300,000 hours of work went into honing the design but the result in scientific, pure aerodynamic terms, was far more advanced than was obvious, or has been widely recognized.

How wedded to the ellipse was Mitchell? His initial reaction was the famous Mitchell statement that Shenstone repeated to all comers: 'Mitchell said, I don't give a b_____ whether it is elliptical or not, so long as it covers the guns.'[33]

After the Type 244 debacle and with the sound but staid Hurricane as competition, Mitchell knew he needed something special to win the Air Ministry contract for the new fighter. Mitchell's mind was open, and searching. However practical he was, it is obvious that Mitchell cared what this, his most vital of aircraft, looked like. The design and decoration of the Supermarine Schneider Trophy racing aircraft surely proved that Mitchell did care to some extent about aesthetics. And after all, if an aeroplane *looked* right, it *flew* right. Mitchell would have one chance at the new fighter specification, everything had to be right, no gambles, no hunches were acceptable – everything had to be calculated to work.

There is no suggestion that Mitchell was not aware of the elliptical wing shape, but there have been suggestions that his Spitfire copied the elliptical wing from the Heinkel 70 (He 70). This can be debunked if the facts are properly researched (see Chapter 11). The ellipse was neither introduced by, nor unique to, the Heinkel 70 – which unlike the Spitfire, used a basic symmetrical ellipse and retained a gull wing design. Neither was the Heinkel new, nor 'unveiled' in 1934 at the Paris Air Show, as some Spitfire commentators have claimed. The Heinkel 70's first flight was on 1 December 1932,[34] its first Paris Show in 1933. It took its major design features from a previous aircraft by the same designers – the Bäumer Sausewind of 1925 and, the later Heinkel He 64 of 1931. The He 70 was also very much a work in progress and its fuselage, canopy and nose shapes were changed and significantly altered between 1932 and 1936 across numerous variants, from the He 70 A to the He 70 G: these changes significantly affected its aerodynamics and its weight and wing loading.

Supermarine's modified ellipse was a different shape and was far more exotic, far more scientifically advanced – *it* was unique and went back into early aeronautics to gain its advantage.

Mitchell's racing float planes – notably the S.4. – had already hinted at the thin winged, elliptical form and his 1929 still-born six-engined flying boat to specification 20 /28 had an elliptical wing. In 1927, the Shorts-Bristow Crusader float plane designed by W.G. Carter of Glosters under the supervision of a Colonel W. A Bristow for the Schneider Trophy contest featured a broad bladed, fully elliptical wing with a recessed trailing root edge (a feature later perhaps aped by the Heinkel 70 and specifically the Heinkel 111).

Of even more interest, yet uncited by most Spitfire commentators, was the stunningly advanced design of the 1929, Italian, Piaggio Pegna P.C. 7 – a special design for the Schneider Trophy contest of that year. Designed by Giovanni Pegna for the Piaggio company, the P.C. 7 was a revolutionary low drag hydrofoil aircraft without traditional floats. Its design was unique in that its fuselage or hull rested within the water – rising up on elliptical hydrofoils as a rear-mounted propeller powered it out of the water – whereupon a front-mounted engine would engage a propeller for flight. Despite the fact that this aircraft only achieved water trials and never flew in the Schneider contest, it brought to the aeronautical world's attention one other important, revolutionary feature – a stylish, pointed tipped, symmetrical elliptical wing.

Here in 1929, in front of an international audience, was a sharp, ellipsoid wing that was even more 'pure' in geometric terms than the elliptical wing of the Shorts-Bristow Crusader or the Bäumer Sausewind

– that 1925 German ellipsoid monoplane that had inspired its designers into latterly shaping the Heinkel He 70 in 1932. The Piaggio's design caused a sensation at the same time that German and British designers were exploring the ellipse.

Long before that, from the 1870s onwards, Lilienthal had made gliders with parabolic, semi ellipsoid wings, and in 1876, the French designer Alphonse Pénaud produced one of the most stunningly advanced all-wing designs – one that featured a modified elliptical wing shape.

After study from 1880 to 1920 into the benefits of the ellipse by Zhukovskii (Joukowski), Frederick Lanchester, and Hugo Junkers, the elliptical shape was back at the centre of research.

The young Shenstone, with his fascination for boats and flying boats, had a keen interest in hydrofoil design and was soon to publish articles discussing the work of hydrofoil pioneers such as Guidoni, Forlanini, Crocco, Pegna, and Tietjens. Shenstone's area of focus was upon the efficiency of hydrofoils through their shape and boundary layer behaviour. The first winglets were seen on hydrofoil designs in the 1920s, and Shenstone was particularly interested in solving the problem of hydrodynamic cavitation – the destruction of the lift effect by the recirculation of water at very high speed over the lifting surface – where the water effectively 'boils'.

In 1930–1931, Shenstone had also discussed hydrofoil designs and wave-skimming aircraft ideas with another proponent of their benefits – Alexander Lippisch. By the time Shenstone arrived at the home of racing float plane design at Supermarine in Southampton, there was much international research into the ellipse, which both Shenstone, and Supermarine were fascinated by. Shenstone's hydrofoil enthusiasm may well have helped secure him Mitchell's consideration. Shenstone also worked on advanced, powered-sail theories and created an idea for set of elliptical sails that, correctly set and masted, could create a natural wind power unit for large ships. This idea was to be highlighted again in the 1980s using modern technology, but young Shenstone was working on it in the 1930s.

In France, Dewoitine had produced the D.513 (latterly the D.520) – an elliptical winged aircraft with elliptical tail surfaces, yet with a poor drag coefficient of CD 0.30. And in America, Seversky and Douglas were readying ellipsoid winged airframes for mass production. Even the DC-3 was soon to deploy ellipsoid wing tips and a wing to fuselage fillet as additions to its DC-2 foundations. De Havilland had used an elliptical tail on its biplane DH Moth types and also used an elliptical tail and wing tip taper on the DH.86. The de Havilland Albatross airliner used a fully ellipsoid fuselage, elliptical tail fins and a heavily tapered wing.

It becomes obvious that by the year of the Spitfire's first flight in 1936, the ellipse was in far wider circulation than some Spitfire commentators with their theories of Heinkel 70 influence have revealed (see chapter 11).

In the Second World War the Seversky-influenced American P-47 Thunderbolt fighter used an elliptical wing to great effect, and the Russians produced the Lavochkin La-7 elliptical fighter. The Japanese produced the Aichi D3A1 'Val' and the Italians made the Caproni CR 2000 – both ellipsoid. In 1938 the American air racer Keith Rider, who had produced a series of smooth-lined racing monoplanes, produced an elliptically winged racing machine – the R6 'Eightball'. This looked for all the world like a modified version of a Miles Sparrowhawk (one of which had been sold to America...). Of great note, the R6 featured the addition of an elliptical wing – a forward swept, distorted ellipse that was nearly identical in planform to the earlier Spitfire. Still in America, by 1941, Lockheed's first jet prototype, the L-133, was also fully elliptical and perhaps had subtle shades of the Piaggio Pegna PC.7 design. Heinkel used a modified, forward swept ellipsoid wing on his later jet fighter design, the He 176, and again on his He 280 twin-engined jet fighter – surely a recognition that Supermarine's pioneering modified ellipse was far beyond the basic ellipse.

Such realities dismiss recent claims that the ellipse never caught on and was a fad, or unproven and unrepeated.

Similarly, the German gliders of 1928–1936 with their ellipsoid wings and advanced fuselage fillets, were a major factor in the ellipse's acceptance; the research behind them was soon seized on in America where it was published as a series of NACA technical memorandums. However, as early as late 1927, the Shorts Bristow Crusader was proving that the ellipse was being investigated in Britain as well.

There had also been that pretty little German wooden aircraft of late 1925 – the Paul Bäumer / Walter Günter-designed Sausewind ('Rushing Wind') with beautiful, polished elliptical wings. This, via the elliptically tailed Heinkel He 64, gave birth in late 1932 to the near-identical Heinkel 70, and as stated, some have since focused on that aircraft as an alleged basis of the Spitfire's wing. Given that the He 70 itself was a direct Bäumer Sausewind 'copy' and that the He 64 had been a stepping stone in design terms with its smooth skin and elliptical tail surfaces, and that the ellipse was the centre of international development, the suggestion that the Spitfire copied or cribbed the mail plane Heinkel 70's wing is self evidently in error, not least as the Spitfire's distorted or modified ellipse was unique and very different from the Heinkel's gull winged, more symmetric ellipse. The He 70 was a late addition to the study and use of the ellipse – not the new or incredible design of 1934 touted the by ill-informed commentators of today – even if its entire body was smoothed over with layer upon layer of filler and paint in a perhaps 'new' manner.

The fast He 64, designed to compete in a 1931 European air race and to provide a basis for a sleek high speed, touring aircraft, was a stunning design with the input of the Günter brothers, and with Karl Schwärzler as chief engineer. This very fast aircraft was the subject of NACA Memorandum No. 175, and had a wing loading of 11.8lb/sq ft, leading edge Lachmann-type slots, and a speed range equal to then current racing aircraft. This was achieved through elliptical tail shapes, a smooth body and very careful detail design. It was a real coupé of an aircraft and a German-registered example, D-2205, was purchased in 1932 by Handley Page and fitted with a Gypsy Major engine, prior to being bought by the Air Ministry in late 1935 as K3596.

So the He 64 – reflecting some Bäumer Sausewind ancestry – was clearly a significant aircraft employing ellipsoid and smooth surfaced design, and both it and the Sausewind created the He 70, which by default of these facts, cannot therefore be called new, incredible or revolutionary nor of have having influence on the Spitfire from being cited as such. The He 70 was fast – but so too were the He 64 and the Sausewind.

Shenstone's uniquely modified ellipse reached much further back than the Bäumer Sausewind, the He 64 and the He 70.

Above all, it was making the ellipse work on a *fighter* to fly at over 20,000ft and 450mph, making it justify its use, and trying to use it with a thin aerofoil on a high-speed fighter, that was Shenstone's part in Mitchell using it, and, modifying it for use on the Spitfire. Clearly the Spitfire wing was indeed very different from the Heinkel, even if the layman saw the elliptical shape and jumped to erroneous, perhaps even defamatory conclusions.

The Spitfire needed speed and, vitally, falcon-like manoeuvrability. It also needed to house retractable wheels and an array of armament. Above all, as envisaged by Mitchell, it needed to climb fast and have a wing that worked in the thin air of high altitude combat circa 15,000–25,000 feet – the new post biplane era, fighting height. As such the wing was going to have to perform a very different task to that of the low-level flight envelope of the Schneider Trophy aircraft where Mitchell had learned his stuff. New thinking was needed and new thinking was what Beverley

Shenstone, however young he may have been, offered. Who else amongst the designers had witnessed and worked within Junkers and been part of Alexander Lippisch's design team researching into the outer reaches of the unknown – the all-wing and delta wing? No one was obvious – except the young Canadian, Shenstone. Did not Mitchell's own letter offering employment effectively admit that Shenstone had knowledge that Mitchell wanted? Had not Chamier grabbed Shenstone before someone else did?

The issues of wing loading, span wise flow, lift distribution, twist or 'washout', stall and spin characteristics, aerofoil thinness, aileron flutter, and structural loading all had to be solved for the development of the Spitfire's ellipse. Of particular note was the requirement to tune the ellipse's span wise flow and to solve the tip stalling issue for which it was known. But the ellipse had the lowest induced drag: that is why it was chosen. By 1934, Shenstone had even published a paper dealing with the efficiencies of adding twist and other techniques to the the non-elliptical, tapered wing – the ellipse's rival – as seen on the Bf109 and the Hurricane. Given this knowledge, the choice of the more complicated ellipse was not taken lightly; the secret lay in its modification from its basic shape.

How Shenstone managed that feat had its roots in the totality of his training in Canada under Professor Parkin, and his time in Germany allied to his own natural talent. And what about all those years carving the sculptures that were his model boat hulls? Had those moments contributed to Shenstone's thinking? Of relevance to that possibility, Shenstone privately wrote of the Spitfire:

> The fuselage was an entity, a sweet set of lines faired like a ship's hull from stem to stern.[35]

So maybe the influence of his boat building youth *was* an inspiration for him, and through flying boats for Mitchell. Clearly Shenstone saw a link between the Spitfire's shape, its hull, and boats. Boats were a Shenstone passion that stemmed from the float plane and flying boats that had been the focus of his postgraduate work with Professor Parkin in Toronto and from a boat building childhood. R.J. Mitchell and his men were also immersed in boats, floats, and flying boats – this team of designers and detail shapers must surely have all shared the same intuitive design skills and factual learning to jointly create the Spitfire's elegant hull.

But, for the essential Spitfire, the big question had to be, why the ellipse? According to Shenstone it supplied the perfect theoretical form, and he wrote:

> The elliptical wing gave us what we wanted – the lowest possible wing

aerofoil thickness to chord ratio allied to the lowest induced drag.[36]

Few Spitfire historians have gone beyond this quote to explain its basis or what it really means in depth. Some even claim that a tapered wing with washout was within a few per cent of the Spitfire's wing performance – yet fail to frame the ellipse's broader advantages. To truly understand the Spitfire's wing, surely we need to do look in depth at the how of the ellipse, allied to the why.

Firstly, we need to know all about the ancient art of the ellipse.

6

The Mystical Ellipse

The geometric form of the ellipse was not new, it had been around for a very long time and is part of both ancient and sacred geometry. As a wing planform, the ellipse had a long history prior to the 1930s – as also had the all-wing or tailless design concept with its roots in nature that was the curved and near-ellipsoid shape of the Zanonia Macrocarpa seed.[1] Other applications in nature's arsenal also saw elliptical wing shapes applied to a host of flying seeds, insect wings, and birds.

Early records depict Chinese kites with ellipsoid wing sections, and the form of the ellipse was first studied by Menaechmus and even Euclid the ancient philosopher cited a cone-shaped, pointed geometric form that was the origin of the shape. Apollonius is said to have created the name 'ellipse' (Greek ἔλλειψις *elleipsis*) for the shape that we know today. Pythagoras also investigated the geometric ellipse. Ancient Mayan records not only show renditions of elliptically winged flying machines, they also depict perfect delta winged aircraft. These have recently been constructed in model form and successfully flown.

Around 2000 BC the ancient Egyptians made carvings in wood, and renderings in art, of elliptically winged flying machines. For the Egyptians, knowledge of the ellipse stemmed from their study and use of the geometric ellipse, the vesica piscis, used in calculating the Pyramids' construction. The ellipse and the science of the numbers behind its conic points lie at the heart of ancient geodesy and metrology. Archytas of Tarentum, a Greek mathematician of 400 BC is also reputed to have investigated the ellipse as a wing, in model form. Eratosthenes, the third century Greek who was keeper of the Library of Alexandria, also realized that the earth itself was not a sphere but a distorted curved shape, which he claimed to have measured. Here began the science of using polar co-ordinates and plotted points – essentials of the ellipse. And what of Australia's indigenous Aborigines with their boomerang, which was often elliptical, and whatever the carved shape of its all-wing planform followed an elliptical trajectory?

In the 1480s, Leonardo da Vinci concentrated on flying machines in his design work and the ellipse clearly made its mark – his studies noted that the dragonfly and flying fish used elliptically shaped wings to achieve their natural aerodynamic efficiency. The parabolic oval or ellipsoid shape was also cited by Kepler in 1600 and, in 1705 Halley said that the comet that was to latterly bear his name followed an elliptical orbital track. Across millennia, the ellipse took on mystical qualities, from stone circles to astrology, to pure mathematics, and onwards to sails and wings, the ellipse offered properties that were unusual.

The Middle Ages also saw furtherance of ancient Chinese rocket experiments. In the 1530s, Conrad Hass proposed triangular fin shapes in a work on rocket technology and, in the seventeenth century, the Polish-Lithuanian engineer Kazimierz Siemienowicz had recorded his thoughts on swept delta-type wings.

In the seventeenth century the English mathematician John Wallis worked on the development of infinitesimal calculus, and produced a work on the integration and length of the ellipse in 1659. The separate fields of elliptical integrals and, elliptical functions, were Wallis's fascination. The true study of the properties of the ellipse stemmed from Wallis's work in the Middle Ages: Isaac Newton also studied the ellipse, as did the aerodynamic future vision of Jacob Bernoulli in 1679. Bernoulli advanced the art of elliptical calculus and authored the lemniscate elliptic integral methodology.

The calculus of the curve even touched Einstein who, after consulting the famed theorist Hermann Minkowski sought to express the forces of nature through geometric calculus. Einstein's principal theory of relativity relies upon the curve of space to attain its basis. Previous ideas were to be found in the nineteenth century mathematical works of Carl Gauss who framed the idea of multi-dimensional calculus and Hermann Riemann who developed mathematical tools for calculating curved areas which transformed Newton's laws into expression via geodesic movement. Within this mathematical world of curved expression via numbers, lay the geometry of the ellipse, and also the gateway to research into gravity, anti-gravity, and beyond. The ellipse even appears as the hyperbolic node point within the distribution of matter in logarithmic scales. From wing design to gravity, fusion, and the mathematical beyond, the curved, ellipsoid, hyperbola is a fundamental element of science that has been studied for centuries.

Further mathematical research into the quantification of the ellipse's lower induced drag and smoother wake vortex, came from the work of the German Erich Trefftz (1888–1937). He created a method of assessing numerical variations and transformations taken from calculations based on measuring induced drag effects *behind* a wing rather than *upon* a wing. His work was an early precursor of the later finite element techniques now so common. He also worked on glider design and elliptical wing planforms in the late 1920s German gliding design revolution and his theories were used by the Akaflieg Darmstadt design group.

But what was the ellipse? If a circle is consistent – or 'concentric' – then an ellipse is 'eccentric' in its deviation from a norm, and this deviation from the circular norm can be measured, yet is most obvious in the form of the parabola and the compound curves that can spring from it. Without entering into the precise details of cardinal calculus, involute, evolute, caustic and pedal curves amid cartesian equations and formulae – all the very stuff of the ellipse – it is important to know that the ellipse, a mystical offshoot of the circle or sphere, has fascinated man. Its properties seem to have entranced mathematicians and designers throughout history.

As early as 1804 Sir George Cayley was building curved wing sectioned, parabolic kites and gliders, and as late as 1915 physicists and mathematicians were striving to create further calculus for the curves of the ellipse.

In 1876, Frenchman Alphonse Pénaud proposed an elliptically shaped all-wing machine. This flying wing craft had an elliptical wing that had a straighter leading edge and a more curved trailing edge. Pénaud's machine also had a glass domed cockpit canopy and retractable undercarriage. It was incredible, and may well be the genesis of the elliptical fashion. Pénaud 's design, long forgotten now, was remarkable in the way that its geometry blended the quarters of the ellipse into a flying wing and used an early form of elevon control surface. Nine years earlier, Pénaud had also designed an aircraft which he created a model of – it had a sharp elliptical wing with curved, low angle winglets – a remarkable accurate precursor of today's aerodynamic developments.

In 1879, Victor Tatin produced an aircraft that made a successful test flight – it had two wing-mounted propellers powered through a compressed air power supply. Of note, Tatin's design had wings that were nearly ellipsoid and a combined tailplane that was a blend of parabolic curves.

In nature we find an interesting combination of both the all-wing tailless design and the curve in the form of the crescent-shaped Zanonia seed and its near ellipsoid planform.

The astounding stability of the glide qualities and aerodynamic performance of the Zanonia seed were studied in great depth in Germany by Professor Friedrich Ahlborn (1858–1937) who published his paper *Uber die Stabilitat der Drachenflieger* (About the Stability of Dragonflies) in 1897. Ahlborn had studied zoology and went on to study aerodynamics and hydrodynamics. The academic aerodynamic community seized upon his discussion of the aerodynamic performance of the small Zanonia seed. Ahlborn was not alone in having visited the Far East at this time to study biology, however it was Ahlborn who researched the Zanonia seed in great detail. Of particular note was the all-wing, curved shape and its incredibly accurate, built-in wing twist or 'washout' across the wingspan – creating the amazing stability of a flying form that had neither fuselage nor tail – as conventional 'perceived wisdom' would later decide was essential for man's flight…

Lilienthal, Etrich and Wels, were the names of early German designers who took on board Ahlborn's observations, to great effect. Ahlborn had also created the idea of extending the seed's wingspan by adding a parallel centre wing section and distorting the crescent shape; as such he effectively created the flying wing concept and mimicked the ellipsoid form.

Ahlborn's research work was noted in Britain and is referenced at the Royal Aeronautical Society (RAeS). J.W. Dunne (1875–1949) – a leading figure of British flying wing work noted Ahlborn's swept wing, tailless design work in his paper to the RAeS, entitled 'The Theory of the Dunne Aeroplane', in 1913. The designs of Jose Weiss (1859–1919) in England also partly resembled Ahlborn's Zanonia-inspired creations, but were claimed to have been arrived at independently.[2]

The all-wing theory and the ellipse were, even as far back as 1900, linked.

In 1867 the British designers J.W. Butler and E. Edward patented an ellipsoid delta-type wing shape. Otto Lilienthal in Germany had also based his monoplane glider designs on the curved design principle – with a suggestion of all-wing theory thrown in via Ahlborn and his Zanonia studies. Percy Pilcher, the Scottish hang glider designer, also used the parabolic wing and his *Hawk* glider – in which he was killed in 1899. Glauert in England, with his fundamentals of aerodynamic design, also studied the ellipse, as did one of the key figures in elliptical research, Frederick Lanchester, whose work on lifting line theory and the concept of a trailing vortex wake was an essential of the early art of aerodynamics.

In early 1894, Lanchester build a series of large, flying models with sharp, thin-section elliptical planforms. He called these 'Aerodrone' models. Of significance to the Spitfire and Shenstone's 1934 work,

Lanchester also built in wing twist or 'washout' to these elliptical wings. In June and July 1894, he successfully flight-tested the models and proved to himself his elliptical development theories – the models flew long and stable test flights of up to 290 yards in less than ideal winds. Later testing at Gottingen in 1913 revealed a lift /drag ratio of 17, which was an improvement on the then best score of 15. Lanchester's work was published in his aerodynamics research book, *Aerodonetics*, a follow-up to his earlier book *Aerodynamics: constituting the first volume of a complete work on aerial flight* (Constable and Co., London 1908), which provided an early basis of elliptical research.

Jose Weiss was the Frenchman from Alsace who came to live in England in 1870 where he settled in Sussex and produced oil paintings of the English landscape to earn a living. But within a decade he was designing and building parabolic and ellipsoid all-wing tailless gliders. Eric Gordon England flew a Weiss glider for a 58-second flight in 1909 and this remained a record until after the First World War. Weiss's prophetic machines, gliders and powered, were elegant and aerodynamically sound – many were curved, all-wing machines.

The elliptical wing and the all-wing theory were also joined together to form a successful flying craft in 1906 by the forgotten but influential Danish designer Jacob Christian Ellehammer of Lindholm Island. The Danes also claim that Ellehammer was the first man to fly a powered aircraft in Europe. In 1912 he also invented a form of helicopter with an early form of cyclic control, but it is for his stunning ellipsoid all-wing design that he may be cited as another forgotten design pioneer.

Just like Blériot's machine, the early elliptical designs were mostly, monoplanes, yet thanks to design choices and technical fashion trends, it was the square-shaped and square-rigged biplane design that claimed the rights to the art of powered flight through the efforts of the Wright brothers – no doubt influenced by the works of Octave Chanute who abandoned the parabolic wing and established the trend for square, box-kite type biplane design. Some argue that this square-winged biplane choice, set aeronautical development backwards from the potential of the monoplane and the drag-reducing potential of curves: streamlining had to wait it seems, despite the later efforts of many – notably Henri Coanda from France.

Despite wonderful design moments with aircraft such as the curved and streamlined Bristol Monoplane of 1916, the 1911 Morane-Saulnier, and the Deperdussin racing monoplane of 1913, which set a dozen world speed records and flew at 124 mph in 1913, the monoplane and the parabolic or elliptical wing shape, were overshadowed, as perceived wisdom clamped its blinkers upon aircraft design for decades. Dutchman Anthony H.G. Fokker did, however, stay almost faithful to the monoplane – a certain tri-plane, notwithstanding…

More widely, the monoplane, the all-wing, and the ellipse would make a comeback. And Hugo Junkers would spearhead the revival of the monoplane. Lippisch, the Horten brothers, and others would soon build upon the all-wing theory, and they and others would also use the ellipse. By 1910, Junkers had investigated the lifting qualities of ellipsoid shapes during experiments with the effect of an elliptical form upon the flow of water. Hydrodynamic studies, the roots of aerodynamic studies in terms of flow analysis, revealed that the ellipse had beneficial properties of smooth lift distribution and low induced turbulence.

The short jump from fluid flow to air flow around the ellipse was best grasped by Nikolai Egorovich Zhukovskii – known in the West as, Joukowski or Joukowsky. He was born in 1847 and died in 1921 and became a founding father of Russian hydrodynamic and aerodynamic studies – notably beginning with his work on stability of motion, and peaking with his work on what was, in effect, the boundary layer of airflow, and behaviour close to the skin of a body, wing or fuselage. Zhukovskii also taught Tupolev, perhaps the greatest of the Russian designers. Zhukovskii also pioneered research into underwater shock waves and dam wall construction, long before the 'bouncing bomb'.

In 1890 Zhukovskii started experiments with the effects of the concentric shape of a disc in fluid and in airflow and soon moved on to study the eccentric shapes of the oval and the ellipse. He also travelled to Germany to visit Otto Lilienthal and returned to Russia with one of Lilienthal's curved-winged gliders. Associated with the work of German mathematician, Martin Wilhelm Kutta, Zhukovskii delivered his method for calculating the mathematical expression of lift over an aerofoil – today known as the Kutta-Joukowski theorem. Kutta had published his views in 1902 and he and Zhukovskii reached the agreement that led to a joint citation of their aerofoil and theories. Kutta, who spent a year in England at the University of Cambridge, also went on to study John Wallis's work and to pursue the aerodynamic ellipse from a German perspective.

From around 1900 to just before his death in 1920, Zhukovskii made an intense study into airflow behaviour, notably in ellipsoid wing shapes and blended wing-fuselages. His work on conformal mapping, and displacement of the circle led to the transformational formula. This was world class, pioneering work that placed Zhukovskii and the Moscow

Technical School at the forefront of aerofoil research. In fact, it allowed the Moscow institute to offer the world's first course in aeronautics. Zhukovskii's work resulted in a theory of airflow study that was called the Zhukovskii transformation – a means of designing aerofoils.

In those early years of the twentieth century, Zhukovskii drew what he thought would be a wing and fuselage shape that would represent the lowest form of both induced and parasitic drag. He drew an elliptical wing that seamlessly joined itself into an elliptical fuselage; the shape featured a wing trailing edge that curved into the fuselage boom and, of greatest significance, the wing's upper skin surface had a concave filled-in 'fillet' panel to extend the curvilinear shape of the wing and its lift pattern gently into the fuselage join – curing the normal fuselage's 'interference' effect. This was the first true, wing to fuselage fillet.

As can be seen from the accompanying drawing, this flying fish-like, elliptical form shape, Zhukovskii section number 747, dated pre-1920, provides us with a defining aerodynamic reference point for the ellipse: it also, almost manages to incorporate a wing to fuselage interference drag reduction theory of preserving curvilinear lift distribution, and it is clearly a possible moment of inspiration for subsequent designs of the later decades. Shenstone certainly cites Zhukovskii as a point of inspiration long before he turned up in Germany or at Supermarine.[3]

On a parallel track, the next major steps in the development of the all-wing and tailless design theories were to take place in Germany at the Wasserkuppe gliding centre. Gottlob Espenlaub, Friedrich Wenk, and Alexander Lippisch were to be leading figures in the art of all-wing and tailless design: Lippisch moved from the inspiration of the Zanonia seed, to the flying triangle – the delta shape.

There, the all-wing, the crescent shape and the ellipse, all came together.

A near all-wing design with a Zhukovskii style, wing to fuselage fillet, emerged in Britain in 1923, as the Westland Dreadnought – designed by the Russian M. Woyevodsky. The British Westland company had come to embrace the all-wing theory through its connections with the designer Geoffrey T.R. Hill (1895–1955). Hill and his brother Roderick, designed and build their own glider in 1913. After being apprenticed at the Royal Aircraft Factory at Farnborough, Geoffrey Hill served as a pilot in the First World War. He returned to the field of design and returned to Farnborough and the Royal Aircraft Establishment. Hill worked for Handley Page and continued his interest in glider design. He then went to work for the Westland company and began his studies into aircraft safety and stability, which led him to his own interpretation of the all-wing theory and resulted in his Pterodactyl designs. He teamed up with many leading figures in gliding and flying wing work – Robert Kronfeld being his test pilot. Like Lippisch, Hill was also to touch the career of Beverley Shenstone and during the Second World War both men worked for the Air Ministry and the MAP, with Geoffery Hill even turning up at the Canadian National Research Council in its all-wing aircraft project development under the direction of no less a Shenstone link than a certain, Professor John Parkin.[4] The de Havilland company also produced the elegant Albatross airliner in the 1930s, which was elliptical in fuselage shape as well as wing sand fin surfaces. The famous engineer Stanley Hooker[5] also made a study of the effects of the ellipse on hydrodynamic flow in his early career. The ellipse was more than just a fad.

The hidden history of the all-wing and the ellipse, both singularly and in combination, and their theories of lift low drag, and stability, remain a significant part of aeronautical heritage. Clearly, the ellipse has a long history of aeronautical study reaching back far beyond the late 1920s and early 1930s. And it was not just in the air that the ellipse was studied.

For the effectiveness of the ellipse was also noted by sailors – large sailing ships used sails with elliptically shaped trailing edges – they provided powerful, smooth suction and when arrayed in a staggered formation acted rather like slots or flaps – increasing local airflow velocity and therefore concentrating their effect. The key to efficient sail design lay in curvature, tension, angle, centre of pressure. For many centuries, the extra power of the elliptically shaped sail had been known. The fastest sailing boats, notably the large tea-clippers, also had elliptical hull shapes – as the shape was found to be the fastest due it producing less turbulence.

What has the Eiffel Tower got to do with the Spitfire? The answer, beyond the concave ellipsoid shapes of its vertical design, was that its designer, Gustave Eiffel, pioneered wind tunnel work on sails and wings and had noted the enhanced dynamics of parabolic/ellipsoid forms.

Elliptical sails have a different function – a differing lift/polar ratio – than an elliptical wing, but one nonetheless that offers significant aerodynamic advantages,

As a young sailor and student hull designer, Beverley Shenstone had already encountered sail power and was soon to investigate the possibilities of creating a sail-based power unit design for large boats. As early as 1934, he and Stewart Scott-Hall founded the Hamble Yacht Club Design Research Group and, as late as the 1960s, Shenstone was cited by the University of Southampton and its committee on yacht design research. Seventy-five years after Shenstone's elliptical research work, an

Australian design company launched a Spitfire-inspired elliptically hulled catamaran with elliptical sails, and one of the world's leading surfboard designers created an ellipsoid surf board with an elliptical keel fin. The ellipse has assisted architects in producing aerodynamic skyscrapers with bowed surfaces to cheat the wind.

Car makers have also explored the ellipse's qualities, notably Jaguar aerodynamicist Malcolm Sayer in the E Type and XJS. Citroen used an ellipsoid rear windscreen on its cars to tune the wake vortex behind the car. Ellipsoid curves and fillet panels were also used extensively by the designers of the streamlining movement of the 1930s, notably Nigel Gresley in his A4 Pacific Class stream locomotives of the late 1930s. The Peugeot 802 prototype car of 1936, engineered by Jean Andreau, deployed elliptical curves to reduce drag. These manifested in the Peugeot 402 saloon and convertible, inspired perhaps by the American Chrysler Airflow, which also deployed ellipsoid sculpting. Perhaps Guiseppi Figoni, Georges Paulin and Sixten Sason were the Art Deco leaders in the use of the ellipse in car design. The Swede Sixten Sason designed the Saab 92 in 1946 and it was full of elliptical themes developed from Sason's training as a pilot and Saab aircraft designer and draughtsman. Jaguar's Malcolm Sayer had also worked for the Bristol aircraft company in the 1940s and he transferred elliptical knowledge to car design. More recently, the famed designer Luigi Colani has extensively deployed parabolic and ellipsoid shapes in his industrial design portfolio – one often inspired by nature.

As Gustave Eiffel knew, the ellipse has also been shown to have structural benefits – it avoids the concentration of stress in a radius and like its lift qualities, ensures a more even spread of forces across its shape. This was why the Vickers Viscount used elliptical apertures for its doors and windows – to avoid stress concentrations and resulting cracks. The origins of the NACA duct – the very low drag NACA-designed, intake vent for aircraft (later seen on racing cars) – traces its origins in the qualities of the ellipse, as did many aero engine intakes, notably the ellipsoid air inlet mouths seen on the Handley Page Victor crescent-winged bomber aircraft. An ellipsoid light aircraft, the composite built Twister, featuring an elliptical wing, has been launched in recent years, as has a recreation of the Spitfire itself – the Mk 26B from Australia. In 2010, the re-born Junkers company in Germany launched an elliptically winged glider.

Far from being a 1930s fad, the ellipse and its properties go back thousands of years and remain of fascination to this day. This diverse history proves that the ellipse is ancient and that man has studied it across the centuries. It remains a form of alchemy, a blending of elements to produce an effect. Back in the late 1920s, as a young student in Toronto under Professor Parkin, Shenstone had been taken with Zhukovskii's work on drag reduction and boundary layer control and was aware of his ellipsoid wing studies. Such studies were also clearly evident in the developments in German gliding circa 1928–1930.

So, the ellipse really was unlike other shapes and in wing form it had unique and proven properties; it offered something that was physically different not just in shape, but in its action and effect. The lift produced by the ellipse was actually different to the lift produced by other wings. The ellipse it seems had remarkable properties – no wonder insects, flying fish, and some high performance birds used it for their wings. Just after 1900, man had tried it and rejected it – but only temporarily.

Plotting the essence of the ellipse, and then uniquely modifying it, was soon to become a major story in the development of man's flight.

7

Supermarine's Modified Double Ellipse

Creating a perfect geometric ellipse would have been easy. In simple terms, to draw an ellipse, all the designer has to do is consult a text book of mathematical tables and calculus, plot some key cardinal points, and the conic geometry springs to elliptical life. A normal elliptical wing is usually relatively close to being symmetrical – its leading edge and trailing edge may match and are mirrored from a centre reference line. Normally, there is neither forward nor rearwards sweep – the wing simply delivers its ellipsoid benefit across angles, incidences and speeds. This is the type of 'off the shelf' ellipse seen on the Bäumer Sausewind – Heinkel 70, and Dewoitine 513 and other aircraft, but *not* on the Spitfire.

The Spitfire's ellipse is utterly different – it is in fact a unique collection of conic, ellipsoid values. No other work on the Spitfire has detailed this 'first' in aerodynamic design – one that stemmed principally from Beverley Shenstone's mind and was contributed to by the core members of the Spitfire team, notably in structural terms. It is the very essence of how and why, the Spitfire's non-standard, or irregular ellipsoid wing works, that is, the point of its function rather than simply its iconic form.

Of particular importance, the Spitfire wing's leading edge is straighter in comparison with the more obvious curve of its trailing edge. The Spitfire's wing is, in fact, composed of two differing elliptical sections of equal span, with differing root chords, that have been woven together in a unique manner. It is a deliberately distorted, pulled or swept forwards ellipse. This was the first use of such a deliberately distorted ellipse – one very different from earlier elliptical wings circa 1925–1933. The forward sweep took the shape nearer to a part-crescent shape; adding an effective forward sweep enhanced the ideal elliptic flow patterns and span loadings. This added quality also meant that when the wing was twisted, the adverse effect upon the low induced drag qualities of the basic ellipse, which wing twist would normally impose, were lessened. Outside the wing centre line, the two ellipsoid elements are asymmetrical – they do not match in the manner of a normal elliptical wing (they are not a mirror image). The Spitfire's almost-ellipse is a parabolic geometric sculpture that is hand crafted, actually *invented* in terms of both its shape and also in its varying aerofoils.

This is the *essential* difference between the Spitfire's ellipse and any other ellipse of the time and specifically that of the Heinkel 70. The two are *not* generally similar in planform shape – as Shenstone himself pointed out.

For the Spitfire, it was principally Shenstone who created the aerodynamics of this unequal, modified ellipse – or near ellipse. Crucially, inspired by glider design and delta wing studies, and in conjunction with the structural works of Joseph Smith, Alfred Faddy and Harold Smith, who wanted a straight, spar to fuselage join, instead of a weaker swept spar angle, Shenstone calculated a forwards distortion and created the shape.

Few of the Spitfire's ellipsoid values and plots, or cardinal points, were standard – they could not be simply taken from a text book of known calculus and drawn: Shenstone had invented them and the plotting of the wing's unique geometry. His elliptical shape lies just the tiniest fraction outside the elliptical textbook norm. It reflected the curves that he, Mitchell and the team had sketched out in pencil. As such it was an invented ellipsoid creation – a sort of elliptical, parabolic, conic entity of rare brilliance. The scientific significance of this has been ignored for decades and gone unmentioned in many works about the Spitfire.

Underneath the wing's skin, via Alan Clifton in the technical office, it was the drawing office's Joseph Smith with Alfred Faddy, and others including Messrs Fenner and Fear,[1] who did much original work to create an advanced and strong structure to carry the loads of Shenstone's aerodynamics. They also, along with Arthur Shirvall,[2] carried out detail design work on the shape. It seems obvious that the two functions, aerodynamics and structures, worked with each other as a team effort in order to create the smoothest, strongest wing. Getting the main spar forwards – towards the leading edge and making it unswept against its fuselage pick up points, imparted great strength against failure or twisting under high dynamic loadings. Working in conjunction with the aerodynamics, meant that the upward bending of the wing's centre of lift was also optimized inboard, for structural needs to reduce bending loads. However thin the wing may have been, it was a safe wing.

Modifying the basic ellipse created a wing with the best aerodynamics of all worlds, across a far wider set of speed and incidence values than

than even the normal ellipse could deliver. Shenstone tuned the 'mean aerodynamic centre' from the outcome of joining two differing elliptical sections together – balancing lift with the needs of strength. He refined the aerodynamic lift within a wing of multiple curves and two different aerofoils, and made sure that the purer, more effective elliptical lift retained its efficiency despite the addition of a touch of wing twist –'washout'. Every aspect, from downwash to wing-to-fuselage interaction, was calculated, plotted, sculpted and tuned to the highest degree of efficiency possible. Shenstone created a high-speed wing that also worked at very low speed for take-off and landing – without any need for leading edge lift improvement devices. This was a remarkable feat that is ignored by many commentators, especially those that say the wing was over-engineered, too complex and could easily have been a simpler, tapered affair.

Shenstone's brain went beyond even the creating of the shape – he brought swept wing, all-wing and delta wing vortex tuning experience and analytical knowledge, to creating and plotting a curved wing that built upon the ellipse, cured its tip-stalling problem, and controlled its vortices. And he added a series of tuned, forensically calculated hand designed or 'fair' curves that interacted with wing 'washout' twist, aerofoil, curvilinear lift distribution, forward sweep, boundary layer work, and a host of angles and effects to produce a unique wing performance that the world had never seen before. He also tuned the wing and slim fuselage to aerodynamically interact with the small, low drag tail fin.

Shenstone used all he had learned to create this wing, and even though by 1934 he was Mitchell's chief aerodynamicist, he carried on studying advanced aerodynamic calculus by working with Professor Raymond Howland. As we now know, Shenstone had the aerodynamics experience, but Howland was the advanced mathematics professor – the two exchanged knowledge, with Shenstone's calculus improving to keep him up to speed as the new Type 300 wing progressed rapidly. He had to be able to come up with answers – the correct ones.

In thousands of hours of work from mid-1934 though to final prototype sign-off, Shenstone's entire focus was the creation of the Spitfire's wing, and its overall aerodynamic design. He consulted trusted friends, ranging, for example, from Alexander Lippisch, to Geoffrey Mungo Buxton, and Stewart Scott-Hall, who was the Air Ministry's resident technical officer at Supermarine. Shenstone listened to all that Mitchell, and men such as Clifton, Smith, Faddy, Fenner, Fear, Mansbridge, and others, including

Squadron Leader Ralph Sorley who was the Air Ministry's operational aircraft requirements specialist, had to offer. They in turn, listened to him; they all worked together and the result was a never-seen-before, hand-created, ellipsoid wing of such qualities that it was years ahead of its time. This wing and its theories were not based on a hunch, nor the product of an unproven idea or unproven theory. Mitchell would never have taken such a gamble, especially as this was not his last design; there was more Air Ministry work to be done. The Air Ministry did not gamble on its requested fighter designs either.

The Spitfire's elliptical details bear deep analysis in order to understand their effects.

Because the ellipsoidal wing has a far more balanced pattern of lift distribution, more equal downwash patterns, and lower drag, it has a higher efficiency factor than a normally shaped wing, but it does suffer from sharp reactions at the stall with consequent tip-stalling dangers – it does after all have no real wing tip in the traditional broad-bladed sense. Beverley Shenstone's long hours of calculus not only created a wing with the best low-drag features of the ellipse, but he also managed to tune out the limiting and harmful tip-stall and consequent spin characteristics. But the ellipse's lack of a broad wing tip meant less drag in level flight and much less drag in a tight combat turn – giving the Spitfire wing its vital advantage of retained energy, in contrast to the Hurricane and Bf109 and their turbulent wing tip flows.

Shenstone also resolved the wing's spanwise airflow circulation control in a manner that reflected what he had observed when working on the early Lippisch swept wing (later used by Lippisch on the Me 163) and delta wing shapes – the effect of vortices, lift distribution patterns and trailing edge sweep being very relevant. Shenstone altered the aerofoil section along the wing and created a tip shape that although essentially elliptical, did actually vary from the pure mathematical ellipse – to balance his other tuning effects. His boundary layer work concentrated on localized curvature effects, streamwise flow fluctuation and speed and layer effects.

A vital question is, how did a wing for a propeller powered fighter, designed in 1934–1935, for around the 350mph figure, still function efficiently and correctly at speeds of 500mph+ or Mach 0.90? For this is what the Spitfire's wing achieved. Was it an accident that the wing also worked at a speed far beyond its original design speed, and in the transonic region? Was this capability an unintended benefit that just happened? Some commentators insist that the Spitfire's wing designers could not, in 1935, have known about designing wings for the transonic, near supersonic, region and that this aspect of the Spitfire was accidental. This opinion, of course, fails to realize that the man who designed the Spitfire's wing aerodynamics, had just been closely involved with, and contributed to, the creation and testing of the first delta wing – itself the secret to transonic and supersonic flight. Swept wing research had also been part of this work, and Shenstone was credited for such by Lippisch in print.[3]

Given that Shenstone had this unique knowledge and work experience, it is clear that his advanced calculus and wing shaping for the Spitfire's distorted ellipse, must have benefited from what he had discovered about delta and swept wing effects. Surely, in the light of this, the Spitfire wing's ability to 'work' at the transonic speed regime cannot simply have been an accident. If it had not been for the limitations of the structural integrity (or lack thereof) of the humble propeller at above Mach. 0.92, perhaps the Spitfire wing could have flown even faster?

The advanced techniques used in the Spitfire wing were the essence of the rare science of airflow control and analysis that took place in a mind that could think in three dimensions, and visualize flow dynamics, at the edge of the transonic and supersonic gateway – in 1934.

However, for the issue of twisting the wing, adding wing twist – 'washout' to one aspect of the wing's performance, would have detracted from another – it could have ruined any ellipsoid benefits of lower induced drag by adding angles of resistance to the airflow and altering the ellipse's pattern of action. Shenstone spent hundreds of hours blending the wing's shape and form to create a geometrically and helically twisted wing that was aerodynamically unique in that it balanced wing twist with planform effect and lift distribution needs. In fact, it traded pure lifting ability with performance ability. To this, he worked specifically on the wing to fuselage join area, to improve the wing's curvilinear lift distribution pattern – that is preserving lift and smooth airflow near the wing to fuselage junction where, on a normally shaped aircraft, lift degenerates and speed-sapping turbulence and drag occurs, especially under high propeller power effect. The combination of addressing all these factors in one wing, was advanced stuff – way beyond anything then seen. And yet these achievements have never been credited – until now.

To cure the tip stalling, a crude aerodynamicist would have simply put a sharp, drag-inducing, protruding horizontal strip or fence, along the leading edge at the wing root to trigger an earlier stall at a specific point and this could have ruined the ellipse's low induced drag benefits. Equally crudely, a vertical wing fence across its upper surface – chordwise, would have been a cheap cure to any spanwise airflow problem, but would have caused a loss of lifting area. Instead, Shenstone spent hours working out by just how much he could twist the wing and vary that twist along it, without massively degrading the ellipse's low induced drag figure.

By adding twist, the ellipse's stalling issue was solved for the smallest of penalties and, in a feature so often overlooked, Shenstone added that touch of forward sweep or distortion that further benefited the ellipse's as it moved the stall, forwards and inboard – away from those sensitive pointed wingtips – reducing the risk of stalling and spinning. The ailerons kept 'working' too – beyond the stall – this was amazing stuff. Forward sweep meant the washout angle could be smaller – upsetting the ellipse, less and speeding up the boundary layer.

The key to Shenstone's tuning of the ellipse was to identify where the centre of lift would occur as all the modifications were incorporated into the design – not afterwards. By creating a combination of lift coefficient with a known circulation of lift, the modified ellipse was given lift across a broad range of wing at a semi-span location. This was lift that remained attached (not degraded) at an incidence just below the stall – therefore making it impossible for the wing tip to stall first. Through this calculus and through the ellipse's smoother, less peaked, lift gradient, the wing's perfect efficiency was preserved from 50mph to 500mph – with no movable leading edge needed. This had not been done before by any aerodynamicist.

Importantly, Shenstone added the Spitfire's unusual, large wing to fuselage infill panel, which reaped massive benefits in preserving curvilinear lift distribution – that is continuing the wing's lifting effect, and lowering fuselage interference drag turbulence to astounding levels, delivering that vital low drag, high speed characteristic of the Spitfire. This added to the wing's lift coefficient – helping retain vital energy so that the pilot could remain on the offensive with a 'working' energized wing at higher bank angles than the Bf109 (and the Hurricane). After working on this in-fill or fillet technique in Germany, and studying the significant literature on the technique that was focused on by Muttray and his paper[4] being translated and published by NACA as Memorandum 764 in October 1934, Shenstone used the winter months to calculate and design this vital wing root panel. It was formally adopted into the Spitfire's design in April 1935.

The other vital development of the Spitfire's specific ellipse was to work out the levels of drag as they vary as a square of the lift coefficient. With a conventional wing, more lift means more downwash and more lift-induced drag. Hundreds of hours of work were needed to tune the wing's efficiency, and deep calculus into the ratio of drag and lift, known as the efficiency number, were required. The ellipse was known to even out the peaks and troughs of lift pressure distribution – therefore yielding the smoothest lift and the lowest induced level of drag being produced as a result of that lift. Also, with the ellipse the vortices are more evenly patterned and less concentrated and less drag in turns is evident.

Shenstone did not trust small-scale wind tunnels, especially those roughly shaped and finished tunnels that could deliver results unrelated to full-scale wing performance in pure air. Shenstone's time with Lippisch had revealed these issues. Neither did Shenstone (nor Mitchell) trust the pronouncements of British experts on wing thickness – immersed as such experts were in the perceived fashionable wisdom of the thick wing section. When the National Physical Laboratory (NPL) stated that there was little benefit from creating a wing with less than 20 per cent chord ratio, Shenstone (aided by his studies and NACA information), knew that the NPL was wrong – and time revealed this to be so. The Spitfire's aerodynamics were mathematically predicted, and key items were wind tunnel tested using a small, one-fifth scale model. Shenstone recorded that there was remarkably little wind tunnel work undertaken on the aircraft, and much time was saved by taking previously designed and tested ideas from the Type 224, and improving upon them.

A low wing loading was another vital achievement of the Spitfire's aerodynamic performance. It was this low wing loading design that allowed the Spitfire to fly and climb faster and higher, as well as to turn tighter, and to have a faster rate of turn (the two being separate factors) than any other fighter. It also assisted the wing at the low speeds of landing and take-off without the need for any leading edge devices (such as the slots fitted to the Bf109) and aided only by the convention of flaps. The sharp, responsive, aerobatic, 400mph wing was aerodynamically stable at that speed and on the landing approach at 60mph. In both situations, it neither stalled nor dropped a wing unexpectedly. This feature placed the Spitfire and its design, far ahead of the known aerodynamic conventions of the day, no other wing behaved so well at such extremes.

The famous Spitfire test pilot Alex Henshaw often praised this particular aspect of the Spitfire's behaviour; he realized that this achievement was incredible, and that Shenstone had achieved aerodynamic stability across a speed range never before considered.[5]

The advantage, the sheer efficiency of the ellipse, was why the ellipse was chosen and then tuned as it had never been tuned before. Adding it to an ultra-thin aerofoil was another tweak that raised the Spitfire's ellipse above all others. If the ellipse was an ancient mystical geometric form, then the Spitfire's wing shape was unique and magical. Scientifically, it was a major step and a wing that remained competitive for over ten years at the height of rapidly advancing wartime aerodynamics work.

Indeed from 1943, a wing that was a close reflection of the Spitfire's wing shape and mounting fillet found its way onto the leading Hawker fighters – the Tempest and specifically the Fury. The Spitfire wing was 'faster' than even the P-51 Mustang's laminar flow wing and even the early jet wings. The American Thunderbolt P-47 fighter also used the elliptical wing as did several other airframes, notably in Russia and was also seen on Dewoitine and Seversky monoplanes in France and the USA, and Lockheed's L-133 jet prototype also used a sharply elliptical wing as early as 1941.

The fundamental advantage of the ellipse is that in comparison with a normally shaped wing, the ellipse had a smaller tip blade, which reduced the problem of lift-induced drag being caused by the spilling of low and high pressure air off the normally shaped, square, broad, wing tips and wing trailing edges. Normal wing tips allow the differing air and pressure flows to mix across a wide area and create induced drag vortices of distinct types. The pressure difference between the top and bottom of the normal square wing causes spillage and turbulence when they meet – principally at the wing tip and along the trailing edge. This spillage also reduces the aspect ratio of the wing by rendering its outer tips less efficient. The spillage effect is also characterized as 'downwash' from the wing tip and trailing edge, causing localized angles of attack to the airflow, which vary along the trailing edge and create drag, thus harming lift and speed. Today, the familiar upturned winglets on airliners reduce these problems by funnelling the spilled air. But by the 1920s, the ellipse, with its much smaller wing tip or wing end, formed as it was, nearly to a point, was proven to significantly reduce this spillage and create less of the resulting induced turbulence or drag, as well as having a smoother lifting pattern along the entire wing.

Whether a wing is short and stubby, having a low aspect ratio, or long and thin and possessing a high aspect ratio, induced drag still results at the end of the line. Long thin wings, such as those on gliders, do have less induced drag, but they are not good for a fighter as they would limit speed and manoeuvrability. Seen within general parameters, the earliest square wing and the square tapered wing, dependent on shape and twist, have been said to have anything from 5–20 per cent more drag than an elliptical equivalent – a significant factor. In later years, the advantage *could* be narrowed to less than that, down to 2 per cent for specific heights and speeds, but at the expense of other performance parameters – notably wing loading and drag.

Developments in tapered wing design eventually meant that the normal tapered wing, when tuned with 'washout' twist and various effects, could, at very high altitudes, come very close to matching the ellipse's lift pattern and behaviour. Ironically, it was Shenstone himself who published papers on improving the standard tapered wing's performance by such methods of applying twist.

But adding twist to a tapered wing was not a *guarantee* of efficiency. Shenstone wrote:

> A combination of taper and twist can be found giving an induced drag scarcely greater than that of an elliptic wing. When comparing these curves (results) with the corresponding results for untwisted wings it should be borne in mind that the latter are dependent on the aspect ratio... But the advantage is not always with the twisted wing. For moderate (wing) tapers, the twisted wings have as low or lower drags than untwisted wings... But for greater tapers, the drags increase very much more rapidly for the twisted wings than for the untwisted.... In practice the question of weight also has to be considered and the optimum taper is then slightly greater than the purely aerodynamic optimum.[6]

So, ditching the harder to build ellipse, for a tapered and twisted wing, was not as easy as some subsequent commentators have suggested. Wing loading was the issue and those Spitfire commentators who have argued that, as a tapered wing could have come close to the ellipse, that Mitchell could have saved himself a lot of trouble by producing an easier-to-build, tapered wing, rather than the ellipse he chose, ignore this and other points – notably weight and wing loading.

There were those who claimed that a standard, tapered wing shape, such as that applied to the Hurricane or Bf109, could, with the addition of 'washout' wing twist, nearly equal the ellipse's stall performance and lift efficiency. But this was theoretically so at very high altitudes, and it was also the case, that for a tapered, non-elliptical wing, the degree of twist or 'washout' needed to match the performance of the ellipse, was so much greater, that it invoked penalties upon the airflow that put it at a great disadvantage in terms of drag. The often suggested, twisted, tapered wing, would also have to be stronger and heavier, and it would have less chord width – so it would have an even higher wing loading – to the detriment of climb, turn and stall performance – a fact proven by the fact that the ellipsoid Spitfire climbed faster and turned tighter than its tapered wing competitors on both sides. As those 1942 American stall tests showed, the Spitfire had a safe stall in a wing that could be used by the pilot right up to the edge of its lift efficiency. Not using the ellipse would mean that leading edge devices would also have had to been added, creating weight and drag. Similarly, the tail fin would have to been increased in size as the wing loading went up – adding more drag and reducing speed.

Thus, the anti-ellipse argument utterly fails to understand or convey the fundamental, core advantages as known at the time. These advantages are the reasons Mitchell used the ellipse, and the results tend to speak for themselves. The arguments of hindsight suddenly seem very weak.

The tapered wing Hurricane did *not* have wing slots, but then it could not match either the Spitfire's ellipse nor the Bf109's tapered wing in terms of lift, retained energy rate, and speed. The Hurricane also needed a longer wingspan than the Spitfire to achieve a similar wing loading. The Hurricane took a minute longer to climb to a set height than the identically powered Spitfire, and was 40mph slower than the earliest Spitfires. It was slower and heavier on the controls – it was more stable, but far less instantaneously reactive. These deficits stemmed from the Hurricane's weaker aerodynamic performance: more drag, less lift, slower velocity.

As any Second World War or current Spitfire pilot will testify, the Spitfire's magic is its wing – its ability to climb, and to roll and turn in instant, reacting and working faster and more efficiently than any competitor, German or British. It is the lift pattern, wing loading, and the *retention* of wing energy that is key to the unique science of the Spitfire's flying ability and its instantaneous responses.

Proof of the theory is further framed by the fact that no other aircraft could match the Spitfire's Mach speed numbers: Mach 0.90 was a known Spitfire descent speed achievement. The fighter specification Spitfire had a tactical Mach number of around 0.82 Mach. This was higher even than the later, laminar flow-winged P-51 Mustang, which managed 0.78 Mach. The Spitfire had a tactical Mach number advantage over the German fighter with its Mach 0.75. The Spitfire's Mach speeds proved that its wing airflow and wing structure characteristics were unique and highly advanced. The Spitfire's wing worked at low and high speeds and it stayed attached to the airframe at very high Mach numbers of up to Mach

0.92. It is known that a Spitfire in PR Photo Reconnaissance specification, easily got to 40,000 feet, but on 5 February 1952, a Spitfire Mk 19 of No. 51 Squadron RAF, based in Hong Kong reached 51,500 feet / 15,712 metres and also claimed 0.94 Mach in descent – but this Mach number may have been the result of aerodynamic effects upon the instruments sensors and the shock waves off the cowling, and canopy, must have been relevant.

As early as 1937 the one-off 'Speed Spitfire' extended the knowledge around the Spitfire's speed potential. A racing variant, it had wing tips that were a slightly broader ellipse in their curve, whereas the mid-1940s special photo reconnaissance 'PR' Spitfire variants featured longer, more pointed wing tips that gave more lift at high levels and which were another version of the ellipse's geometry. The ellipse, with all its attendant benefits as a lifting shape, offered the chance of fine tuning and development.

Prior to all this, in order to win the government contract to supply the RAF's new fighter, Supermarine had to beat off the competition. That meant that their aircraft had to break new ground – something its predecessor the Type 224 had not.

The Supermarine Type 224 had not delivered. In plain English, it was a failure. For the Type 300 (the Spitfire), what Mitchell and his team had to do, was produce something special, something nobody else had even thought of, prove it, and then make it perfect, utterly perfect. The true depth of the Spitfire's wing science, so obvious to those that actually flew it, with all its differing aspects of tuning and shaping and principally calculated by Beverley Shenstone, was the key to breaking that new ground.

8

The Spitfire's Vital Advantage

If, after the failure of the gull-winged Type 224, the second attempt from Mitchell's Supermarine concern – the Type 300, was going to win, there were some fundamental points that had to influence the design to achieve the qualities required.

Above all was the question of manoeuvrability allied to speed – yet the Air Ministry specification suggested 250mph was deemed adequate. In that, maybe it reflected known conventions of fighter design from the First World War. RAF fighter pilots were taught to fly in a tight, controlled and unexpressive manner and to do so in ever tighter formations that reflected the conceits of known aerial warfare using biplanes. By 1935, this know-it-all policy left Great Britain in the position where its air force had no aircraft capable of more than 300mph, and new biplanes such as the Gladiator were seen as the future, not the past. Bombers not fighters were the focus of the RAF's top brass – a top team that was locked into Edwardian thinking and the First World War psychology of Lord Trenchard, valuable in 1916, but irrelevant against Hitler's *Luftwaffe* in 1930s.

But thanks to men such as Air Chief Marshal Sir Wilfrid Freeman, the up and coming Hugh Dowding, Sir Robert Vansittart, Sir Henry Pownall, Lord Swinton, Viscount Weir, R.J. Mitchell, Sydney Camm, and a host of private and political supporters, the status quo, was altered – just in time.

Although official financial sanction came for what was to become the Spitfire, in December 1934, and although formal draughting drawings of its wing were listed from that time, it is clear from several reference points, not least Shenstone's own diaries,[1] that Supermarine had been working on the airframe that was to become called 'Spitfire' and its ellipsoid wing shape, from earlier in 1934.

Wing armament (guns and cannons) were not the only reference point – the retracting undercarriage, cooling system, and lift coefficient requirements all had to be worked in – and the broad chord ellipse solved those issues. As early as 19 July 1934, there was a meeting at Supermarine with the Air Ministry to discuss the further developing of the failed Type 224 into something altogether more lethal.

Many have suggested that it was the need for more guns that prompted the change to a wider, elliptical wing that would house these eight guns – in early 1935. Although this reflects the record of official dates of announcements, other records suggest that the elliptical wing was in the frame before the need for extra guns was *officially* announced.

The Air Ministry's Squadron Leader Ralph Sorley's thoughts on the need for more guns and then canons, cannot have been secret. They were aired from as early as that 19 July 1934 meeting at a Supermarine design conference when Sorely discussed the case for more guns – the Air Ministry had even been testing cannons on a Dewoitine 510 that it had purchased. Thus, this early influence upon the Spitfire's design process, with more guns being needed, is established before the subsequent dates and events that some have since allied to the choice of the ellipse – notably the erroneous claims about the Heinkel 70 being unveiled at the November 1934 Paris Air Show and influencing the Spitfire's choice of wing design just at the moment in December 1934 when the Air Ministry made the need for eight guns more obvious – resulting in a final official pronouncement as late as April 1935.

Shenstone's personal notes provide an illuminating description of the reason the eight guns were not evenly placed within the wing. He suggests that the extra guns were added *after* the ellipse was chosen and had to be fitted in around pre-existing wing ribs:

> Specification F.37 /34 had called for a four gun fighter, like its predecessor. But when work was well advanced the RAF changed its mind and asked if we could fit eight guns. After a bit of a struggle we managed to squeeze all eight into our thin wing, with just a hint of a bulge round the two outer weapons. The rather uneven spacing of the guns was because the Spitfire was originally designed for only four guns and only when it was in advanced stage were eight guns decided upon. Had it not been for this, the installation would have been neater.[2]

From this, it seems that if Shenstone's record is correct, the intervening years have confused the issue – with some commentators suggesting that it was the need for *eight* guns in total that drove any *subsequent* selection of the ellipse. But Shenstone's notes confirm that it was the combination of the original need for four guns in total and the undercarriage etc., that lay behind the need for a broad chord wing – a wide wing design that, in steps, became elliptical, with all its aerodynamic advantages. The blurring of the actual dates around the ellipse's relevance to the Type 300/Spitfire's design and the various dates related to the decision for eight guns stems from a combination of circumstances and coincidences. The above extract adds a new dimension to an old argument as it is evidence from the wing designer himself that when Shenstone later told others that it was the need to house the guns and (other items) in the wing that led to the consideration and use of the ellipse, he meant the four guns not the later eight that have so often been cited as the starting point for the ellipse.

Once again, new evidence offers a new perspective amid the froth of debate.

'Officially' the Type 300 Spitfire became an Air Ministry supported design reality in December 1934. Officially, more guns were then needed and a wing to accommodate them had to be found. This has led to a theory that has a flaw – one that relies upon the instantaneous appearance of the ellipse as an idea, and the sudden creation of production-related ellipse draughting drawings within days of the need for 'official' change taking place. The theory also assumes that once the failings of the Type 224 became obvious in early 1934, Mitchell and his men sat around for over six months and then they suddenly sat down and started draughting elliptical wing drawings in early December 1934. And if Vickers were to formally approve work on a revised design, as they did in early November 1934, there must have been informal proposals on hand to achieve that very decision.

But then came the basis of the falsehoods created by certain commentators ever since – the gross erroneous claim that just prior to the events set out above, the Heinkel 70 was unveiled as a new design at the November 1934 Paris Air Show where Shenstone, we are told, supposedly saw it for the first time, and within days the ellipse was suggested for the Spitfire. An alternative 'theory' is that the Heinkel 70 influenced the Spitfire designers before that date, or that Supermarine copied a Rolls-Royce-engined Heinkel whilst designing the Spitfire. Both these claims are factually, historically false – utterly incorrect (see chapter 11) – yet they have been repeated by many and continue to be so.

The reality was that in early 1934, as soon as the failings of Type 224 were self evident at first flight, Mitchell's mind turned to a modified design. We know that this was when the rough ideas, the freehand sketching, and the more formal design discussions were started by Mitchell and resulted in a series of revised, ever more tapered wing designs, and then Shenstone suggesting the ellipse – one that would not have been be ready to draw as a formal, plotted and calculated geometry without a series of lengthy design stages, submissions and agreements.

Clearly, to achieve all this in a matter of days between November and December 1934 would have been impossible.

Therein also arises the fallacy that this earlier design work, must have meant that the Spitfire was begun as a privately funded venture prior to Air Ministry official approval. Shenstone's records clearly state that having been funded to create the Type 224 – or Ministry specification F.7/30 – upon its failure Mitchell negotiated with the Air Ministry the continuance of funding as an extension of the original remit, F.37/34, in order to modify the design and search for a more successful outcome. Whether that outcome and officially funded status was in late 1934 or later in 1935 has long been argued over. In late 1934, the Vickers Board (overseeing Supermarine) approved the continuing work of the refinement of the Type 224 – notably a thinner wing and then a reshaped wing (the beginning of the ellipse). The Air Ministry, via Stuart Scott-Hall, their then Resident Technical Officer at Supermarine and a friend of Shenstone's, were fully informed as to what was going on.

Questioned in 1959–1960 Shenstone said that, in his view, the private funding story was a myth. He stated that the idea of modifying the Type 224 F.7/30 design was Mitchell's and that Vickers' own Sir Robert McLean had been less than keen – possibly preferring another design idea, and that it was Mitchell who kept the modification idea (which led to the Spitfire) alive. Shenstone's words make it clear:

> The idea of taking the F.7/30 and improving it was certainly a Supermarine idea, so you can say it was a private idea, but this venture was by no means private, considering that the whole thing was paid for by the Ministry under a Ministry specification.[3]

Shenstone stated:

> Without seeming to lack respect for Sir Robert McLean's ability and energy, in my opinion the Spitfire would not have been born if Mitchell had not been willing to stand up to McLean, particularly in the era when McLean quite clearly preferred the Venom concept to that of the Spitfire. Because it was cheaper and lighter.[4]

Of great note, Hugh Dowding assessed these defined Type 224 F.7 /30 modification proposals in the first days of November 1934, and issued written correspondence on 8 November 1934 after his discussions with R.J. Mitchell on the matter. This coincided with the 1934 Paris Air Show – as discussed above, so often and so erroneously linked to the timing of the ellipse. It was at this time, ready for further meetings, that the Supermarine drawing office with Alfred Faddy, under the aegis of Messrs Clifton and Smith, drew up the early ellipsoid ideas with Shenstone. On

5 December 1934, a full design conference at the Air Ministry was held and R.J. Mitchell was present.

If the design revision work was a private *idea*, it was perhaps only a de facto private *effort* within the factory for about four weeks – yet still under the frame of the F.7/30 Type 224 modification work – framed by drawing 300000/4 through to 300000/12. Dowding's letter of 8 November 1934 to Major James Buchanan confirmed the issue of an ITP order (Intention To Proceed) twenty-one days later.[5]

The real chronology further reinforces the evidence that the modified wing design and its elliptical studies existed informally *before* the dates in late November and December that some commentators cite as the birth or genesis of the use of the ellipse – and contradicts the suggestion made by several commentators that it was the1934 Paris Air Show sighting that started it all. As we know, Shenstone first inspected the Heinkel 70 at the *previous* year's 1933 Paris Air Show in the year of the Heinkel's full launch.

For the Spitfire, the revised wing studies must stem from the Type 224, begun in mid-1934, and the ellipse existed as an idea around the time of Mitchell's meetings with Dowding and the Vickers Board. There is much supporting evidence that the spring and summer of 1934 were defining periods in Supermarine's wing design thinking process – leading to the ellipse in the autumn of 1934 – but nothing at all to do with the chronologically flawed, erroneous Heinkel 70 Paris Air Show influence theories.

Just before leaving Germany in 1931 for Supermarine, Shenstone had visited Heidelberg and had discussions with Ludwig Prandtl, who developed the concept of the boundary layer in 1904. Shenstone had also researched the boundary layer, and wing shapes ranging from the ellipse to the delta wing. Then, before leaving on the Vickers-Armstrongs tour of the American aeronautical industry in the late spring of 1934, Shenstone's notes[6] clearly record discussions on the Type 224's revised wing design. While in America, Shenstone visited Theodor von Karman and discussed Von Karman's and Robert Millikan's works on wing design – notably laminar flow and boundary layer turbulence, which Shenstone says he was 'entranced' by. While in America, Shenstone also got to talk to NACA and examine its new 2220 range of ultra thin aerofoils and their behaviours. Also on his mind were the smooth wings and elliptical and delta shapes of Lippisch. The Americans had also grasped smoothness criteria and NACA reinforced to Shenstone the need for a very smooth leading edge and aerofoil finish.[7]

All this meant that when Shenstone returned from America to the

Supermarine works in late summer 1934, his mind was buzzing with the thoughts to create a wing far in advance of that seen on the Type 224. In his absence, the Supermarine team at Woolston had also been busy thinking about their options and Shenstone was soon adding his thoughts and ideas. The idea of using the ellipse (an early form of the ellipse) must have been born at this time – late summer 1934. This was when Alfred Faddy's drawings,[8] post-drawing number 300000/4 and up to 300000/11, demonstrated the development up to first versions of the heavily tapered and then elliptical wing, and must therefore have been drawn by early November 1934 in time for the range of meetings with Vickers and the Air Ministry to secure further development. The final, forward distorted ellipse shape, drawing 300000/12, being formally draughted a few weeks later in early December 1934.

If Shenstone's inspiration for using an ellipse stems from anywhere, it has to be way back (circa 1900–1910) with the work of Zhukovskii (Joukowski), Hugo Junkers, and others. But Shenstone did not simply suggest the simple ellipse, or an ellipse such as that found on the Sausewind or the He 70, or as per the Shorts-Bristow Crusader or even the Piaggio Pegna PC 7. Instead, he took the ellipse and re-shaped it to become a unique wing planform.

Wing Loading – the Vital Factor

Wings do not just happen – thousands of hours of aerodynamic and structural work are needed. For Shenstone, after the selection of the ellipse for the wing shape of the revised fighter – that became the Spitfire, the wing loading factor was to be the vital ingredient because turn rate as well as turn radius were directly affected. Here is where the detailed work began.

A crisp, short, low-cross sectional area wing shape that flew fast in a straight level line was not going to be enough. The Spitfire had to handle like a racer and its level of wing loading was the key because no pilot, no matter what level of g-force he can stand, can pull as tight a turn in a highly wing loaded machine, no matter what its speed advantage, as another pilot can in a lightly wing loaded aircraft. The new fighter had to have a lower wing loading because, in Shenstone's own words:

> To produce a lots of g force one does not need a fast machine. Tight turns on a slow (but strong type) gives one as many gs as one may wish… A very definite limitation is given by the effective stalling speed of an aeroplane in a turn. One cannot, no matter what 'g' one dares to use, make as tight a turn on a highly loaded type. In fact for every wing loading there is a minimum radius of turn which can be flown.[9]

The basic problems of fighter design were, that the greater the increase in speed, power, and armament, the higher wing loadings became, and therefore, the larger the minimum possible radius of the turn became. The new higher speeds were self-limiting in the turn. Counteracting this was one of the core foundations of why the Spitfire was designed the way it was.

The limitations of g-force were an area of research in the 1930s. In Germany, the brothers Reimar and Walter Horten had built several gliders with the pilot in the prone position. This would allow the human body to accept higher g loadings (beyond 6g) than when sat upright and therefore, pull tighter turns despite any given wing loading limitation. However, the Spitfire was not about to be given a prone pilot and today's pilot g-suits did not exist. And the day of the jet fighter with highly loaded, deliberately unstable wings and a computerized brain to juggle it all, had not dawned. In 1936 the answer had to come from the wing design.

Shenstone's belief was that the Spitfire must be fast, but not be fast at the expense of manoeuvrability. Fast aircraft are not necessarily tight-turning aircraft. The Spitfire needed to be able to turn tightly; it also needed to be able turn and roll quickly – the rate of roll, that flick of a stylish arc, so familiar to Spitfire pilots, was vital in the manner in which the Spitfire could be made to change direction. Just as in a racing car or a racing yacht, the steerage, the reaction, the rate of change of attitude was what counted. The Spitfire's rates of roll and turn were to be vital.

This rate – or the time taken to change the attitude of the aircraft – notably in bank angle and in climb and descent, were the areas where the Spitfire's advantage was found. This came not just from the wing's performance, but also its interaction with the fuselage, the tail and its qualities. Knowing that a set wing type and set wing loading weight gives a known level of wing performance, specifically in the rate of turn, allows the designer to tune the wing to his best advantage. There is no point in having a fast aircraft if it cannot turn as sharply as a slower aircraft due to having a higher wing loading, the speed advantage becomes wasted in combat, if not in a straight, level line. Shenstone's vital work for Mitchell was to produce a fast aircraft that also had a low wing loading and resultant better turning capabilities – giving it the best of both worlds.

Shenstone did this by creating the balance between turning ability of the wing's chord and wing loading (the width of the wing and its weight carrying lifting ability), with the speed gains of the thin section aerofoil and the lift distribution and lower drag benefits of the ellipse. These core efficiency elements were the foundations of the Spitfire's success:

Shenstone drew these separate elements together for the first time in a fighter aircraft, and the result was the Spitfire's unique advance. The success of this can be measured in comparison with the Bf109 (which was very fast in a straight line) because the Spitfire's advantage was that it could be fast as well as turn faster. The Spitfire's wing gave it the best of both worlds – speed and agility – not part of one and some of the other.

This was because the early Bf109E had a wing loading of 32lb/sq ft+ whereas the Spitfire's wing loading was just 24lb/sq ft (the prototype and early models having achieved 22.3lb/sq ft). This gave the Spitfire a wing loading of around 8lb/sq ft *less*, than the early Bf109, and over 10 lb/sq ft less than the later model Bf109 – a benefit, which allied to the thin wing and the ellipsoid lift benefits, gave the Spitfire its winning turn rate advantage, and fast climb rate. As Spitfire and Bf109 variants appeared, the wing loading figures changed – but the Spitfire had room to increase its wing loading without losing its advantage. Later Bf109 variants were to exceed 35lb/sq ft as a wing loading.

To Shenstone, the rate of turn advantage from a lower wing loading outweighed the quest for ultimate top speed, yet the ellipse provided both. At a given speed and based on wing loading (as opposed to wing lift coefficient – see below) the earlier model of Bf109 would, according to Shenstone's 1941 calculations,[10] take just under 12 seconds to make a 360-degree turn, but crucially, it required a turn radius of 720ft to do so at a speed of 275mph. The Spitfire, with its lower wing loading and thin ellipsoid section, would however, take just over 8 seconds and a turn radius of 580ft to complete a 360-degree turn at a set speed of 275mph. Of interest, Shenstone cited a 6g limit, suggesting that above that any theoretical turning ability was limited due to g-force limitations. So actual speeds in the turns were likely to have been lower. But by flying slower, and not stalling or spinning before its enemy did just that, the Spitfire's advantage was that it could make tight turns and still be flown right up to the very edge of the stall – it was all about retained wing energy and a benign stall and achieving it within a set tolerance of g-force. Keeping the ailerons working, allowing full roll control into the stall, was an incredible achievement and one created without wind-tunnel testing.

This deliberate method of adapting lift to wing loading, speed and stall behaviour meant that the Spitfire could turn tighter and stall later. With the Bf109, increasing speed in an aircraft with a higher wing loading as it turns, leads to a loss of manoeuvrability. Therefore, the smallest, fast aeroplane, such as the Bf109, is not necessarily the best for tight turns.

Later versions of the two types revealed similarly interesting figures.

Wartime Royal Aircraft Establishment (RAE) figures of May 1941 published in RAE Report BA1640, and latterly cited by Green,[11] stated that for a turn of minimum radius without height loss, at non-specified maximum speed in bank angle at 12,000ft, the Bf109E had a turn radius of 885ft. In contrast, the Spitfire 1A, did it in 696ft. The Bf109 took 25 seconds to make a 360-degree turn, as opposed to the Spitfire's 19 seconds. The Bf109 could manage its turn at a maximum of 129mph, compared with the Spitfire's 133mph. Arguable though such figures may have been, not least being based on a captured Bf109E, the turn radii results amply illustrate and confirm Shenstone's 1941 statements about wing loading, and underline more recent findings. Bank angles should not change with altitude below a certain level of height and air density, but clearly at high altitudes this may have been a contributing factor.

But could the Spitfire's turn advantage really be well over a hundred feet better than the small winged Bf109 with its slots? Were the British favouring their machine and undermining the Bf109? Were the Germans equally guilty of the same tactic in reverse?

The arguments have raged across the decades. One thing is for sure, the Spitfire *did* out turn the Bf109, but by how much is an argument that the bare figures may not reveal. If wing area and wing efficiency are added to the calculus, as opposed to just the factor of wing drag coefficient and wing loading, the difference between the Spitfire and the Bf109 becomes smaller in pure numeric terms. But this theory does not take into account the elliptical lift pattern and greater retained lift energy of the Spitfire's wing, and importantly the Spitfire had a unique, varying aerofoil – the NACA 2213 and 2209 being dovetailed together. If the calculations for the Spitfire are based on the coefficient of lift number of just the 2213 section alone, and do not include the thinner 2209 section that forms the Spitfire's outer wing, allied to other Spitfire features, are theorists doing the Spitfire a disservice and adversely slewing its wing lift coefficient in reaching their estimates? The same argument can be applied to the use of the Spitfire's wing root fillet, which massively reduces its wing to fuselage interference drag factor in comparison with both the Bf109 and the Hurricane. Calculating drag and lift for all these aircraft using identical lift coefficient factors, arguably *might* have missed something…

To underline that point, the 1942 stalling tests by the US Army Air Force, in the NACA report previously cited,[12] state that the Spitfire VA tested, had a wing lift coefficient (C_L) of 1.68 when measured in cruising flight at an engine speed of 2650rpm with 36.9 / 3¾ lb/sq in. of boost (under 200mph). In a 180-degree turn from level flight with the flaps up at 174mph, a C_L of 1.22 was recorded. These lift coefficient C_L figures contrast with those cited by others – notably Mason,[13] which used lift coefficients of C_L 1.0 not just as one lift coefficient, but as a maximum assumed lift coefficient value for the Spitfire (and its competitors). Clearly, the 1942 NACA figures taken from a test aircraft fitted with relevant testing sensors and aerodynamic tuft indicators, provide evidence of a lift coefficient higher than that which some later authors have credited the Spitfire with in the comparisons with other Second World War fighter aircraft.

The stubby little Bf109 wing, belting out a rough and altering lift gradient with its slots snapping in and out automatically, meant that its wing had less energy, and less bank angle performance up near the combat relevant stall regime, as well as having variable lift. But was the Bf109 really *several* hundred feet behind the Spitfire's turn performance as stated by the numbers? Many argue that it was not that far behind, but surely they cannot deny that the Bf109's turning performance was inferior.

More recently, in the paper referred to earlier when discussing drag coefficients, and entitled, 'Comparison of turning radii for four Battle of Britain fighter aircraft', Ackroyd and Lamont[14] recalculated the basis of past claims. These new figures in one sense correctly reinforced the crucial wing loading claims that Shenstone noted in 1940[15] that being that the speed and bank angles used for these calculations were critical – so citing a very high speed or vertical bank angle was not realistic, the tightest turn took place at a lower speed and the issue of retained wing energy and loading near the stall was very relevant – yet missing from some other calculations. Few aircraft, not even a Spitfire, could turn tightly at 300mph, at 90 degrees vertical bank and with high g acting upon the pilot and airframe. In 1940 Shenstone also noted the wing loading and turning radii capacity of the Heinkel He 112 – the single-engined elliptically winged fighter derivative of the (now much lauded) He 70 dating from 1932. The He 112's broad, symmetrical wing planform, allied to a new body shape, had a wing loading of 31lb/sq ft.

In his book *Fighter*, Len Deighton[16] provides a diagram showing the turning radii of the Bf109, Spitfire and Hurricane, which claims the Bf109 had the tightest turning circle at 770 feet – and with a wing loading of 25lb/sq ft. This wing loading is nearly 10 lb/sq ft *less* than the Bf109's *true* wing loading. Vertical 90-degree banked turns at 300mph – virtually impossible to achieve due to g build up and the gravity effect upon the banked turn seems to be cited as a basis of the claims. But no amount of 'top rudder' to keep the nose up could possible solve the raw physics of this problem! Deighton was citing the turning figures of Mason, yet they appear to be interpreted via a combination of very high speed, high bank angle and resultant g force higher than could be tolerated by the pilot. The speed cited of 300mph by Mason is above the speed figures Shenstone presented in 1941[17] as being self limiting (250mph), where the g force is likely to be very high. Height, speeds, g and air density are all crucial parameters, and the more recent Ackroyd and Lamont review is interesting in that it cites Mason's figures as in error.

The Spitfire's turning advantage may have been less than some claims at certain flight profiles, but clearly if the Bf109 could have out turned the Spitfire, the Spitfire and the RAF, would have lost against it.

But argument still rages. Surely we should also ask ourselves if, with wing slots deployed, in the hands of an expert, the Bf109 *might* with extreme care, and an unloaded, low-energy wing, teetering on the edge of an in-turn stall and spin, have been able to carve a tighter turn radius than has been suggested as possible by bare numbers? But of great note, the Bf109, however well flown by an expert, and even with slots deployed, would in a slower speed, tight combat turn, have stalled *before* the Spitfire – irrespective of the actual difference in the radii of their turns.

Despite this key factor, there are tales of Bf109s managing to out turn Spitfires, but these tales rely on pilot performance not aircraft performance. A highly experienced Bf109 pilot with many combat hours logged, may well have out-flown a novice teenage boy flying a Spitfire with under twenty hours of piloting experience and unable to push the wing to its limits. In the main, for the Spitfire pilot, the wing's turning performance was superior and usable against the Bf109.

Another key factor was to keep the wing energy intact so that the aircraft retained the capability to fly offensively as opposed to simply defending itself – avoiding a 'bleed off' of wing energy, the Spitfire led by a significant margin in this parameter too – just as it did over the Hurricane even if that aircraft did have a similarly low wing loading. It all came down to the science of airflow.

There was, however, a Spitfire versus Bf109 performance argument that few have investigated. The tighter turn of the Spitfire is attributed to its lower wing loading compared with the Bf109. Yet, argue the Bf109 enthusiasts, the Spitfire needed a much bigger wing area of 242sq ft, (22.48m^2) than the Bf109 with 172sq.ft, (16.06m^2) to achieve its gain. Therefore, in theory, the smaller-winged Bf109 is more efficient in its lift coefficient say the Bf109 proponents. The suggestion has always been that the Bf109 has a higher lift coefficient from a smaller, non-elliptical wing, and that therefore the Spitfire's design advantage and turn radius advantage is not as decisive as claimed.

However, the small-wing-is-best theory of the Bf109 proponents, although it correctly cites wing area size, as opposed to a basic wing loading figure, is flawed by the fact that the Spitfire was deliberately designed to use a bigger wing – yet crucially, one that was elliptical and not square tapered like the Bf109. The Bf109 small wing theory falls apart when the exact nature of the difference between elliptical (Spitfire) wing lift and square tapered (Bf109) wing lift is appreciated in terms of lift quality and lift-induced drag. The smaller Bf109 wing may have less size and therefore less cross-sectional drag area, but it does not have the more efficient, lower induced drag, longer lifting properties of the Spitfire wing – added to by its wing fillet. The Bf109 wing has to resort to leading edge slot devices to stay in the sky and has higher induced drag, a higher wing loading, and a more turbulent boundary layer. It follows that its area-to-lift efficiency ratio cannot be the defining factor.

Speed is a vital arbiter, the Spitfire 1 reached 354mph (570km/h) at 20,000ft, and the Bf109E reached 343mph (544km/h) at 20,000ft, yet theorists say that its much smaller wing area should have seen the Bf109 with a decisive advantage – comparing like with like, but that was not the case. The elliptical Spitfire had much less drag of all types – induced and parasitic or profile related.

Thus, the Bf109 proponents' claims of higher efficiency through smaller wing size, fall at their wing's failings and at the altar of the ellipse's unique lift characteristics and also Shenstone's work on drag reduction. The Bf109 wing slots, their mechanism and the drag triggers of their fittings were drag inducing. The Bf109's slots also tended to open automatically and repeatedly 'bang' or 'snatch' open and subject the wing, the aircraft, and therefore the pilot, to considerable vibration and dynamic change at a vital combat moment, therefore unbalancing the pilot and his aeroplane. So, by using the tuned, larger chord, modified two-part elliptical wing, the Spitfire did not need to resort to moveable leading edge slots like the Bf109, and, vitally, the Spitfire's lift was cleaner, more efficient with lower induced and parasitic drag and the lift stayed attached long after an Bf109 wing had stalled. Neither was the Spitfire's aspect ratio reduced by wing tip turbulence. Slots or no slots, Bf109s stalled and fell out of the sky when attempting to match the Spitfire in a tight turn.

The point about the Spitfire aerodynamics, is proven by the fact that the Spitfire started out as an aerodynamically clean, optimised shape, whereas the wing-slotted Bf109 had to go through a number of 'cleaning up' exercises to reduce its induced and parasitic drag. Of great note, later Spanish built Bf109's, also featured the addition of a large, tall, chordwise wing fence in order to reduce the spanwise flow from which the small tapered wing had always suffered. This wing fence markedly improved the Bf109s wing lift patterns and its fitting proved the point that the Bf109 'small wing, high lift' argument, was flawed when it came to turns and manoeuvres.

Those who argue that the Spitfire could have had a simpler, tapered wing, never mention the above issues. Wing loading was a crucial contributor to performance. With less induced drag, the high lift elliptical wing climbed faster too. In addition, the low wing loading allowed a smaller tail fin – adding speed through less drag. Combat proved that by concentrating on getting a better turn radius for better lifting capacity, Shenstone and Mitchell had given the Spitfire its vital advantage. And once the early Spitfires had been cured of the fuel feed-related engine stutter when rolling inverted to chase Bf109s, they could make even more of its aerodynamic advantage: ultimately, the Spitfire was faster than the Bf109, as well as being more agile. And when the Focke-Wulf 190 (FW190) came along, the Spitfire's original wing carried the development of its engine, power and airframe to match the FW190.

The FW190 achieved a speed advantage over earlier Spitfire variants by using the Bf109-based small wing theory. Again, this delivered speed in a straight line, but in the FW190, with a wing loading of 39lb/sq ft it also delivered lethal, 'flick' stalling in the turn. Small, high-lift tapered wings were fast, but what happened in a turning dog fight, especially in a tight turn?

From 1925 to 1940, the crucial, fighter plane 360-degree turn rates, as measured in speed of time elapsed, had worsened as aircraft became faster and heavier with thicker wings. Earlier biplane fighters had a 360-degree turn time of around 7 seconds, yet by 1939 the quest for ultimate top speed had created turn rate speeds of around 11 seconds – the Bf109G at 12 seconds being the significant example of the trade off between top speed and turn manoeuvrability. With the Spitfire wing, Supermarine managed to reverse this trend but not at the expense of top speed. The Spitfire had both the high top speed and the best, winning, turn rate of 8 seconds in a much tighter radius – reversing the previous trend of 1930s fighter development. The ellipse's lift characteristics were vital in achieving this.

For sheer speed, the addition of various propeller and reduction gear changes to the Spitfire's engine and prop drive soon saw its top speed in

Beverley Shenstone as seen at Junkers, Dessau in 1929. (Photo: *Shenstone family*)

Beverley in the 1950s as Chief Engineer at BEA. (Photo: *BEA via Shenstone family*)

The Class of 1928. Toronto University with Prof J.H. Parkin. Bev is front row far right seated on the floor. (Photo: *Shenstone family*)

Beverley and his then favourite - the sleek Junkers Junior in 1930. (Photo: *Shenstone family*)

Netley 1936. Beverley was a keen sailor. Uffa Fox sought Bev's advice on yacht design for his book in April 1935. Bev's close friend Thurstan James, editor of The Aeroplane also sailed with him. (Photo: *Shenstone family*)

In a very rare image, Alexander Lippisch, father of the delta wing, leans on his drawings as his team, including Beverley Shenstone (far left) look on. Ursinus House, Wasserkuppe, winter 1930. (Photo: *Shenstone family*)

Bev's first wife, Helen Shenstone about to take off in a primary glider at the Wasserkuppe, summer 1930. (Photo: *Shenstone family*)

Spitfire inspiration? British elliptical pioneer Sir Frederick Lanchester with his 1894 flying test model that proved the ellipse's advantages long before today's misguided commentators focused upon the 1932 Heinkel 70. (Photo: *Courtesy RAeS /NAL archive collection*)

Two great scientists and old friends - Alexander M. Lippisch and Beverley S. Shenstone meet up again at Lake Constance, Switzerland, 1972 during Lippisch hydrofoil design tests. (Photo: *Shenstone family*)

The Lippisch D2 flying wing test model photographed in flight at the Wasserkuppe 1931. (Photo: *B.S. Shenstone*)

Whilst the rest of the world was playing with biplanes, Lippisch was creating the flying wing/delta wing as the stepping stone to a jet age future that Beverley Shenstone helped create. D1 test, Wasserkuppe, 1930. (Photo: *B.S. Shenstone*)

Alexander Lippisch and test pilot Gunter Groenhoff with the D2 test flight team.
Wasserkuppe 1931. (Photo: *B.S. Shenstone*)

Woolston, Southampton in the 1930s: German visitors at Supermarine as a Dornier flying boat
is moored on the River Itchen during a visit. (Photo: *B.S. Shenstone*)

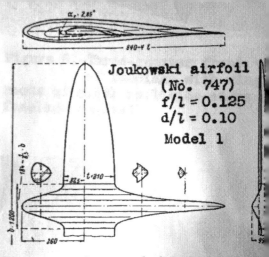

Figure 4.—Wing and fuselage with fuselage faired smoothly into the wing. (Model n

A rare photograph of Arthur Shirvall at his desk at Supermarine in 1934: Shirvall did the detail design for the Spitfire body and created the later float plane version. Like others, he is an unsung hero of the Spitfire's design. (Photo: *B.S. Shenstone*)

Joukowski (Zhoukovski) had his elliptical ideas circa 1900. Here we see an integrated elliptical form. Again, this was long before the 1932 Heinkel 70 - an aircraft so often erroneously cited as an elliptical pioneer. (Photo: *via B.S. Shenstone*)

Type 224 in late 1933 – the Spitfire's ungainly forefather and such a shock compared to a Schneider Trophy winning S.6. Note cranked wing, corrugations and high-drag shapes. (Photo: *B.S. Shenstone*)

K5054, the very first Spitfire Eastliegh March 1936. (Photo: *B.S. Shenstone*)

A view never before seen in the public domain, the experimental wing fillet was tested out on the Type 224 and tuft tested using propwash on the ground. The Spitfire's subsequent wing fillet was one of its key Shenstone-designed advantages. (Photo: *B.S. Shenstone*)

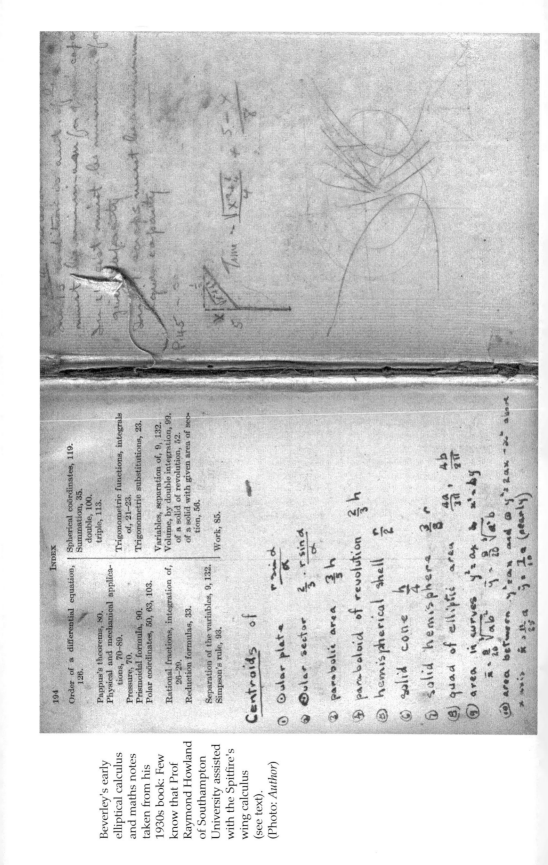

Centroids of

① circular plate $\dfrac{r\sin\alpha}{\alpha}$

② circular sector $\dfrac{2}{3}\cdot\dfrac{r\sin\alpha}{\alpha}$

③ parabolic area $\dfrac{3}{5}h$

④ paraboloid of revolution $\dfrac{2}{3}h$

⑤ hemispherical shell $\dfrac{r}{2}$

⑥ solid cone $\dfrac{h}{4}$

⑦ solid hemisphere $\dfrac{3}{8}r$

⑧ quad of elliptic area $\dfrac{4a}{3\pi}, \dfrac{4b}{2\pi}$

⑨ area in curves $y^2=ax$ & $x^2=by$ $\bar{x}=\dfrac{9}{20}\sqrt{ab}, \dfrac{9}{20}\sqrt{a^2 b}$

⑩ area between $y^2=ax$ and $y^2=2ax-x^2$ about x axis $\bar{x}=\dfrac{3}{15}a$, $\bar{y}=\dfrac{1}{10}a$ (nearly)

Beverley's early elliptical calculus and maths notes taken from his 1930s book. Few know that Prof Raymond Howland of Southampton University assisted with the Spitfire's wing calculus (see text). (Photo: *Author*)

Seen on an un-camouflaged airframe, Bev's Spitfire wing fillet was an advanced feature that drastically lowered aerodynamic drag yet is rarely recognised nor credited. (Photo: *Author*)

The modified double ellipse and the integrated body form – largely the work of Beverley Shenstone, captured in a classic Spitfire pose. (Photo: *Author*)

The thin wing and narrow, smooth lines, influenced by Supermarine Schneider Trophy aircraft, sailplanes and advanced delta wing research, are clearly shown on this Spitfire. (Photo: *Author*)

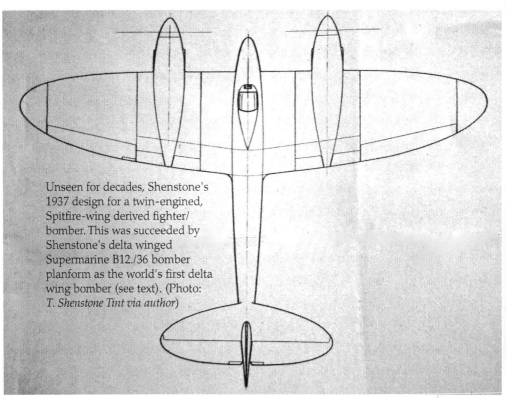

Unseen for decades, Shenstone's 1937 design for a twin-engined, Spitfire-wing derived fighter/bomber. This was succeeded by Shenstone's delta winged Supermarine B12./36 bomber planform as the world's first delta wing bomber (see text). (Photo: *T. Shenstone Tint via author*)

1938 not 2008! Beverley Shenstone's amazing design for a blended-wing fighter, drawn and published in 1938: Clearly, the designer of this 1930s aircraft was a man of prescient genius. (Photo: *Author*)

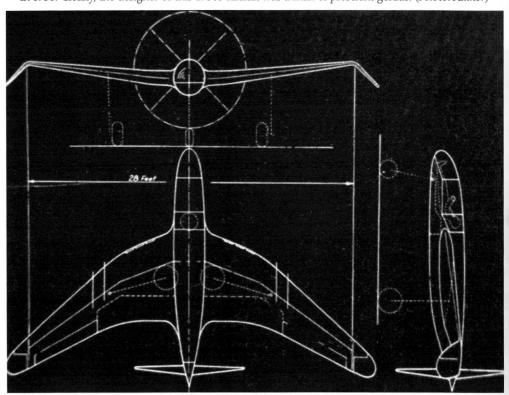

1937 – flight test of a more contemporary Shenstone flying-wing model. Shades of the Mosquito wing perhaps? (Photo: *Shenstone family*)

A stern-looking Beverley at the top-secret Wright Patterson AFB research facility 1942 during his war time posting to the heart of advanced American design. (Photo: *Shenstone family*)

Bev and his son Blair, seen in the late 1940s with a model of the Shenstone/Czerwinksi designed Harbinger glider. (Photo: *Czerwinski for Shenstone family*)

Bev holds the wingtip to launch the University of Toronto's *Loudon* glider, circa 1950. Bev's brother, Douglas, became Chairman of the Soaring Association of Canada (SAC) and Bev was also a senior, founding figure in SAC. (Photo: *Shenstone family*)

The long-nosed variant of the *Harbinger*. Now in-store at Bicester gliding club. (Photo: *Shenstone family*)

BEA days. Sir Peter Masefield and Beverley inspect the latest de Havilland offering for the airline in the 1950s. (Photo: *Shenstone family*)

Vickers Viscount 1949 flight test from London Airport to Dublin. Left to Right: Handasyde, Shenstone, Edwards, Bryce, Buckley. Vickers offered Shenstone their senior design role (see text). Beverley said Sir George Edwards did a much better job than he could of done. (Photo: *BEA /Shenstone family*)

By Royal Appointment: Beverley Shenstone, Lord Kirtleside - BEA's Chairman AM Sholto Douglas, and HRH The Duke of Edinburgh. (Photo: *BEA via Shenstone family*)

BEA Vickers Viscount in the early livery seen in a serene cruise, displaying its Shenstone influenced elliptical elegance. (Photo: *BEA/Shenstone*)

In one of the rarest of historical images, this is Bev's own photograph of the Supermarine Type 224 pre-Spitfire prototype in early 1934. From the mistakes of the Type 224, grew the sleek and smooth Spitfire with all its advanced science of airflow management. (Photo: *B.S. Shenstone*)

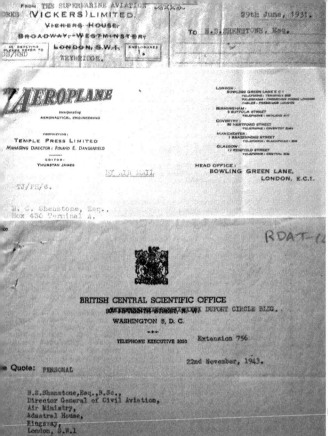

Correspondence – Bev's first pay slip from Supermarine dated 27 June 1931: A letter from his closest life-long friend, Thurstan James the editor of *The Aeroplane*: A Letter citing Bev and his wartime title and official role. (Photo: *author*)

☆ ☆ ☆

Toronto University published a wartime story hailing their hero as a 'co-designer' of the Spitfire – which Beverley in his quiet modesty, disliked and denied at the time. The media repeated such claim, and one famous test-pilot had no issue with the veracity of that claim (see text). (Photo: *author*)

I Fly Overnight to England

Famed Co-Designer of Spitfire Gives Impressions of Air Trip Across Atlantic in Liberator II

By BEVERLEY S. SHENSTONE ('Toronto '28)

IT was cold in Montreal and the snow was banked high along the runways at Dorval. Snogo cleaners were blowing plumes of powdered snow off the tarmac and the snow underfoot was so cold that it creaked when I walked on it.

We turned up at noon as requested and were fitted with oxygen masks and parachute harness. Then down the passage to be fitted for flying kit. A man looked at me, scribbled some numbers on a paper and said, "O.K."

"Are you going to fit me?" I asked.

"I've done it," he replied. "Those are your sizes on the paper."

We were all set to go next morning. We got our clothes and mine did really fit. A double flying suit, great thick overshoes, two pairs of gloves and a leather helmet and the parachute harness. In fact, everybody's fitted, except that one chap thought he couldn't get into his flying suit. But he did.

FITTED IN LIKE SARDINES

Eleven of us trooped across the tarmac to the black Liberator II (B-24), looking rather silly. Most of us carried our ordinary overcoats and perched on the top of our flying helmets we had stuck our hats, which looked quite ridiculous. We crawled up through the trapdoor and were greet-

and blankets and a cabin otherw completely bare. We lay like sardin athwart ships, one man's head to p and the next man's to starboard, a so on. We struggled into the blank and lay down. The trap door bang shut and we took off at 10:15.

It was cold, terribly cold; we did dare move out of our blankets. couldn't talk because of the noise

BEVERLEY S. SHENSTONE

excess of the earlier, faster Bf109's straight line speed. The early Spitfire's straight line speed of 349mph rose to 362mph once the engine and prop issues were sorted out, then rose again in the MkIX variant to 409mph at 28,000ft and a 43,000ft service ceiling.

The Hurricane's low wing loading was achieved though its use of a lightweight fabric-clad rear fuselage and its early canvas skinned wings – wings that were also longer than the Spitfire's broader wings. In theory, the Hurricane's large tail gave it more steerage way, but its longer, thicker wing with higher induced drag and slower aerofoil tended to quickly bleed lift energy and also negate the rudder's effectiveness. With large, ailerons and a thick wing, the Hurricane's roll rate was strong at low speed and low altitude, but suffered at higher speeds and flight levels, leaving the Hurricane on the defensive by having to rely on its minimum turn radius as opposed to being able to use lift energy and a low drag turn rate, to act offensively – as the Spitfire managed. And neither could the Hurricane attain the high, level flight speed of the Spitfire. Effective at lower altitudes, the big-tailed, thick-winged Hurricane with its large cross sectional area fuselage paid a high price as its inherent drag consumed its speed and lift, even after it was given alloy-skinned wings.

Only at very high altitude did the Spitfire encounter heavy aileron response, as also afflicted the Bf109 – so on that front honours were even… But it was that low wing loading that let the Spitfire turn as tightly it did – beating all comers and aided by its rate of turn, which was down to airflow control.

The proof of Supermarine's aerodynamic and structural work is also underlined by the fact that nearer the speed of 0.82 Mach and above, the Spitfire's wing continues to perform and, stays attached to the airframe. Normally, as speed increases, drag increases *beyond* the normal square ratio of speed; this is due to airflow compressibility and the designer must avoid localized compressibility affecting the wing or controls. Bumps and lumps in, or on, the aircraft's skin need to be avoided, otherwise they will set off a localized aerodynamic disturbance that can affect not only lift and drag, but also control responses.

Shenstone wrote an article on the wing loading battle, and for reasons of then professional practice he could not do it under his own name. So, writing under his pen name of Brian Worley in Oliver Stewart's *Aeronautics*, Shenstone allowed himself a rare moment of opinion, or was it Air Ministry-supported propaganda? We will never know, but Shenstone wrote of the Spitfire's advantage over the Bf109, thus:

(The Bf109)… has the same indicated air speed as our Spitfire but due to a higher wing loading cannot get around a turn as fast. They are in fact, not as good, due to the high wing loading. Yes, wing loading is the vital point.

No matter how fast one can fly, if the wing loading is high, one is caught by the more lightly loaded aeroplane when manoeuvring. What the Germans should have done was to pull down their wing loadings to those of ours and given a little away of their top speed… But perhaps they were afraid to do it in view of our fast bombers. On the other hand, the fact that they have not done it, enables us to put up our loadings if we wish, and since we seem to be able to produce more speed than they do, we ought, at their loadings to be 50 miles an hour faster than they are.

So the Germans have not been too clever have they? But they have a long line of continuous fighter development behind them, so if they have gone wrong we must not be surprised or derisive, for it is bound to be hard for people who try to muscle into a racket at the top. We shall only say that it is just too bad, or should we say just too good?

The wing loadings of present German fighters are higher than they ought to be and they are thus inferior to our own fighters in manoeuvrability.[18]

This language was indeed a rare moment of proclamation for the quiet Canadian, who was also writing in the context of 'our' British fighters. Was he the Air Ministry's wartime propaganda's servant perhaps?

Of note, Shenstone, had in the early 1930s worked on the Lotz method of wing taper study, and through publication introduced it into British aeronautical debate. He had also worked on the aerofoil performance, boundary flow, lift distribution and span wise airflow characteristics of the Lippisch swept flying-wing Stork, and his delta wing D1, which evolved from it. Shenstone had also spent over a year at Junkers – and despite his fame for 'corrugated' thick-winged aircraft, Junkers had been at the forefront of elliptical, swept and all-wing aircraft design. Junkers patented his first, swept, all-wing design as early as 1913. His research files were packed with wind tunnel tests and calculus on the behaviour and performance of such wings – notably a small model of an ellipse dated 1910.

These experiences of the early 1930s were confirmed by Shenstone's 1930s published papers. In 1930 he wrote: 'A Study of the Inter-relation of Weight and Drag'. And in 1932 he wrote: 'A method of determining the twist required on a Tapered Wing in order to attain any desired lateral stability at high angles of attack'. What it amounted to was to ensure that at these 'high incidences' the spanwise shape of the lift coefficient curve did not suffer at the wing tip.

In 1934, with Professor Raymond Howland, Shenstone researched and wrote: 'The Inverse Method for Tapered and Twisted Wings', which in essence, described methods for solving the twist or 'washout' for a wing of predetermined plan form and taper to satisfy the stalling characteristics. The pair wanted the paper published in the *Royal Aeronautical Society Journal*, but at that time, records Shenstone, the editor insisted that all mathematical expressions or formulae should be printed linearly instead of the usual form. This made even the most familiar expressions, unfamiliar. Regretfully, in terms of aviation profile, the paper was published in *The Philosophical Journal*.[19]

So Shenstone knew just how good a conventional tapered wing could be, the ellipse would have to offer more. Shenstone also postulated in 1934 that aileron design was vital to wing performance and that having the ailerons extend too far out towards the wing tip would reduce their efficiency; smaller ailerons, mounted further inboard were in his mind and he used that theme on the Spitfire's modified ellipse. Mitchell also knew all about aileron trouble from his Schneider Trophy experiences. He and Shenstone were in agreement about ailerons – their size, shape and location.

Through his 1930–31 delta wing work, and through studying advanced German glider designs, Shenstone knew that it was the behaviour of the airflow over the wing at varying velocities and angles, as well as the actual wing loading itself, that were the two key factors to creating an advanced wing that offered significant advantages beyond a normally shaped, square tapered wing. The ellipse could also provide high altitude efficiency – combined with a thin aerofoil section. As with the Zhukovskii research work and that of the Junkers, and Lippisch wings, it was the pattern of lift distribution, boundary layer, and fuselage interaction that was the focus of Shenstone's work on smoothing the Spitfire and providing it with its unique aerodynamic qualities.

Shenstone's notes state that even Mitchell commented that the wing looked huge in comparison with that of the Hurricane's. But it was a visual illusion of the ellipse that made it appear so. Revealed here for the first time, are Mitchell's words upon returning from Weybridge after his first sight of Sydney Camm's excellent Hurricane, saying to Shenstone:

'My God, Camm has a tiny machine and ours looks too big.'[20]

In fact, the Spitfire had a 3ft *shorter* wingspan and one that was far thinner, with less area, than the conventionally shaped Hurricane.

In 1936, the Spitfire's wing was uniquely thin – against all accepted British aeronautical design practice at the time. Again this choice of thin wing stemmed from Shenstone and the Schneider design team's men. To go out on a technical limb like this shocked many contemporary designers, even some at the Royal Aircraft Establishment, advised against the thin wing idea of the young Canadian. Sticking with it was perhaps the boldest of steps taken by Mitchell and his men. In order to prioritize the design choices, Mitchell's men – principally, Alan Clifton, Alfred Faddy, Ernest Mansbridge, Squadron Leader Payn, Beverley Shenstone, Joseph Smith – held meetings where they allocated points to each feature based upon its importance. High-scoring design details were included, lesser items were sacrificed. Alan Clifton, Alfred Faddy, and Joseph Smith put in many hours of work making the thin wing's structure strong enough to resist the intense combat forces to which it would be subjected. The thin wing was safe, sound, and gave pilots total confidence.

Shenstone's diaries of early 1934, when the Type 224 was taking to the air and yet being a failure, and Spitfire work was proceeding long before official sponsorship in late 1934, demonstrate that it was a constant battle to stay on top of research and developments:

> Evening with Prof Howland. And we discussed the Lotz method. In the evaluation I have apparently made an arithmetic error… I have begun a collection of wing data and associated items, such as aerodynamic controls including balance areas. From now on, I must be ready to be able to produce such data without much searching. It is clear that this is of importance, but of course it can easily be taken too far, but that would take a long time. I do quite a lot of work in the evenings, but there is always more to do…. Letter from Lippisch.[21]

The phrase about having to be ready to produce such data, clearly illustrates the role Shenstone was expected to perform in terms of the Spitfire's design process – *he* was the person who was going to be asked the questions, and answers were expected.

The thin aerofoil section was a key factor – indeed Shenstone says in his private diaries that he could have gone thinner still.[22] As it was he chose the NACA 2220 series aerofoils – using 2209 and 2213 – and then varied the thickness-to-chord ratio. At the tip, the chord ratio is just 6 per cent – far thinner than any contemporary wing and, thinner than the 12 per cent tip chord ratio of Hawker's developed Hurricane replacement, the 1944 Fury – also fitted with an ellipsoid derived wing… The later P-52 Mustang used 13.8 per cent root thickness and 11.4 per cent tip aerofoil thickness.

The Spitfire's modified or double ellipse gave it the best of all worlds – a unique high performance wing, yet one with extra footage in its width or chord, into which could be packed guns, wheels, and radiator scoops. It didn't look like it, but the Spitfire wing was a low aspect ratio, aerobatic wing. Perhaps if it had been short, stubby and square, the wing's performance would have been more obvious to the opinions of the era, but instead, Shenstone swathed the square footage of the wing in the exquisite visual deception of the ellipse.

There was more: the Spitfire wing was also unique in its minimal degree of 'washout' – this is the amount of twist along the wingspan from wing root to wing tip.

'Washout' was a science that had been developed in the early days of wing-warped aviation, yet was eschewed by many designers. 'Washout' was wing twist and stemmed from early research into swept and warped wings by J.W. Dunne, Geoffrey Hill and his Westland Pterodactyl type, and by Lippisch in his early glider studies. It was also explored by the early glider designer Jose Weiss, and significantly by Frederick Handley Page in his powered types. Wing twist or 'washout' stemmed from the observations of Professor Ahlborn and his Zanonia seed studies – where naturally applied 'washout' was evident.

Handley Page's pioneering work, which reached its peak in the 1920s, included his support of the monoplane principle, and his use of swept crescent and part ellipsoid type wing planforms, with the use of the 'washed-out' angle of incidence (as early as 1919 in his monoplane type No. 2). Handley Page's use of the safety feature that is now a universal jet aircraft feature – the leading edge slot – which became the slat, was another of his pioneering feats, albeit derived from the work of Lachmann. The Handley Page Gugnunc of 1928 being the first production monoplane aircraft in the world to be fitted with an automatically moveable leading edge high lift device.

Handley Page used German knowledge to develop the slot, as it was Dr Ing. Gustav Victor Lachmann that became Handley Page's leading aerodynamic boffin. Lachmann patented his leading edge slot device in 1919 and worked in Germany and spent time in the often forgotten Japanese aviation industry. In the 1920s, Lachmann moved to England and joined Frederick Handley Page's company. Latterly Lachmann had also researched and published work on wing design. But the slot was his motif.

Here again was evidence of German design influence being accepted into the British establishment and yet there was also an irony. In 1936, Lachmann published his paper 'The Stalling of Tapered Wings'[23] and stated that the Lotz method of calculus had been 'introduced into this country in a very instructive article published in the *Journal of the Royal Aeronautical Society*[24] by Shenstone'.

Lachmann, however, created one of the largest public arguments in aerodynamic research ever seen. From the publication of his paper in late 1936, arguments about the benefits of the ellipse over the tapered wing raged in the aviation press. The letters pages of *Flight* magazine were buzzing with a mix of vitriol, opinion and research. From November 1936 to March 1937, *Flight* magazine saw heated debate about wing shapes and even had to print regular editorial opinion and updates on the claims being made.

Some contributors even called the ellipse a 'fetish' or a 'fad'. Lachmann, it seems, based his tapered wing research on early theoretical calculus and scale-related findings. He was, it appears, not a proponent of the ellipse. Others (notably Stanley H. Evans) claimed that the benefits of the ellipse were significant. As theorist confounded theorist, the ellipse supporters and detractors marched on. The likes of famous names such as, R.P. Alston, G.M. Buxton, S. Evans, W.E. Gray, G.T.R. Hill, P. Nazir and N. Piercy, were all cited. Ultimately, *Flight* magazine challenged Dr Lachmann's opinions and a great deal of research followed – there were many unanswered questions and many questions of once hallowed theories. As an example of Shenstone's brilliance and Supermarine's work, it is worth noting that this aerodynamic debate raged long after the Spitfire and its modified ellipse had taken to the air and displayed its massive leap forwards in aerodynamic terms.

As for Lachmann, in typically British fashion, having accepted Lachmann and his skills into the British aviation establishment, upon the outbreak of the Second World War, the British then interned him as a possible spy! Gladly, sense prevailed and he was returned to Handley Page.

Twisting the wing in the manner deployed on the Spitfire between root and tip created airflow that stayed attached longer and flowed better. The Spitfire's in-flight loaded wing had a 'washout' of +2 degrees at the root and –0.5 degrees at the tip – creating a twist axis of 2.5 degrees along the wing. Any more 'washout' would have seriously affected the very reason for using the ellipse by creating, not reducing, drag. The 'washout' twist meant that, unlike many contemporary and subsequent fighter wings, the Spitfire did not suffer from a sudden and unexpected stall, and neither did it drop a wing at the stall – so often a feature of high performance wings of all shapes. Instead, the Spitfire wing signalled the impending stall with feedback through the stick, giving the pilot plenty of warning and time to redress the situation.

Spitfire pilots could outturn the enemy and also got a unique level of warning before the wing stopped flying. Pre-stall buffet occurred right next to the cockpit – at the wing root whilst the wing tips remained 'flying' – allowing continued aileron effectiveness and roll control. The unequal chord aileron design also helped the ailerons retain their effectiveness for far longer – a vital factor for the pilot in extremis; this was achieved through calculus, not simply by making the ailerons bigger, which would have made them heavier to use. (Early Spitfires had canvas-covered ailerons; these were soon changed to alloy to match the wing and avoid surface tension problems at high speeds, which quickly became apparent in combat.)

Also remarkable, was the fact that the curved ellipse did not suffer excessive spanwise flow. There was no need for a wing fence to funnel stray, lift-destroying spanwise flow back on course. The small amount of forward swept distortion in the Spitfire's wing deflected the spanwise airflow circulation and lift distribution in a beneficial manner, and added stability. Reduction of drag from an aircraft's skin, was a major element of glider, delta and all-wing design philosophy. Shenstone's application of such knowledge, gained firsthand at Lippisch's drawing board, to the Spitfire's skin, and to its ellipsoid wing and small-tail design, was a key factor in its success. The role of body skin shape and tail design plays a significant part in the work of Shenstone to reduce drag and add speed to the Spitfire.

* * *

The Details of Design – the Boundary Layer and the Wing Root Fillet and Tail Designs

The tuning of the ellipse, of creating a uniquely re-shaped and reformed ellipse and adding to it the boundary layer effect, was to become Shenstone's forensically minded area of focus in the 1930s. Intriguingly, at the same time, his uncle, Allen G. Shenstone, FRS, who went on to become one of the twentieth century's leading atomic physicists, worked on the gaseous boundary layer in his atomic physics research at Princetown USA – where the world of mathematics and science in the 1930s saw many advances. Beverley Shenstone's diaries record contact at the time between the two families, and he visited America in 1934 as part of the Vickers delegation, but it is impossible to know if the two Shenstone men shared any of their thoughts with each other over the subject in 1934. But one thing that is obvious is that both men were operating at the leading edge of research thinking.

Shenstone studied the boundary layer and aircraft skin design with Junkers and Lippisch, and talked with Prandtl and von Karman, two of the leading boundary layer gurus of their time.

By January 1937, Shenstone had published a major paper[25] that he had spent some time researching and writing during his Supermarine years on the theory of boundary layer control techniques, and ultimately that of mechanically sucking airflow from the boundary layer through holes in an aircraft's wing or fuselage. Before that, from 1929, he had begun a close study of the boundary layer – the thin sheath of air that lies very close to an aircraft's skin that is subject to friction-related, localized speed changes, which in turn affects airflow further out from the aircraft's skin. Some of this airflow slows down and stagnates above it, and the airflow increases it speed. Between these layers is the 'boundary' layer.

By creating an especially smoothed and shaped skin surface, by tuning the movement and speed of airflow patterns and their behaviour across the wing's skin, Shenstone tuned these factors to reduce localized turbulence and drag by altering and speeding up the boundary layer airflow – this was why Shenstone insisted on the flush rivets of the Spitfire's construction.

Prior to experiments with perforated or sucking wings, this smoothing and sculpting of the Spitfire's skin friction boundary airflow was the first step in applying boundary layer thinking to a high-performance fighter aircraft wing. Shenstone was inspired by hydrodynamic studies he had made as a post graduate student in Canada, and by hydrofoil research. The effects of the Junkers designs' skin corrugations, and the smooth skin criteria on advanced German glider designs and on delta shapes, only served to confirm to Shenstone that the effect of aircraft skin surface design on the boundary layer, was the key to improving performance. It would be nearly a decade before the first boundary layer laminar flow wing, that of the P-51 Mustang, would see production.

Shenstone was also quite happy to admit that the smoothness of the Heinkel 70's total body form inspired him to pursue such criteria for the Spitfire, but he also pointed out that this was the *only* way in which the Heinkel 70 influenced the Spitfire – as the Spitfire's ellipse was a different shape, a completely different planform to that of the Heinkel, and had a different aerofoil.

The idea of a perforated wing – of mechanically sucking (or blowing) air from the boundary layer –was to take years to be perfected, but the Spitfire's ellipse benefited from Shenstone's early work on the tuning of the speed and direction of boundary layer airflow and his forensic attention to the quality of skin shape and smoothness criteria to reduce the airflow stagnation effect by making the boundary layer as thin as possible. Shenstone's work also delayed the separation of airflow across the camber of the ellipse's aerofoil by increasing the localized airflow speed – moving the separation point downstream in the airflow and delaying the loss of airflow smoothness – thereby avoiding a loss of lift and, in effect, adding lift. Perhaps the Spitfire's wing was as close to the laminar theory as a pre-laminar wing could get...

Shenstone could not apply boundary layer suction via mechanical devices to the Spitfire, but he could apply sculpting and smoothing to reduce shear layer friction and increase the speed of that localized boundary layer airflow. By improving the wing to fuselage junction, by tailoring every part of the wing and hull, airflow separation and turbulence could be delayed or minimized. A significant yet forgotten example of this work can be found underneath the Spitfire – between the rear of each wing root – where two U-shaped channels tune the airflow off the underbody and each wing as it leads back under the fuselage boom. Here, this local shaping stops the air stagnating or becoming fully turbulent and also reduces the wake vortices spilling off the underwing junctions. Suction effect is actually created.

In fact, it was the underwing area that presented problems that were not fully solved. The Spitfire's various add-on radiators protruded beneath the wing, fouling the boundary layer, and despite the Meredith design effect of ram air through the radiator, created underwing turbulence and boundary layer bubbling. The scooped channels and swept wing join reduced these losses, but it was a battle not entirely won at the edge of the then unknown.

The fine detailing of design work was unique to the Spitfire and can only reflect the combination of Shenstone's studies and the hydrodynamic expertise of Mitchell and his Schneider Trophy racer and flying boat, design men – notably Mr Shirvall. Such sculpting – seen all over the Spitfire and invisible to the untrained eye – is yet another example of the collection of design techniques incorporated into the machine, where every tiny aspect has been thought about and forensically tailored to perform a function, by a team of experts.

For those who doubt the application and efficacy of the Spitfire's boundary layer-related skin smoothing work, on its wings, upper surfaces and fuselage boom, there can be no better proof of its achievement than the speeds that the wing and airframe achieved. How did a wing designed in 1934–35, get to regularly perform at Mach 0.82, reach Mach 0.90+ and handle double the engine power for which it was originally designed? How did such a wing and hull remain aerodynamically competitive for a decade against the scale and rate of design development during the war, and still exceed the performance of later aircraft? Structural improvements to carry more weight and more speed, are normal within the development of any airframe, the Spitfire included, but the Spitfire's aerodynamics remained constant across a vast speed range – thanks to Shenstone's skills and the very real likelihood that his swept wing and delta wing work in 1931 had placed him and the subsequent Spitfire wing far ahead of anyone or anything else.

The Spitfire in total took over 300,000 man hours to design and Shenstone spent thousands of hours working out every inch of the aircraft's aerodynamics. He tuned the localized boundary layer velocity, tuned the diffusion of vortices, assessed friction and pressure changes. He altered the Spitfire's NACA 2200 series aerofoils with localized re-shaping – using the NACA sections 2209/4 near the wing tip and NACA 2213 near the root. Blending these aerofoils was revolutionary in itself, and the way in which Shenstone smoothed them into their junctions – avoiding localized peaks and troughs in the aerofoil – required hours of calculus, plotting and structural consideration. Smith, Faddy and the 'loftsman' colleagues, had to work with their aerodynamicist, as every wing rib had to be tuned for height, curvature and effect upon the smooth skin that would lie above its station.

Shenstone tuned out the imperfections of the aerofoil shape – issues that could lead to what are termed 'source' and 'sink areas on the aerofoil where airflow and its behaviour, changes, to make it flow away from, or towards, set points or effects. Shenstone and the team also tried to make the aerofoil/rib shape alterations occur within a pattern – not randomly spread out over the wing. This tuning explains why the wing's structural ribs also had to be tuned with varying high points, and why the tailoring of the stressed metal skin across the wing's span, was so vital to making all aspects of the wing 'work'. Localized curvature, streamwise tuning and tailoring airflow speed fluctuations were the essentials of Shenstone's Spitfire wing skin work where advanced mathematical theory was critical – methods to quantify effects and changes measured as 'skewness' and 'kurtosis' being applicable.

By shaping the wings and hull to speed up local airflow close to the Spitfire's skin, sweeping the air off the panel, Shenstone invoked an early form of suction – speed effect that was a stepping stone to boundary layer control – without mechanically sucking or blowing through the airframe.

With a speeded up surface airflow, a minimally thin boundary or transition layer less than one inch in depth was achieved at a time when up to three inches depth may have been expected. The adverse, speed sapping effects of airflow bubbling – detachment and reattachment of the layer – was removed by such work and the wing's skin friction related airflow, was as smooth as it could be. Later attempts to compromise and use domed rivets, disturbing the airflow, showed a loss of over 20mph, proving that the smooth wing design really did deliver the benefits claimed.

Through the combination of ellipsoid shape and boundary layer design, Shenstone drastically reduced drag over the wing, improved lift, and reduced the turbulence coming off the wing as the aircraft's wake vortex. Wake vortex control, and the reduction of it, is today a core theme of civil and military aerodynamics. In 1936, the Spitfire was unique in having been subjected to techniques to reduce its boundary layer and its consequent wake.

The combination of these effects was to decrease drag, increase lift and give the Spitfire's ellipse its extra efficiency or slipperiness and the speed that Mitchell craved.

The smooth air and smaller wake coming off the wing and the fuselage also allowed the tail to be small – its smaller size, further reducing drag. The small tailplane and empennage would never have worked so well if they had been sitting in a large, downstream, fully turbulent airflow wake. The sensitivity and responsiveness of the Spitfire's elevators, given their small size, showed that they were working in efficient air delivered to the tail in the best 'used' condition possible. The elevator was clearly not sitting in a turbulent funnel of a massive wing and body wake.

No other contemporaneous wing, be it ellipsoid or tapered, had the Spitfire's unique boundary layer effect tuning work. The forward swept, distorted ellipse was and, remains, unique. Adding an early form of boundary layer control only added to its brilliance. Shenstone's work on the Spitfire's ellipse, the full details of which are revealed here for the first time, can now be seen for the advanced, ground-breaking aerodynamics that it was – this was akin to computerized finite element fluid dynamics work. Shenstone's subsequent rapid rise to the top of aeronautics clearly demonstrated that within the closed and narrow constraints of the industry, his achievement was recognized if not publicized.

Boundary layer control was to dominate Shenstone's thinking for years to come, right up to his man-powered flight design research of the 1960s. His son, Blair, recalled to the author:

Dad was fascinated by nature, he studied the wings of birds – sea gulls and falcons, and he often used to tell us boys about the wing surfaces of insects. He told us about how he had noticed very early on, that the dragon fly and other highly efficient insect wing types, featured wing surface shaping and had shapes protruding upwards from the wing skin to control the boundary layer.[26]

As late as 1966, Shenstone was citing research into insect aerodynamics in his published papers.

* * *

The Wing Root Fillet

Another vital area of Shenstone's advanced study for the Spitfire, rarely discussed by Spitfire commentators, was its massive wing root fillet or infill panel that can be seen as the sculpted curved panel that smoothes out the wing to fuselage join in two axes – increasing in size and radius towards the rear. This was also an advanced aerodynamic tuning device that could, if correctly shaped, reduce drag and improve the curvilinear circulation of the wing lift – adding lift where before there was decreasing lift. By smoothing out turbulent airflow and lift disturbance where it normally occurs as the monoplane wing sticks out of the fuselage junction – the 'interference' drag effect and smoothing this join out, less lift was lost and less turbulence created at the wing root – actually creating vital wing energy. The idea had its roots in the observations of Zhukovskii (Joukowski) whose drawings circa 1900–1910 illustrate the benefits of wing to fuselage shaping for the preservation of lift near the junction of wing and fuselage.

Subsequent research, particularly the reports of H. Muttray,[27] showed that wing fillet design was a crucial art, and it was important to ensure that the radii of the fillet increases towards the rear – opening out the curve of the panel. By doing this, the airflow is smoothed and stopped from breaking away and forming a secondary flow pattern likely to cause drag and upset the tail with buffet. Tuning this to the aerofoil's thickness and the wing lift pattern was no simple matter – one mistake could massively increase drag and reduce speed and stability. Shenstone spent hours working out a shape with an expanding root radius fairing that gave the correct air pressure gradient at the vital junction of wing and body – yet without adversely affecting the position of the aerodynamic centre of lift on the wing or causing any instability. Getting this right, could (and did) lead to a reduction in the normally expected rapid deceleration of airflow towards the rear of the wing, and achieving this would add lift, reduce drag and add speed.

An indication of the importance of the advantages of a wing root fillet, was framed by the later research published in 1965 by Sighard Hoerner,[28] where in an in-depth analysis of the Bf109 (an aircraft that *lacked* a wing root fillet), Hoerner stated that over 5 per cent of its total drag stemmed from its wing root to fuselage body drag. He also suggested that if the Bf109 had been smoothed and cleaned up, with attention paid to scoops and panels, the aircraft could have gained nearly 20mph.

Shenstone's work on the Spitfire's wing root fillet benefited its boundary layer and its wing lift coefficient and reduced the overall drag figure. Given the size of this fillet, it could also be argued that it represented an early attempt at the 'area rule' aerodynamic technique, which although in technical terms applies to design for the transonic speed range, may have assisted the Spitfire not just in its handling and lift, but also in its actual ability to approach the transonic speed range.

A careful look at the Spitfire's wing to fuselage join area will reveal the sheer size of this fillet feature; by the time it approaches the rear of the wing, it is a major body panel – a large curved device several feet long and wide, and looking more like something that had come off a boat or a flying boat. Its angles and interactions were carefully calculated to create the smooth transition of airflow between the horizontal wing and the fuselage's upright join. Camouflage paint schemes tend to hide its size, but when studied on a non-camouflaged Spitfire, the significance of this often ignored design feature, this vital panel, becomes more obvious. Spitfire restorers know that it is important to set this panel correctly and ensure smooth joining to gain the best aerodynamic benefits.

By using this panelling to reduce the type of interference drag normally associated with wing-to-fuselage junctions, the Spitfire gained a significant benefit. The device was particularly effective at low speed when extra lift is vital and the propeller's wake is weaker. Shenstone also tuned the fillet to the wing twist so that the stall occurred inboard near the wing root – triggered nice and cleanly by the rear of the wing root fillet. At higher speeds, the effects of the swirling airflow stemming from the propeller's revolving action, would affect the lift pattern on the wing directly behind it, but the tuning of the wing trailing edge and the fillet into the elegant splayed curve, also reduced cavitation and turbulence from the propeller wake – reducing drag. This vital fillet panel was designed over the winter of 1934–35 and officially added to the Spitfire design in early April 1935. By this time, in America the large and rotund fuselage of the single radial-engined Northrop Gamma Express monoplane had also employed the very latest wing fillet design techniques to similar effect – as far as its thick fuselage section and thick wing would allow.

Creating a wing fillet that preserved the ellipse's low induced drag was a major mathematical and theoretical exercise, but Shenstone had studied the Lotz method of calculation, which was relevant to the fillet calculations, and he had introduced it to British aeronautical literature. He was therefore ideally placed to make the most of such theories, to create the Spitfire's wing fillet. Professor Howland's help with the calculus was to be vital.

The task was made much more difficult because of the localized effects of the variable aerofoil and variable wing chord. Exact angles that preserved low induced drag, and which stopped airflow breakaway, had to be worked out by shaping the camber and incidence of the fillet. All corners had to be removed and the ratio of fuselage cross sectional area to wing thickness had to be tailored accurately to a theoretical best value. By solving all this and fitting this sculpted fillet panel, Shenstone achieved another massive leap forwards in wing lift and boundary layer low drag design and performance for the Spitfire. Neither the Hurricane nor Bf109, or any other combat type, contained such advanced aerodynamics.

How did Shenstone know about this at his young age?

The answer is broad experience early in his career. While working at Junkers in 1930–31, he had been involved with experiments on Junkers aircraft with the wing root infill panel and knew just how effective they could be. Secondly, Shenstone also worked with Lippisch and Jacobs on the wing design of the Fafnir glider. Something was wrong with the elegant glider; despite all its fairings and curves, it had an airflow and lift problem. The issue was found to be in the wing to fuselage infill panel shaping. The three men worked on altering the wing to fuselage interference and the result was the Fafnir II, which had a differing wing root and cockpit fairing design.

One of Shenstone's further basic lessons in his wing design learning came from Junkers. The famous Junkers-type wing surface corrugations acted as multiple chord-wise wing fences – funnelling airflow straight back across the wing at maximum lift effectiveness, as seen on the Ju 52. However, when Junkers removed the corrugations for the Ju 86, spanwise or transverse airflow migration occurred along the tapered wing, and the channelling effect of the corrugations was lost. This spanwise flow reduced the lift effectiveness and adversely altered the handling of the aircraft – 'wing drop' occurred: Yet on the Ju 52, the extra skin area of the Junkers hallmark corrugations also added to the cross sectional C_{Da} drag figure and wing to fuselage interference occurred – just as it also had on a previous Junkers design. These were vital lessons for a young designer such as Shenstone and few had had the chance to be exposed to such tests and techniques.

In the Spitfire, by smoothing out the wing to body join, and by reducing the fully turbulent boundary layer drag, speed went up, and by streaming less turbulent wake air off the wing root, the wing was more efficient and so too was the tailplane, and thus could be made smaller. It is accepted aerodynamic fact that wing-induced drag can account for a very large percentage of overall drag, and that the wing to fuselage interference factor can have a pronounced effect on the drag and lateral stability and manoeuvrability of an aircraft, especially in turns and at the stall, and it must be obvious that the successful tuning of this effect by deliberate design of the Spitfire's wing root fillet helped deliver the aircraft's handling and speed advantage over all competitors

* * *

The Tail Design

Beverley Shenstone was also occupied by the Spitfire's tail fin, he and Mitchell worked closely together on its design. Both men wanted the tail kept very small – again to reduce drag, Shenstone had learned this technique at Junkers and Lippisch, and Mitchell, Simmonds and Mansbridge had moved towards it through the Supermarine racing designs.

Along with the wing design and slim fuselage boom, the tail design was another vital element to the harmony of the whole design. In comparison with the Hurricane's large, biplane legacy tail fin, the smaller size and area of the Spitfire's advanced low drag tail empennage is very obvious. Tail design is vital to stability and controllability and can be best achieved by tuning the fin, to the fuselage design and length – known as the moment arm – as well as to other factors. Just as with the wing to fuselage work, the fuselage and tail fin relationship were vital to low drag and responsive handling.

The Spitfire tail fin and tailplane design was advanced because, instead of making it a proportional size to the wing (in the traditional manner of the time), it was designed to reflect the properties of the slim fuselage and tuned wing wake spillage. This was another vital example of new thinking in design.

The Spitfire's low wing loading also helped towards having a small tail because a higher wing loading from a smaller wing would have required a more efficient and bigger tail with all its disadvantages of increased weight and drag. Once again the ellipse, contrary to its recent detractors, proved its worth by assisting the success of the small tail idea. The Supermarine team, with Shenstone's aerodynamic work, created a small tail yet one with good fin and rudder efficiency. The Spitfire's rounded canopy (as opposed to the Hurricane and Bf109, square-cornered or flat-sided canopies) also yielded significant aerodynamic advantages by making sure that the boundary layer remained intact as possible – and did not pass broken, unattached airflow down the fuselage onto the fin and rudder.

For the Spitfire, controlling the airflow off the wing and fuselage was vital to the efficiency of the tail, and to controlling the adverse effects of vortices and sideways acting forces around the wing and fuselage. The evident, class leading handling qualities of the Spitfire – that instant and sharp response – clearly demonstrate that the efforts of Spitfire's aerodynamicist were successful. This tail design and its resulting control effectiveness is another unsung facet of the Spitfire's design.

Having a larger tail fin would also increase drag and create a problem of aerodynamic side loading – the effects of sidewash and stability. Nearly eight years after the Spitfire was shaped, the early P-51 Mustang suffered tail fin failures in flight due to its large fin being affected by these fuselage, wing and fin related sideways acting forces – and alterations had to be made.

In mid-1935, R.J. Mitchell received criticism of the Spitfire's small tail design from the Air Ministry's observers, notably R. Alston and H. Stone at the Royal Aircraft Establishment (RAE) after scale model spin tests suggested that the tail fin was too small and that the tailplane was set too low. These views were based on the theories of then perceived wisdom, or as they said at the time, 'past experience'.[29] Such experience was based on biplanes and thick-winged, broad-fuselage monoplanes with large biplane type, 'barn door' tail fins such as the Hurricane. Perceived wisdom, it seems, was, quite understandably, at it again.

Attempting to apply such traditional thinking to the Spitfire's new scientific thinking was typical of the era. With little knowledge of the tailless, delta, or all-wing design advances, which Shenstone had brought to Supermarine, or of Mitchell's racing designs, the outside 'experts' wanted to stick a large, old-fashioned biplane-type tail fin on the sleek low-drag Spitfire and increase its rudder area by 40 per cent! After all, they had just seen the Hurricane's large tail fin and, perhaps reacted against the shock of the new that the Spitfire presented...

Shenstone was clearly concerned as his notes show, yet it was suggested that the low-drag tail was too small to effect quick spin recovery. A spin recovery chute was latterly attached to the Spitfire prototype as a precaution. A larger rudder area was tried on scale model form, yet showed only a small improvement. Mitchell stood firm, backed his own thoughts and Shenstone's, and refused to fit a larger tail fin, but decided that the tailplane should be raised[30] – by a smaller amount than observers had suggested, but still by 7 inches to a point where any possible blanking effect on the rudder was reduced. This would offer some increase in spin recovery reaction. Shenstone's diaries clearly record internal debate about the tail designs with Mitchell and it was the boss who took the decision to raise the tailplane slightly. It seems the boss got it right.

The tail fin and tailplane issues took up many hours of precious time, yet Mitchell and Shenstone had stopped attempts to stick a large, traditional, 'agricultural' tail on the design. The pair resisted huge re-sizing. In the end a compromise was reached – the Spitfire fin was kept as it was, but the tailplane was raised up a touch. Shenstone knew from his work on Lippisch's design team, that a very small tail (or no tail at all) gave significant drag reduction advantages. His notes about the Supermarine tail debate tell us that:

We knew that the tail caused drag. We wanted a small as tail as possible.[31]

The Spitfire's tail fin and tailplane, were ellipsoid as well – aping the ellipse's traits and preserving its Mach flow numbers. However, the later, longer-nosed Griffon-engined Spitfires did receive a larger tail fin in order to provide better directional stability for the type's greater torque and length. Joseph Smith, as Supermarine's great wartime chief designer, had no choice other than to enlarge the tail and extend the fuselage, but true to the Spitfire's original calculus, he did it by balancing size, drag and effect, to perfection. Shenstone's original work was not diluted, but enhanced – the increased drag of the larger fin was offset by the lower drag of the longer fuselage and the handling benefits were significant when allied to the larger engines, and notably also for low-level combat, the clipped wings. Joseph Smith also oversaw the design and production of the later variations of wing shapes for the Spitfire – notably the cannon installation and the 'universal' wing variant.

* * *

The key elements of the Spitfire's modified double ellipse and its overall aerodynamic performance were:

- Uniquely modified unequal and asymmetric ellipsoid wing shape providing greater chord than conventional tapered wing, yet with lower induced drag and higher lift in a smoother lift distribution. Shorter wing span than the Hawker Hurricane.
- Low wing loading (21–25 lb/sq in.) allowing the tightest turn possible and good general lift ratios.
- The wing design reversed the 1930s design trend towards wider and slower turn rates and achieved a class-leading turn performance without sacrificing top speed, a unique achievement in design terms.
- Elliptical knife-edge wing tip to provide better lift and tip vortex patterns, especially at higher altitudes.
- Advanced safe stall characteristics with ailerons effective deep into stall pattern – proven by later tests in 1941.
- Advanced NACA 2213, 2209/4, thin wing aerofoil sections uniquely modified across the span to calculated thinness.
- Unique, early boundary layer control tailoring delayed lift reduction and separation across the aerofoil; this added lift, reduced wake drag and added speed.
- Tuned leading edge allied to ultra-thin wing section allowed greater high-speed ability and low-speed safety without need for wing fences or leading edge slot devices – a major factor as the wing worked safely at both ends of the speed range. This was an aerodynamically unique achievement at the time.
- Minimal 'washout' twist moves tip stalling in-board to root section and gives very safe stall and spin characteristics with advance warning of airflow buffet and separation.
- Forward sweep effect to assist lift patterns and negate spanwise flow, as well as reduce structural problems.
- Sculpted wing root to fuselage fillet fairing adds lift and retains curvilinear lift circulation, reducing fuselage interference effect and turbulence and tunes trailing edge airflow downwash prior to delivery to tail.
- Very small tail design significantly reduced drag and added speed.
- Minimal trim changes from flap deployment and retraction. Minimal airflow changes from gun ports.
- Tuning of underwing shapes and radiators etc to add speed.

- Fuselage uses slimmer section 'waisted' fuselage-tail-arm boom and sees wing set below the fuselage's under-curve in profile plan form, reducing interference drag and adding speed: the slim fuselage significantly reduces parasitic drag.
- Minimal frontal area reduces drag coefficients.
- Intuitive control response and feedback – minimal control stick inputs reflected glider handling techniques – fast rate of reaction to controls.
- Attempt in 1935 to create lowest ever piston monoplane drag coefficient target of C_D 0.20.

These defining factors were the essence of the Spitfire's wing design, overall aerodynamics, and associated flying qualities. They are examples of the Spitfire's unique mastery of airflow, unmatched then or since in the context of the design parameters.

As discussed above, there were many influences upon Shenstone. The ellipse was not the preserve of one man nor one designer, it was a researched and known wing plan form shape from as early as the late nineteenth century. From the Zanonia Macrocarpa seed to Zhukovskii's designs, the ellipse and the flying wing were known, referenced and intimately linked, Shenstone, and many others had studied them. Beyond this, there was the fact of Beverley Shenstone living at the world-leading Wasserkuppe gliding centre in 1930–31. From this moment, there was gliding, pure unadulterated sailplaning and a trip to the land of Zanonia seed research: Gottingen was getting in on the act – again.

9

Sailplanes and the Spitfire?

Shenstone knew how far ahead German monoplane designers were because he had been amongst them. He knew Britain would stand alone. Both he and Professor Parkin and Wing Commander (later Air Vice Marshal) Stedman back in Toronto knew that going to Germany in 1930 would be a unique learning curve. But little did they know of the advances in glider or sailplane design that were, at that very moment, manifesting themselves in Germany. The leap forwards to elliptical, swept, all-wing, and then delta wings, stemmed from the advanced aerodynamic studies of the German gliding movement.

Shenstone likened gliding to sailing, as many have. Gliding and glider design are, perhaps, the most exquisite manifestation of the aerodynamic art. As we know, Shenstone became a glider pilot who worked with Lippisch and supplied him with theoretical research calculus for his new all-wing and deltoid wing shapes. Lippisch would give the world the delta wing and the swept wing Me 163 fighter. A key question is, how did Lippisch get to the swept wing and the delta wing? The answer is via the ellipsoid and all-wing shapes. These were the stepping stones to the swept wing and delta planform.

In the mid to late 1920s, Lippisch and other German designers, glider designers, turned to the ellipse to improve upon the soaring and flight characteristics of their gliders

As Germany had been banned from having an air force by the Treaty of Versailles on 28 June 1919, all its designers turned to advancing the art of sailplane (*segelflug*), design. Germany had no fighter force – by order – so it threw vast resources on a scale greater than any other nation, into advancing the art of powerless flight design. Some powered aircraft work took place through the Swedish Government using licence-built German designs for its air force, but in the main, gliders or sailplanes became the centre of focus. The situation also created a reserve of highly skilled pilots. There was even a German national research institute for glider design – the Deustche Forshungsinstitut fur Segelflug (DFS) at Darmstadt. This was headed as early as 1930, by Professor Dr Walter Georgii. Of note, in

1939, Georgii wrote to Shenstone inviting him to be a committee member on the selection of the glider type to be chosen for the ill-fated 1940 Helsinki Olympics.[1]

Back in late 1929, just at the time the young Shenstone had turned up in Germany, a glider wing design revolution was underway – via the Darmstadt and Gottingen institutes. Previously, gliders of the early 1920s were solid stately machines with thick wings, which had to be turned in long, slow arcs of flat flight. High bank angles immediately resulted in the wing suffering a change to airflow and lift patterns, leading to a major loss of lift and a loss of height due to the limitations of the wing designs. Designers such as Lippisch and his contemporaries, such as the members of the Darmstadt group, realized that better lift patterns, lower drag, a smoother fuselage-to-wing junction, and a lower wing loading were vital improvements that could be applied to glider design. The ability to make sharper turns (to stay within thermals) without losing lift, was a leading aerodynamic consideration. Sharp turns at very high altitudes were also to become the needs of fighter aircraft before long…

The solution to getting this manoeuvrability and more lift, was the combination of the elliptical type wing form – with its knife edge tips, wider wing root chord area and its better lift distribution and vortex patterns, with lower drag and better boundary layer control. Smoothness of skinning and a generally smooth finish was to become a major part of increasing aerodynamic efficiency – at a time when the rest of the world was turning out wire and strut-braced aircraft with roughly finished wings and fuselages.

It was within these developments that use of the ellipse or semi-ellipse became a major feature in glider German design – as did smoothing out the join angle between the fuselage and the wing. These factors, allied to the gull wing anhedral /dihedral effect, and the influences of where the wing was mounted upon the fuselage – the interference effect, which altered wing lift distribution and flow, especially when close to the stall, and in cross winds or cross angles – became the major areas of aerodynamic study. Revised aerofoils and revised shapes soon ensured that glider wings no longer stopped flying when pressed into tight, high incidence turns. Lowering drag of all types added lift and speed: it was a sailplane revolution.

Suddenly, German gliders were the best in the world – with much better lift ratios and vastly improved turn rates and handling. Soaring ability was transformed.

Gliders such as Professor Madelung's design, the Vampyr, and then others such as the Fafnir II, the Wein, the Rhonsperber, Rhonadler and Condor all demonstrated ellipsoid and streamlined design traits. They were flown by people such as Peter Riedel, Günter Groenhoff, and Robert Kronfeld, men who became personal friends of Beverley Shenstone in the1930s. British glider design was, by its own admission, left standing; later 'British' glider designs of the 1930s such as the Elliotts Olympia and the Slingsby Petrel owed a very great deal to the lines of German gliders.

The Lippisch-designed Wein (Vienna) glider of late 1929, was notable for having a very smooth skin, an elliptical tail fin, an ellipsoid wing planform and a carefully researched wing to fuselage junction. These features created a massive leap forwards in aerodynamic and glide ratio efficiency which Beverley Shenstone was on hand to witness. Pilot Robert Kronfeld (later of the RAF and British tailless developments) achieved flights of over 250km in this milestone glider design.

Lippisch was at the centre of all this advanced work – and when Shenstone arrived at Lippisch's office, straight from the Junkers works at Dessau he was immersed into these arts. Nowhere else in the world offered this chance. The Germans were years ahead of their competitors and Shenstone was living and working amongst them, literally at the leading edge of design. As we know, Shenstone did not 'copy' these ideas, he worked with the team and provided Lippisch with many of the calculus solutions to his advanced delta design proposals, via his own theoretical calculus and an ability to think in three dimensions. Shenstone was there, in Lippisch's Ursinus House office, as part of the delta wing's development.

Shenstone and the delta team worked together on researching a new, simpler method for the evaluation of the spanwise distribution of lift – focusing on gliders and then delta gliders. Even after Shenstone had joined Supermarine in early 1931, he remained in contact with Alexander Lippisch and regular written correspondence between the two is evidenced.[2] With research posted between themselves, and occasional visits, Shenstone contributed to Lippisch's findings. By 1935, Lippisch had presented his *Verfahren zur Bestimmung der Auftriebsverteilung langs Spannweite* (Method for the Determination of the Spanwise Lift Distribution).[3]

This research stemmed from delta research using models and full-size aircraft – all of them glider or powered variants of gliders. It used other findings to create a new methodology that was latterly published as Technical Memorandum No. 778, by the USA National Advisory

Committee for Aerodynamics (NACA), and was an important work on wing lift behaviour.

Of particular interest in development terms, the Germans built small-scale models of their advanced glider design proposals, whereas the British by convention did not. In Canada and at Toronto University, Shenstone had been brought up building small-scale models of boat hull designs – latterly including his own and his hull designs – and he had used Canada's only wind tunnel. Lippisch's technique of building a model and then testing it using smoke, tufts, and even windblown snow particles, was instantly recognizable to Shenstone – as were the pitfalls of the scale to size variations between models and the real thing.

Like gliders, the new powered monoplanes of the same era had, in the main, thicker wings and thicker wing mounting boxes so at their most advanced they had unbraced wings. The advantages of the monoplane had the potential to be undermined if the boundary airflow patterns and wing to fuselage airflow patterns were badly tuned. In Germany, Shenstone had watched the changes in glider design and in powered monoplane design that explored these issues for the first time. Very little research into these problems was then taking place in the USA or the UK. Shenstone had noted this important design aspect in his early flying boat hull design work, and had also noted the hydrodynamic interference and blanketing effect of boat keels and rudders on hull design – this being closely linked to the wing to fuselage effects in aerodynamic terms. Again, he could grasp it quickly.

So well did Shenstone grasp what was going on, that soon after he joined Supermarine, he and fellow glider pilot Stewart Scott-Hall, who was the Air Ministry's resident technical officer at Supermarine, wrote their paper 'Glider Development in Germany'. This was published in *Aircraft Engineering* as a supplement to *The Aeroplane*.[4] Notably, it was soon reprinted as NACA Technical Memorandum No. 780.

In 1931, the wing to fuselage issue was of interest to Shenstone . Of the drag reducing benefits of not only a wing to fuselage glove, but also a slimmer fuselage, he wrote:

> There is a limit to the fineness ratio of a fuselage, but it is not known very clearly what that is. Taking all we know into account it appears that it is worthwhile to make every effort toward increasing the slimness of the aeroplane.
>
> It is known that the drag coefficient (for fully turbulent boundary layer) becomes slightly less as the size of the aeroplane increases. The size in this connection is the length in the direction of motion. Now, a fighter is basically a small aeroplane, but its length can be increased by careful arrangement,

which increases the size, which decreases the drag coefficient.[5]

Shenstone's researches had revealed to him that increasing the length of a fuselage, yet reducing its thickness, gave significant speed gains through drag reduction. A slim fuselage or boom was the ideal form and latterly underpinned Shenstone's suggestion of a long slim fuselage on the Spitfire, and it was knowledge that Mitchell and his Schneider Trophy winning men were in agreement with.

Much of this knowledge came from experiments taking place in the fast advancement of German sailplane design. Men such as Muttray and Lippisch were conducting research into smoothing out the monoplane glider wing to fuselage problems. The earlier work of Zhukovskii (Joukowski) and his combined ellipsoid wing and fuselage section was a major influence on all designers. Junkers, Lippisch, and then the young Hortens, had all seen the advantages of reducing the fuselage interference drag – by getting rid of the fuselage completely; this was the essence of the all-wing design. It was research that few others had considered. Willy Messerschmitt, whom Lippisch was to later work for, was a sailplane designer, and he had the view that to be a good aircraft engineer, a designer must have sailplane experience, both as a pilot and designer. He had both, and so too, in younger context, did Shenstone.

What Shenstone also learned as part of this German change-over to monoplanes and high-lift gliders, was that wing and fuselage skins that were smooth and curved offered great advantages in reducing drag and increasing speed – way beyond the theories of small-scale wind tunnels. The full-scale effect, added to the advantages whereas ill-formed or rough surfaces with awkward wing-to-fuselage combinations, suffered excessive drag that was far worse than a small-scale model test might suggest. Learning about the weaknesses of scale effects between models in small wind tunnels and full size toolings, in flight, was a major discovery. Shenstone wrote:

> It came to this: the monoplane was no better than a good biplane unless the wing to fuselage interference was minimized and the wing profile made precisely accurately and very smooth.[6]

These were, for the Spitfire, prophetic words.

Comparing the perfecting of the Spitfire's wing design to that of gliders and all-wing theory does not occur to many, but in doing so, mindful of the designers' previous experiences and knowledge, it becomes very obvious that the Spitfire design does take some degree of inspiration from its aerodynamicist's previous fascination with the world's best sailplanes and all that he learned while immersed in that world.

After the Second World War, Lippisch the glider designer was hailed as the father of the delta wing, yet few realize that even as late as 1938 he was guest of the British aviation establishment in London where his work was feted and exhibited. On 15 December 1938, Alexander Lippisch delivered a lecture at the Royal Aeronautical Society (RAeS) in London in which he demonstrated his work in wind tunnel development, smoke flow and scale effects and wing design.[7] Questions from the audience came from the likes of Professor G.T.R. Hill, Professor B.M. Jones, Dr Townend, and a certain B.S. Shenstone – who within less than four years would be appointed a Fellow of the RAeS.

Beverley Shenstone had been instrumental in getting Lippisch to the RAeS and, acted as his interpreter. Shenstone states in his unpublished notes[8] that there were discussions concerning the possibility of Lippisch joining Supermarine. How accurate this amazing claim is, and if there are any substantiating records, is now hard to ascertain. Of interest, at the end of Lippisch's London lecture, much cordiality and the desire for scientists to work together for peace rather than war, was expressed. We can, however, know that Lippisch was keen to leave Germany, failed to do so, yet in May 1945, with Shenstone's help, was secured by American troops after travelling from Vienna, and removed to a new career in the USA via some time spent in London and at Farnborough's research facility before going to Wright-Patterson. Shenstone had been concerned that Lippisch might fall into Russian hands and he was keen to assist where he could. Lippisch had been interrogated and no evidence of any political views or actions in support to Nazi idealogy was found. He also had many friends in England and America – NACA in the USA had been publishing his papers since 1935.

For the Spitfire, the influence of the Russian Zhukovskii, the German glider designs, the Zanonia seed and Lippisch's glider design and delta work upon Shenstone have, for perhaps understandable reasons, been obscured, but in the story of Shenstone and the Spitfire, they cannot be ignored.

Some of the definitive theories of the time, stemmed from Prandlt, Glauert, von Karman and Millikan, and then Lippisch. Incorporated into this knowledge were the discoveries of the Supermarine Schneider Trophy designers and the international developments of the series – not least that of the Giovanni Pegna-designed Piaggio P.C.7 and its elliptical wings and hydrofoils. As a boat and yacht enthusiast, Shenstone became fascinated by the hydrofoil and went on to write articles in the 1930s citing

Pegna's work – so the shape of Pegna's 1929 elliptical Schneider racer design was known to Shenstone.

Mitchell and his men were original thinkers as their racing float planes showed, but they were not alone in absorbing everything they could from the worldwide pace of racing float plane development, and they were by 1931 building large flying boats. Supermarine's at Woolston was a repository of advanced knowledge, into which walked Beverley Shenstone and his mind full of flying boats, hydrofoils, flying wings, elliptical shapes and deltoid flying triangles.

It must have been a meeting of minds; if it had not been, would Mitchell have employed him?

Over half a century later, there was to be an intriguing further irony to the whole subject of American, British, and German design knowledge when, on 20 October 1999, Daimler Aerospace Airbus GmbH Hamburg Germany, filed a US patent application number 08/953913 in the names of J. Meister, J. Pfennig and W. Held, for the 'Rudder assembly with a controlled boundary layer for aircraft'. This patent application happened to cite a main reference as: 'B.S. Shenstone, "Sucking off the Boundary Layer" as describes original efforts for boundary layer control. *Aeronautical Engineering* Jan 27, 1937'.

So, in a delicious reflection, Shenstone's Anglo-Canadian-German-Russian, Spitfire-related research made it back into a European Airbus project! The point proves that in 1999 Airbus (Hamburg), used Beverley Shenstone's 1930s work, as a reference point for a boundary layer patent (US Patent Number 5899416). Once again, the advanced brilliance of the quiet Canadian is underlined.

For the Spitfire, however, the facts are clear. The Spitfire was British, conceived by a Englishman with a British team utilizing a vast range of design research and air racing and flying boat experience. The air racing experience had also absorbed techniques and developments from a range of international teams who had all contributed to the development of the Schneider Trophy float plane racing series. Amid the Supermarine Spitfire's core design group was a Canadian of close British lineage with knowledge gained in Canada, Britain, and in Germany who had also studied the work of an early Russian pioneer, as well as the works of a host of other aerodynamicists, and ultimately Junkers and Lippisch.

Shenstone then spent years working for Mitchell under the tutelage of all the experience at Supermarine before he shaped the Spitfire's aerodynamics. The previous aerodynamics work on the Schneider Trophy racers and sea planes by Oliver Simmons and then Ernest Mansbridge, were also major contributing factors to the knowledge at Supermarine's upon which Shenstone drew for the Spitfire. The expertise of Faddy, Fear, Fenner, Shirvall, and others gained on Supermarine flying boats and racers, contributed to the sculpting of the Spitfire.

There was also the influence of British glider design on Shenstone's Spitfire design development to be considered.

The Abbott company produced the Carden Baynes Scud, a glider designed by Mr L.E. Baynes in 1931, which was noteworthy for its smooth finish, aerodynamically tuned wing to fuselage junction, and its wing tip chord ratio – particularly in its later extended span variants. A Mr G.M. Buxton flew a Scud II to a height of 8750ft (2666m) in a thunder cloud over Sutton bank in 1935, thus gaining a British height record. As we shall see, Mr Buxton was to be involved with Shenstone and the Spitfire wing and E.D. Abbott Ltd was to manufacture Spitfire parts.

During Shenstone's time based at the Wasserkuppe, at the heart of the Rhön Rositten Gessellschaft glider bureau (Lippisch was its designer), he met the cream of British glider designers, including Messrs Cooper and Buxton when they visited the Wasserkuppe. A noteworthy visit to the Wasserkuppe in August 1930 came from the British Gliding Association, which sent a delegation of over a dozen luminaries to inspect the rapid of advance of German sailplane design – an advance that had seen the duration of glider flights double and glide to descent coefficients markedly improved. The delegation openly admitted that they intended to see the latest research trends and consider how best such ideas could benefit British gliding.

The principal visitors (including British Gliding Association lead members) were: Sir Sefton Brackner, Mr Gordon England, Colonel the Master of Semphill, Dr Whitehead Reid, Group Captain Gosage (British Air Attaché in Berlin), Mr G.M. Buxton, Mr Hiscox, Captain Needham, Mr Waplington and Mr J.R. Ashwell-Cooke. Beverley Shenstone was resident at the Wasserkuppe at this time and, as with (Air Commodore Chamier's visit), his German language skills were useful as interpreter for the delegation. The German reception team was headed by Dr Lippisch and Professor Walter Georgii.

The previously mentioned Mr G.M. Buxton became significant when Shenstone struck up a friendship with him, as Geoffrey Buxton visited the Wasserkuppe in 1930, and this relationship was to last over a number of years. Like Shenstone, Buxton was also a great enthusiast of the tailless design theory. Buxton went on to design two gliders, including the *Hjordis*, which had a thin wing section and was designed for ultimate glide performance. Flown by another Shenstone acquaintance, Phillip Wills, the *Hjordis* was perhaps the first British high-performance sailplane and had a wing taper ratio of 4:1 and a wing twist of 6 degrees. Buxton married Racy Fisher, daughter of Admiral Sir William Fisher and first cousin to Phillip Wills' wife. Buxton's glider design had an advanced slimline fuselage and was designed in response to the startling design advances of the *Austria*-type glider of Dr Kuppe in 1931. Buxton also designed the King Kite type glider. It and the *Hjordis* were two of the very few original British designs of the era. In the 1940s, Buxton was largely responsible for the design of the Hotspur type troop-carrying glider.[9]

Buxton commissioned the building of his *Hjordis* design from Slingsby Sailplanes of Kirby Moorside Yorkshire. G.M. Buxton was a Master of Art (MA) from Peterhouse College Cambridge, and clearly knew how to think and design for the air. Phillip Wills (from whom Shenstone was later to fulfil the role of Chief Engineer at BEA in 1947), was the designated pilot of Buxton's *Hjordis* when it flew it at the Wasserkuppe in 1937.

Buxton (by 1936 a Squadron Leader) also made several presentations to the Royal Aeronautical Society, notably on 16 December 1937 when the issues of tailless design and wing and fuselage skin smoothness were the main topics. At Buxton's invitation, Beverley Shenstone presented his thoughts to the audience on the importance of smooth skinning and laminar and boundary layer flow control. The incredible aerodynamic efficiency of the Fafnir II glider (85 per cent efficient) was also cited as evidence of the smooth skin argument that, by this time, had been applied to the Spitfire – despite the dilemma of the cost of manufacturing difficulties that might result.

Buxton and Shenstone, underlined the gains for glider designs having a smooth skin, a very slim fuselage and a small tail, or no tail at all. Buxton was one of the leading lights of his day. Geoffrey Mungo Buxton and Beverley Shenstone were both the same age, both highly talented, and were born and later died within days of each other. Shenstone had naval ancestors and loved boats and sailing, while Buxton also came from a naval family, and went on to serve in the Royal Air Force Special Duties squadron in the Second World War achieving the rank of Group Captain. He also became a Fellow of the Royal Aeronautical Society – of which Shenstone became President. In the Second World War Buxton was an RAF pilot and test flew captured German aircraft – it was Buxton who tested a captured Bf109 in the North African desert where it had landed.

It is significant that Buxton, who had already grasped the tailless concept and the importance of smoothness, as well as designing the two gliders, features in Shenstone's Supermarine diaries. In spring 1934, as the doomed Supermarine Type 224 was taking to the air, and several months before the Air Ministry officially endorsed work on the Spitfire, Shenstone notes the involvement of Buxton in his early Supermarine fighter design work.

> Buxton visited our factory. As I was not in the office from ten o'clock until noon, Clifton was rather annoyed. Buxton stayed the night with us. Long discussions about the shape of the wing.[10]

This information, published for the first time, shows us further evidence that a British glider designer, Geoffrey Mungo Buxton, was offering Shenstone input into what was to become the Spitfire's wing design. Buxton had seen the benefits of the ellipsoid wing, the faired wing to fuselage join, smooth skinning and minimal tail or tailless, low drag design. The thought of Buxton and Shenstone, both glider pilots, both avid all-wing, tailless and smooth surface design enthusiasts, discussing the proposed Spitfire's wing shape and body smoothness, late into the night in Shenstone's water side home at Netley in 1934, offers us a further tantalizing vignette of how the Spitfire's ellipse was perfected – of how yet another vital ingredient was tailored into creating the Spitfire's smooth sculpture.

Shenstone himself wrote in his notes of the time regarding the influence of German glider design on powered aircraft that:

> The aerodynamic refinement which is characteristic of a number of aircraft types now in development has obviously resulted from the intensive study in the field of motorless flight.[11]

This was proof then, that advanced glider design, *was* influencing powered aircraft design. If it was beneficial, why would Shenstone *not* apply such knowledge, gained first hand, to the Spitfire? It is now clear, that this sailplane learning, allied to to other influences, notably that of flying boat and float plane racing design, played a significant role in creating the knowledge that designed the Spitfire's aerodynamics and its resultant intuitive handling. Another character in the Spitfire's design genesis was that of famous yacht designer Uffa Fox. Fox and Shenstone were friends, they corresponded regularly and Shenstone's diaries show that in April 1935 the pair discussed Fox's wishes to design and build a glider to take on the Germans. Fox abandoned the idea and turned to yachts, but he was a visitor to Shenstone's waterside home at Netley. So the Spitfire owed much to boats, yacht hulls, seaplanes and to sailplanes.

10

Beyond the Leading Edge

As several commentators have observed, Shenstone was one of the few people who knew what was going in German aviation in the 1930s – both in terms of the advances in design and the potential military threat that would stem from those advances. Shenstone saw it as a warning and made every effort to produce something to counter the threat – his relationship with R.J. Mitchell, Air Chief Marshal Sir Wilfrid Freeman and Lord Beaverbrook underline this.

We know, for example, that during a later trip to Germany in 1938, Shenstone met Willy Messerschmitt and had a glimpse of the still- secret Me110 twin-engined light bomber. Shenstone did not know its details, but on his return to England, he went straight to the Air Ministry and reported his sighting. He noted in his diaries:

> I saw the Me110. On my way back, I dropped into the Air Ministry to have a word with Dancy who had formerly been the resident technical officer at Supermarine and was now dealing with German developments, at the Air Ministry. When I described the Me110, Dancy brought out a couple of photocopies of Messerschmitt drawings. One showed a fuselage less the fore part and a wing showing leading edge cut-out near the fuselage. On that information, the feeling was that this was a single engined machine with heavy cannon in each wing, port and starboard.[1]

Shenstone had told the Air Ministry that the Me110 was twin engined. The British attitude was soon revealed by their response – the experts dismissed Shenstone's views and told him that the big wing pods were heavy gun housings and that the aircraft was single engined!

Shenstone refused to accept this and filed a report stating that the Me110 was a twin-engined bomber. He also estimated its speed capabilities based upon his opinions of what he had seen. Within a very short time the reality of Shenstone's report and predictions were established as correct – indeed his performance estimates proved to be very accurate. He noted:

> My sight of the aircraft showed there were two engines (Daimler Benz 600) and fuselage armament two 20mm cannon, so we had enough data to make

a 3-view drawing and to calculate Me110 performance. One really needs luck sometimes.[2]

The Me110 was indeed a fast twin-engined aircraft and formidable night fighter. Shenstone had been correct. Whilst the Ministry thought differently, the likes of Mitchell, Shenstone, Robert McLean, Beaverbrook, Camm, Churchill, Hugh Dowding and, notably, Wilfrid Freeman, were preparing for the truth.

Intriguingly, in the film of the Spitfire's birth, *The First of the Few*, R.J. Mitchell is portrayed as meeting Messerschmitt in Germany. In fact, Mitchell did not make this trip, it was Mutt Summers, Beverley Shenstone and Stewart Scott-Hall who went to Germany and met the German designers. Shenstone commented: 'It looked better showing Mitchell going to Germany, than me'.[3]

Shenstone knew of the threat, and he put everything he had into the ellipse for R.J. Mitchell. The wing had it all – smoothness, performance, that rate of turn, the tuned 'washout' effect, and an incredibly thin aerofoil section that, thanks to the detail and the structural design work of Supermarine, had the inherent strength to stay attached to the airframe whatever the extremes of flight and combat loadings. Shenstone always made the point that Joseph Smith had created a stiff and strong wing, within 'severe' constraints of space. Shenstone always stated that without the team, his wing would never have been made.[4]

But securing the wing against flutter and spar failure at combat stress levels was no easy task for Supermarine in the firm's first military fighter aircraft. And the smooth metal skinning was difficult to manufacture (the Spitfire prototype had a boat-type overlap on its forward wing skin area – not copied for production). Other work on the wing included a suggested increase in dihedral from 4.5 degrees to 6.0. This was in reaction to questions over stability due to the high centre of gravity. Mitchell rejected such suggestions of possible lateral instability; the wing handled well.

The Spitfire's design in its entirety was all new – for a new task. As such, it is wrong to suggest that the Spitfire was directly developed from the Schneider racers. Lineage there may have been, but recycling of components or calculus there was not. Flying fast in a straight line a few feet above the waves was not the Spitfire's remit. Building a fragile, temperamental machine that would require hourly attention and inspection, as with any racing machine, four wheeled, four legged or with wings, would not have provided a reliable service aircraft. Maybe this is why the doomed Type 224 was made to be simple and strong – a reaction too far perhaps, but one that allowed the mistake to be realized – so that a more agile, yet still reliable machine would emerge from the ashes.

There were many other aspects of the new design that needed tuning – not least the underwing radiator scoops. These proved to be particularly difficult to finalise. The previous Supermarine fighter prototype to Air Ministry specification F.30/70, the Type 224, had employed an evaporative steam cooling system. This had to be changed for the Spitfire, but Mitchell and Shenstone were reluctant to add external radiators as these would increase drag. However, continuing to use a steam-cooled engine bay system was beginning to look potentially troublesome. The original plan had also been to have the oil cooler mounted under the engine. This oil cooler had to be moved under the wing. Use of the D-nosed spar as a condensate tube had also been considered. Thankfully, something simple yet clever intervened.

By careful design and the input of Frederick Meredith[5] from the Royal Aircraft Establishment at Farnborough, Supermarine came up with an underwing ducted system with the radiator set inside a low drag sleeve under the wing, which thanks to shaping and funnelling, featured a ram type effect – exhausting the heat-carrying air charge through an adjustable trailing edge vent that had a small thrust component. Combined with use of an ethylene glycol coolant, the ram air system provided the Spitfire with adequate cooling in-flight without seriously upsetting the drag coefficient. There was not yet a facility big enough to conduct full-scale testing of wings, and Shenstone was very wary of the adverse scale effects of testing models in wind tunnels – a view he had reached via his work with Professor Parkin and in Germany.

Carburettor air intakes were originally planned for citing in the leading edge, but these two were abandoned in favour of a scoop – leaving a clean wing. Shenstone wrote of the changes:

> Change of cooling to glycol and change in carburettor design forced the placing of the radiator and the single large air intake below the fuselage. The glycol radiator remains in the place chosen for the auxiliary steam condenser, which, as an examination of the underside of the wing shows, could not have been varied to any extent without fouling one thing or another.
>
> The rather full breasted appearance of the Spitfire from the side (compared to the Hurricane) was due to the fact that it was intended to install the oil coolers in the nose just ahead of the an above the oil tank. When the latter were moved to just ahead of the port wing before the aeroplane was completed to enable provision of better ducting, the fore

body lines were left full to enable the same oil tank to be used. On so little depends a characteristic feature.[6]

Shenstone, as a result of his researches and previous glider studies, was keen to achieve the smoothest finish possible for the Spitfire's wing (see below for reference to the Heinkel 70). In doing so he specified a flush riveted finish and smooth plating. This was both expensive and time consuming to manufacture. Could it be compromised to speed up production and cut costs?

In order to find out, the now infamous split pea tests were carried out. In these tests, in January 1937, the first flying Spitfire prototype was fitted with hard dried split peas – the same diameter (but slightly taller) as mushroom or dome-headed rivets at strategic points on the flush riveted airframe. By experimenting with the placing (by industrial glue) of the peas on the wing and fuselage, in a series of flights, the effects of using cheaper, quicker, domed non-flush rivets upon the Spitfire's performance were ascertained. Shenstone often told this tale in later life, his sons clearly remember it being a favourite of their father's stories.

The results showed a large speed loss of around 8–10mph when the wing's smooth finish was altered. Nearly 25mph was lost when the false rivet shape was tried extensively across the airframe. However, more acceptable lower-speed losses were found with use of fewer peas as dummy domed rivets at strategic points away from the upper wing. Dome heads on the fuselage, with overall losses of between 1–3 mph, were deemed acceptable as a trade-off between Supermarine's science and the realities of quicker wartime production by relatively unskilled workers. So it was that domed rivets found their way onto the super-smooth Spitfire.

Thus, perfecting the ellipse did at one stage rely on dried split peas and glue to get Spitfires into battle. There were other aspects of the design that required detailed study and development. The famous ellipse was also further modified on a number of occasions. In 1937, with the Spitfire's high, (level flight) top speed of just over 350mph fully recognized, the thought of trying to capture the world speed record occurred. However, the prototype Spitfire could only achieve 290mph at very low levels. Once up beyond 15,000 feet, it went beyond 350mph. But to achieve 350mph at lower level in denser air, some special measures would be needed. Engine development tuning and propeller work soon had the Spitfire racing ahead. The Merlin engine would soon develop around 1500hp. Later, in the forthcoming Battle of Britain and beyond across the war years, Spitfire pilots became used to 400mph. Some, notably the Spitfire PR variants, got closer to 500mph – Mach 0.85+ being easy to achieve and a rarer, harder to reach Mach 0.92 having been recorded in the thin, easier to penetrate, high altitude airs where indicated airspeed and actual ground speed were not the same thing.

But the 1937 idea for a faster Spitfire, was spurred into action in late 1937 when an especially tuned and smoothed, Messerschmitt Bf109 captured the world land plane record at 379mph – mostly down to its power-to-weight ratio, even with strut-braced wooden tailplanes. With Air Ministry support, the forty—eighth production Spitfire airframe was taken from the Woolston factory floor and work began in earnest.

A modified 2100hp Merlin 'Sprint' engine with high octane fuel feed, allied to the Spitfire's first use of a four bladed prop, was supplied. From an aerodynamic standpoint, a glider-style smoothed yet optically flawed Perspex-moulded racing canopy with a narrow, faster raked one-piece windscreen tided up the airflow around the cockpit. Then, the ellipse was also tweaked. The wingspan was reduced to 33ft 8in and the wings were given specially hand-built re-profiled tips that were slightly rounder with a reduced radius arc. With an especially smoothed skin, flush rivets, filled gaps, a tail skid, and low drag underwing radiator pod, and other modifications, this aircraft became the ultra low drag 'Speed Spitfire'.

This aircraft was painted in a stunning royal blue with silver side flashes. It looked every inch the quintessential streamlined 1930s racer. Mutt Summers took it to the air in November 1938 and Jeffrey Quill flew it the following month. A designated RAF pilot, Flight Lieutenant H. Purvis, took the Speed Spitfire to 408mph on 24 February 1939 over the sea off Portsmouth.

Other changes to the ellipse saw a more pointed, tighter wing tip radius (the reverse of the wider, Speed Spitfire tips) applied to versions of the Spitfire Mk VI and VIIs. These sharper tips, giving a wingspan over 40ft 2in, provided better lift distribution at the very high altitudes required by these Spitfire variants. Of aerodynamic interest, these even more efficient wing tips were variants of the ellipsoid calculus of the original design.

As the Spitfire gained more power and higher speeds than ever dreamed possible in 1935, a new issue of a very high Mach number problem manifested as aileron reversal – at speeds far in excess of those the wing was originally designed for. Far from decrying the design for this issue, observers should perhaps reflect that this new problem of theoretical transonic aileron reversal manifested above 580mph – not a speed considered in the Air Ministry's original specification for this aircraft type.

Wing flexibility and airflow effects upon Shenstone's specially tuned aileron design, meant that the wing was strengthened under Joseph Smith's leadership – with an increased resistance to twist of 47 per cent via structural modification not a total redesign. The theoretical aileron reversal speed rose to over 700mph – a velocity unlikely to be met before the propeller disintegrated. Contrary to some opinion, the ellipse was not completely redesigned as a result of any failure, but further modified to keep it competitive with rapid developments – a subtle but important difference of context and quite normal in terms of on-going structural developments to any aircraft as it is developed to higher weights and speeds.

These later Spitfires – the F variants and beyond the Mk 21 – featured the stronger wing and revised aerodynamic tabs on the re-shaped ailerons. But contrary to some claims, the fundamental aerodynamics of the ellipse were unaltered. These measures – taken nearly a decade after the aircraft was designed show that with development the basic design was sound. Supermarine also devised another wing for a Spitfire derivative – that was never produced. Spitfire airframes code numbered EF 644 and EN946 were in 1942 altered to include modified boundary layer trials work and modified leading edges, respectively. Changes to the leading edge provided minimal benefits at only one high speed vector and higher drag at others, and so were abandoned; the original aerofoil and wing shaping had been correct and only minimal revised boundary layer work was evolved, as the first attempt had been very efficient.

Fashionable as it now is to criticize the issues encountered in the latter days of the war as the faster, enlarged, Spitfire was compared with aircraft designed much later, it is perhaps worth considering just how long the basic 1935 wing design lasted in the face of the huge advances in aerodynamics research up to 1945. Did R.J. Mitchell ever consider that the wing would be criticized for its transonic performance at above Mach 0.85, nearly a decade after it was designed? That the Spitfire remained competitive as a basic design platform speaks volumes for the excellence of its aerodynamic and structural design.

As a point of reference, Hawker's Sydney Camm introduced his first thinner wing fighter in 1943 in the form of the Typhoon derivative, the Tempest. This then led to the ellipsoid, thin-winged Hawker Fury/Sea Fury of 1944. So it was eight years after the Spitfire's first flight, that Hawker's Fury took to the air with a thin section wing with ellipsoid design and a curved and sculpted fuselage to wing joining panel – both ingredients having first been seen on the Spitfire nearly a decade before. The tip chord ratio was still double that of the Spitfire's.

Who designed the Fury's wing? Sydney Camm is credited, but Shenstone may have played some role. His records show that he had regular contact with Sydney Camm and his team throughout the war and, after the war, Camm asked Shenstone to modify the Hunter.[7] During the war, we know that Shenstone worked on several projects with Camm. Could it be that the similarities of the Fury's wing – especially its wing to fuselage sculpted junction and the way in which its wing is set in relation to its fuselage in a manner similar to the Spitfire's unique wing set, betray Shenstone's influence? It is clearly possible, but it cannot be substantiated and thus remains just an intriguing possibility or just a coincidence…

Shenstone left more than just design and development notes about the Spitfire, he also wrote a private essay on the nature of its design and development. In the essay, entitled 'An Aeroplane Grows' the emotional attachment to the design, and the manner in which a team of men created it, is framed. Shenstone says:

> Five men are standing around a table looking at a drawing. It is way back in the golden age of the mid-thirties, before war and rearmament were certain to come. The drawing shows an aeroplane. At the upper left of the drawing is a side view, flying as it were, out of the picture. At the upper right is a front view, as if it were flying out of the picture into the faces of the viewers. Finally, at the lower right is a plan view so that it appears to be diving out of the bottom of the drawing. In the space left are a few lines of figures.
>
> The five men are not looking at these figures. They are not looking at any particular part of the drawing, but trying to think of the aeroplane as a whole. This drawing was not turned out in a hurry, but is the result of some months of detailed work and calculations.
>
> To each of the five, every line on the drawing had a, meaning. Every curve had a good reason to be there. Not one thing little thing could be changed without affecting some other aspect. Had any of the five thought back over the significance of any detail shown, he could have written an essay on it.
>
> They had often stood like this around the table during the months before, trying to decide what exactly was the best way to do this or that. The point was that none of them really knew, nor was there anyone who could tell them. This was because they were designing this aeroplane to do its job better than it had ever been done before. They were treading new ground, reaching out beyond their meagre knowledge.[8]

Here in these words, Shenstone captures the lonely enormity of the task facing Mitchell and his men – they had to create the science to be as sure as they could, at the time, of what they were doing. The key phrase being, at the time – hindsight was not an option. Further extracts reveal more:

> The point is that knowledge was always increasing bit by bit and that as a result they, or any men like them, could never be final and say: 'This is the goods. It expresses our final word.' They could only say: ' It expresses all I knew when I did it, but if I were doing it again, I should do thus and thus.'
>
> Some day these men had to say 'Stop now and build the damned thing!' … The decision was felt rather than expressed, for, as nobody had anything more to say, the chief designer, who by the way was under 40, slapped the drawing thoughtfully and returned to his office.
>
> In this odd and inconclusive and distinctly undramatic manner was this aeroplane born.
>
> Each detail was also the subject of numerous calculations and detailed discussions. Each part was estimated, drawn, checked, and issued to the workshops as quickly as possible…
>
> The foreman said this and that could not be done and had to be persuaded otherwise. They said it would take too long if they used flush rivets and had to be told about performance.[9]

Shenstone's article goes on to talk about the building of the prototype, and stresses how the technical office and the drawing office worked together – not with one being subservient, an important factor in the aircraft's design and detailing to its benefit and a point that utterly destroys some more recent, absurd claims that the teams failed to communicate adequately.

> This friendly battle between designer and manufacturer always goes on even in a well balanced and organised establishment and results in much learned by both sides. Only in an unbalanced firm is one side subservient to the other and in such cases the losses are great.[10]

His final words, touch an emotional chord, and underline the essence of the creation – the Spitfire:

> These five produced the basic design and it was undoubtedly their brain-child… At the end of the story when it is a fighting instrument to preserve the country, the designer has no more than a sentimental claim to the aeroplane. It is no longer his. Its name is on the lips of all the world. The whole country has sweated to build it. It is no private thing of his. It is owned by the nation, the Empire. He did not even give it to them. Somehow it did the job by itself. So when this one of the five sat in a restaurant and pretty girl came around with a box, collecting for further production, he didn't even say to himself: 'Why should I give for this, my own little bit of creation?' No. he merely put sixpence in the slot and thanked his private deity for the protection that thousands of work men and hundred so of pilots were giving him.[11]

11

The Heinkel 70 and Other Issues

Debate has raged across the decades about the suggested similarity of the Spitfire's wing shape to that of the Heinkel 70 (He 70) single cabin, six-seat transport airliner. Some observers have repeated a suggestion that for the Spitfire, Mitchell and Shenstone must have 'copied' or 'cribbed' this Heinkel's wing. Others say the He 70 'inspired' the Spitfire's wing. Several commentators have inferred a chronological influence and timing between their claims of the 'unveiling' of the He 70 at the Paris Air Show in 1934 (an inaccurate claim) and the choice of the Spitfire's ellipse by early December 1934.

There is much evidence that the first elliptical suggestions for the Spitfire were discussed *before* the 1934 Paris Air Show, not least as R.J. Mitchell designed a fully elliptical flying boat in late 1929, but the vital, principal point is that, as the He 70 was neither unveiled nor seen for the first time at the 1934 Paris Air Show, the claims of the He 70 being an influence on the Spitfire based on such often repeated statement of date and implied influence, can only be incorrect – or in plain English, utter rubbish. Neither was the He 70 the 'new' shape claimed by some to be so influential upon the Spitfire (irrespective of November 1934 as a claimed date of influence).

The He 70 was based on its designers' 1925 elliptically winged Bäumer Sausewind aircraft, and the interim plot of the 1931 elliptically tailed and super smooth Heinkel He 64 racing tourer aircraft – a speed record holder in its own right. The historical record is that He 70 had its first flight on 1 December 1932. It entered Lufthansa service in March 1933, and Shenstone saw it at its first Paris Salon – the *1933* Paris Air Show.[1] So much then, for the He 70 being 'unveiled' in November 1934 as the Spitfire was being shaped, as so much incompetent research has claimed.

Some have suggested that Rolls-Royce secured an He 70 and that after it was brought to Britain and inspected and wind tunnel tested, that

Supermarine cribbed or stole ideas from this airframe during the Spitfire's design development.

Such claims are factually incorrect, chronologically impossible – they are utter rubbish and could be seen as gross defamation. For some reason a host of recent Spitfire researchers and authors cannot get the dates, facts or aerodynamic issues, correct. There have been many errors of claim and these errors have assumed 'factual' status in the digital age: clearly, a defining correction is needed.

One recent Australian author, Gary Sunderland, writing a history of the elliptical wing, stated that the British obviously obtained the He 70 to learn more from its advanced design and categorically claimed in implied linkage that at this time Supermarine were engaged in designing the Spitfire. The statement is in gross error. Similarly, the Merlin-engine was fitted to the Spitfire long before the Kestrel engine was seen in an He 70 – so the Heinkel could not have influenced the Merlin's early development either…

The facts are that when the Rolls-Royce He 70 came to Britain the Spitfire had already been designed, and flown. In fact, by November 1935, the first Spitfire's wing was being physically completed in the metal, and by late January 1936 the first Spitfire prototype was built and was to fly within five weeks. Meanwhile, Rolls-Royce's He 70 was in bits, awaiting its new engine, at Rostock in Germany.[2, 3] Even if someone had reported back from the Rolls-Royce He 70 with some design ideas, they could not possibly have been incorporated into the, by then, finalized, tooled, and built Spitfire prototype, in the few weeks before it flew. It is worth adding that there was nothing in the He 70's wing aerodynamics that was relevant to, or usable by, the Spitfire. Furthermore, the curved-nose profile of the Rolls-Royce He 70 was all-new – previous He 70s, had had a stepped, square nose profile, so even any engine or cooling related knowledge from the original German-engined He 70 was redundant at the time!

R.J. Mitchell's own diaries cited by his son Gordon in his book about his father, openly discuss the Heinkel 70. Heinkel had shown great interest in Mitchell's S.4 Schneider trophy racer and been impressed with its smooth design – so smoothness did not start with the He 70! Years later, after Heinkel and his designers, the Günter brothers, had created the He 70, Mitchell was keen to see their aircraft. This he did on 21 April 1936 when the Heinkel's pilot Captain Sheppard, then based at Rolls-Royce's Hucknall facility, briefly showed Mitchell the He 70 that he had brought for the first time into Britain on 26 March 1936. But all this was *after* the

Spitfire's first flight, so no design influence nor inspiration upon Mitchell for the Spitfire stemmed from it.

An often repeated gross inaccuracy, including in books, articles, and upon a website claiming to be an attempt to set the record straight – entitled *The Spitfire Wing – a Mathematical Model*, is that the He 70 was unveiled in November 1934 at the Paris Air Show where Shenstone saw it, and within days, Mitchell had chosen the suggested ellipse, which was then was formally drawn up in response in early December. Such claims do not reflect the historical records. Neither was the He 70's ellipse new, defining or a revolutionary influence – as so many have suggested it was at the very time of the Spitfire's wing design choice. It is surely appropriate to cite the 1894 experiments by Frederick Lanchester into elliptical planforms, including with added 'washout' in his flying, elliptical wing models to prove the point that elliptical knowledge did not begin with the He 70 in Germany. Shenstone's modified ellipse and use of washout go back a lot further than the He 70, perhaps even beyond Frederick Lanchester's 1894 elliptical research findings and flying models.

The reality was that the He 70 was a rapid response to American aerodynamic developments that had led to an increase in the speed of monoplanes. In 1931, the Lockheed L9 Orion was announced – replete with smooth curves and a high speed. The Northrop Gamma Express mail plane with its massive radial engine was also on its way. The Germans needed a response[4] and speed was the key factor. Heinkel and his designers the Günter brothers rushed to produce a competing design in weeks. The He 70, created from the He 64 and its own smooth skin and elliptical tail, and mirroring the elliptical wing planform of the Bäumer Sausewind was that response.

As such, the irrefutable facts are that the He 70 was not a sudden 'new' idea that shocked the world and set a fashion, but instead was a competent development of existing elliptical and other knowledge – previously used on two other German aircraft circa 1925–1931 and notably seen in British and Italian designs before 1930. These facts completely destroy the opinions and claims of those who cite the He 70 as a new elliptical design moment of such status that it immediately influenced the Spitfire.

One author, Wayne Saunders, writing in 2010 in an RCAF journal tribute article to Shenstone, correctly stated that the Spitfire did not copy the He 70's wing design, and that the Spitfire's wing was different to the He 70's. But amazingly Saunders then curiously claimed the Spitfire's wing design *was* similar in general planform to the He 70s.

This contradiction, of course, is not the case and the reverse of the proof that the two wings were a different shape! It was Shenstone *himself* who stated when questioned by authors that the He 70's wing shape only 'faintly resembled the Spitfire's'. So from the designer's mouth, 'faintly resembled', cannot become, 'similar' in general planform shape as Saunders states. And the separate fact that the two aircraft had differing aerofoil thickness sections is actually less relevant in terms of disproving the claims about wing shape.

It seems that authors without fundamental knowledge of aerodynamics are prone to muddying the waters.

Saunders also wrote that Shenstone left Germany in late 1931, which is incorrect. The facts are that Shenstone left Germany in May 1931 and Mitchell's letter of offer of employment to Shenstone after an interview in Southampton, arrived on Bev's twenty-fifth birthday – 10 June 1931.

There has even been an article by the design academic Kenneth Agnew who, writing as far back as 1993 in the *Journal of Design History*,[5] in an extended article based on a lecture paper, questioned the concept or use of the ellipse. He seemed to suggest that the He 70 was somehow new, incredible and, crucially, stated that it (and its de facto influence) was unveiled at the November 1934 Paris Air Show, which is factually incorrect. Agnew cites Shenstone as seeing the new shape of the then unveiled He 70 at the 1934 Paris Show, and also of Mitchell and his men of working on an aerodynamic hunch – at the risk of the nation's security. The inherent suggestion of influence by this so-called new Heinkel aircraft just before the ellipse was officially chosen for the Spitfire is implicit in Agnew's claims, but as we know, the He 70 was *not* unveiled in 1934 and in terms solely of the key claim – the elliptical wing shape – was neither new nor an incredible revolution.

Agnew also suggested that the Spitfire wing was somehow over-engineered, and that the aircraft could have got away with a simpler, lighter tapered wing. He tells his audience that, as R.J. Mitchell knew the Spitfire was to be his epitaph as a dying man, his last design, that this may account for the nature and complexity of the Spitfire wing design – the use of the ellipse. This is perhaps Agnew's gravest factually incorrect statement – as in late 1935, after the design sign-off, Mitchell went straight from designing the Spitfire to designing the B.12/36 Supermarine bomber – which had a, deltoid wing with elliptical tips designed by Shenstone. Mitchell worked on this design from *before* the Spitfire took to the air in 1936 – working on the B.12 /36 across the two years prior to his death. Both his records and Shenstone's notes confirm this, as do others. In late 1936, Mitchell also suggested two Spitfire-based, light bombers with two seats and long canopied (one with a turret) as derivatives, which were not commissioned.

The B.12/36 bomber was awarded an official Air Ministry contract in competition with a design from Vickers, as a four-engined bomber for the RAF. Two prototypes were built, but sadly they were later destroyed in a German bombing raid on the Supermarine factory and the project stalled. Sir George Edwards said the B.12/36 wing was an incredible design.[6] There was also a suggested B.13/36 variant suggested by the Ministry, with two engines and a longer bomb bay.

So the Spitfire was most definitely *not* Mitchell's epitaph as his last design, and the claims that Agnew makes and supports about the Spitfire's design, based on stating that it *was*, are in gross error. Similarly, Agnew's opinions about the unveiling of the He 70's so-called new or incredible ellipse at the 1934 Paris Air Show, can only be in error, as must be any suggested influence upon the Spitfire at that time. These errors must be corrected simply in the name of factual, historical accuracy. The record needs to be set straight. Furthermore, Agnew even gets the year of Mitchell's death wrong…

As late as 30 May 2011, a Canadian named Bernie Gotham of Oshowa Ontario managed to get a letter published in Canada's *National Post* newspaper where he made the claim that R.J. Mitchell personally purchased an He 70 in order to study its design more closely – in the context of the Spitfire's design process. Such an outrageous claim, unsupported by any factual evidence, thus became a printed and a web-based on-line claim of 'fact' with no investigation or rebuttal.

Mitchell, of course, did no such thing and the Rolls-Royce powered He 70 came along after the Spitfire's design and first flight. So, once again, the gross errors of such libellous claims based on myth and incompetence amid the agenda of those determined to attack Mitchell and the Spitfire are exposed for what they are.

The fact that the authors of the claims that the Spitfire somehow de facto, 'copied ' the He 70, fail to note that the Sausewind and He 64 (both smoothly finished and elliptical in varying aspects) were previously extant should not go unnoticed by the reader. Similarly, those authors of claims about an He 70 influence also fail to state that there are significant differences between the He 70 and Spitfire wings. This only serves to further illustrate how little those authors knew of the facts before attacking the reputation of the Spitfire and its designers. And that is without mentioning the chronological errors of fact made, or the British, and Italian elliptical designs of the era that came *before* the He 70.

Curiously, no one seems to accuse Heinkel of 'copying' the wing design for the He 70 and the subsequent He 111 from the elliptically winged Shorts-Bristow Crusader, Schneider Trophy entry of 1927, which the wings of the two Heinkels closely mimic. This is probably because to do so would be much less exciting in hyperbole and headlines than claiming that the 'iconic' Spitfire, an aircraft of the victorious side in the Second World War, copied its design from an aircraft of the losing side...

The arguments and permutations could be endless, but it is clear that claims of the Spitfire de facto cribbing or copying the He 70 are historically and chronologically incorrect. Reality is far less exciting than erroneous speculation, incompetent research and conspiracy theories...

In the age of the internet, when any badly informed or lazy layman can propose a theory or opinion based on an erroneous version of fact, and see it become an anecdote or quotation that is repeated until it becomes apparent fact or accurate history, Supermarine, Mitchell, and his men, specifically Shenstone, have been badly served by those making the He 70 'copying' claims.

The inaccurate claims about the He 70 being some kind of new, defining design moment in 1934 (or any date) can only be the result of ignorance or deliberate act. The referenced facts are very simple and accessible, as are the answers to the questions:

• It is claimed that the Spitfire wing was copied or cribbed from the He 70. This is factually and scientifically incorrect – *irrespective* of any parallel personal denial by Shenstone.

• FACT: The He 70, designed by the Günter brothers, used a basic symmetrical ellipse inspired directly from its elliptically winged forebear – the Günter designed Bäumer Sausewind of 1925. The He 70 ellipse was gull winged and was not a thin-wing design; it did not possess advanced aerofoil or skin shape tuning. The wing planforms and aerofoils of the He 70 and the Spitfire were significantly different – they were a different shape!

• Of further significance, there was the Heinkel aircraft that linked the Sausewind and the He 70. This was the high-speed, Heinkel He 64 of 1930–31. Of note, the He 64 had an elliptical tail fin and tailplane and a very smooth finish, which the He 70 then repeated in close form. Therefore, the elliptical tail surfaces of the He 70 were most definitely *not* new and, its elliptical main wing was taken from the Sausewind of 1925. The He 64 had a tapered wing, but its smooth fuselage form and elliptical tail surfaces are clearly the direct precursors to the He 70's usage of the same, just as was the Sausewind's ellipse. The He 70 was rushed through in less than six months – stemming from the He 64, itself a high speed type. Given all these facts and their dated reality, any description of the He 70's use of the ellipse as new, incredible or revolutionary in terms of design and shape, must be in error. Strangely, the proponents of the He 70 as a Spitfire influence, seem to ignore the Heinkel's ancestors...

• Only in its multiple layers of (impractical at high altitude due to possible cracking) filler and paint (that added weight and time to its building), did the He 70 wing and body achieve a level of smoothness that could be cited as innovative in its class. Yet glider, delta wing and racing aircraft had also pursued smoothness criteria in the same era – notably in the He 64. So smoothness was not new either, even the Sausewind in 1925 had used layer upon layer of varnish and been polished to a glossy smoothness. Shenstone was totally open about how this smoothness criteria of the He 70 did influence him, but body smoothness, fuselage included, is not wing planform design related. Wanting to match a total body smoothness criteria and admitting such, as Shenstone did, is not admitting to the copying of an ellipsoid wing planform. Yet Shenstone's admissions about the Heinkel's influence in terms of *smoothness*, may have been manipulated or misinterpreted to suggest that it was the Heinkel's wing *shape* that influenced him, which is untrue.

• It is often claimed that the He 70 was the defining, new use of the ellipse in the early 1930s and that no other use of the ellipse was evident.

• FACT: Heinkel and the Günter brothers did not invent the ellipse, theirs was not the first use of it. Many other elliptically winged (and tailed) aircraft existed, including in Britain and in Italy in 1927 and 1929 respectively. In no sense was the elliptical planform of the He 70 a revolution or unique aerodynamic innovation.

• Numerous other aircraft used the elliptical wing planform prior to the He 70. The He 70 wing's minor differences from the 1925 Bäumer Sausewind are thrown into even starker relief when the He 70 is seen alongside the elliptically winged British, 1927-designed, Shorts-Bristow Crusader. Yet it is not 'fashionable' to suggest that the He 70 reflects the Crusader – notably in its trailing edge wing root design – as later seen on the He 111 bomber. No one seems to have argued that even Mitchell or Shenstone copied their ellipse of the British Shorts-Bristow Crusader (they did not), no doubt because such a claim would not be as 'attractive' as claiming it had been cribbed from a German machine...

• In Italy in 1929, the sharper-winged ellipse of the truly revolutionary hydrofoil flying boat, the Piaggio Pegna P.C. 7, was also seen. Giovanni Pegna designed this ellipsoid wing for the Italian 1929 Schneider Trophy entry and the design was internationally known, even if it did not compete. It even had elliptical hydrofoils. The Pegna P.C. 7 *really* was an incredible elliptical design flying boat concept of international profile, long before the He 70 appeared. In many senses it also aped Lanchester's 1894 elliptical design – as did later jet fighters. In 1930s Italy, Cesare Pallavicino was also a top aeronautical engineer and designer at the Italian firm of Caproni. He too was at the leading edge of aerodynamics and aware of all the developments in wing design. In 1930, long before the He 70 appeared, Pallavicino produced an elliptically winged variant of his Breda 33 class of single-engined monoplane – the Breda Ba. 33 variant had an ellpisoid wing that had overtones of the wing seen on the Shorts-Bristow Crusader and the Pegna P.C. 7 ellipse. Later in the 1930s, the Italian manufacturers, Reggiane and Macchi produced Pallavicinio designs, highly manoeuvrable fighter monoplanes including the superb Macchi C.202.

• R.J. Mitchell had used elliptical type wing shapes on his early S.4 Schneider Trophy racer and in the tailplanes of the later Schneider machines. The Spitfire's tailplane shape closely matches the S.5 and S.6 shape – not the Heinkel's. Indeed, does the He 70's tailplane not mimic the Supermarine racers designs? By July 1929, Mitchell was designing a true elliptically winged giant flying boat to Ministry Specification 20/28 – long before the He 70 appeared. So Mitchell designed a large fully elliptical wing three years before the He 70 appeared. Of note, the Spitfire's wing structural design aped that of Mitchell's 1929 flying boat with its front biased spar design.

• Before the He 70 or the Bäumer Sausewind, elliptically winged aircraft shapes had been drawn, modelled and tested by Hugo Junkers (1910) and Zhukovskii (Joukowski) (circa 1900) these designs had been studied internationally. Indeed, both the above designers had drawn elliptical wings that all the later shapes bear a very similar resemblance to. Prandtl, Kutta and Lanchester had also studied the ellipse. In France, Alphonse Pénaud had built an elliptical flying wing in the 1870s! Many other ellipsoid designs dating before 1932 are known (see chapter 6).

• The Spitfire's ellipse was a unique, modified or distorted ellipse, a parabolic and cubic curved calculus created by tailoring two ellipsoid sections of varying chord, into an asymmetric, forward swept wing planform that had a straighter leading edge in comparison with its more curved trailing edge. The Spitfire wing had a unique calculus, ultra-thin multiple aerofoil camber, 'washout' wing twist and, both boundary layer and curvilinear lift distribution shaping features. Its wing rib design and helical twist, were outside elliptical norms and non linear. As such, it was

173

the Spitfire's application of a modified elliptical wing planform that really *was* a new design and a singular, incredible achievement – as was its ultra-thin aerofoils. The combination of these design elements had not been seen before. No one else had done it!

• It has been variously claimed that He 70 was 'unveiled', 'launched', and 'seen' in the context of first sight, at the Paris Air Show in November 1934.

• FACT: The He 70 design, reflecting its designers' 1925 work on the Sausewind, and the He 64, was built in months in 1932, had its first flight on 1 December 1932, was launched in 1933, and entered Lufthansa service in March 1933. The He 70 first appeared at the *1933* Paris Air Show.[7, 8, 9] Of note, the He 70 also visited Croydon airport on 17 June 1934,[10] long before the 1934 Paris Air Show where it made its *second* French Salon appearance. The allegations that the He 70 was unveiled or new in November 1934 (and immediately influenced the Spitfire design drawings and elliptical decisions of late November and early December 1934), are therefore, in gross error and utterly false. Shenstone's autobiographical notes clearly cite 1933 not 1934 as his sight of the He 70 and the historical records back that up.

• Even if the observer *discards* the flawed November 1934 Paris Air Show theories, it becomes very obvious that Shenstone and Mitchell had nearly ten years in which to copy the source of the He 70's ellipse – that of the 1925 Bäumer Sausewind – *if* they were going to 'copy' its normal ellipse, which they did not. Indeed, one might as well argue that if the He 70's 1932-launched ellipse was the influence on the subsequent Type 300 Spitfire, why, upon the actual weakness of the Supermarine Type 224 in February 1934 at first flight, did Mitchell et al., not immediately, there and then, 'copy' the by then well known and in-service He 70 design? After all, it had been around since December 1932 and in the Bäumer Sausewind lineage since 1925. Mitchell had, of course, designed an elliptically winged monoplane flying boat in 1929, and his S.4 Schneider racer had had an ellipsoid wing, elliptical tailplane and elliptical float strut mounting fairings, so Mitchell had no need to copy anyone when it came to the ellipse.

• If Shenstone was going to copy the 1931 He 70's ellipse, why did he not do it in late 1933 or early 1934 as the Type 224 failed? Surely that would have been the moment to 'copy' the He 70 and achieve 'designer' status? Not that he was made that way, or ever pursued such status. The Spitfire designers got to their *unique* version of the ellipse in their own time and at their own choice, irrespective of the He 70 and various timings – real or imaginary.

• It is often claimed that the British secured, via Rolls-Royce, a Rolls-Royce-engined He 70 airframe and used it for wind tunnel study, and/or to copy design aspects for the Spitfire – by definition *prior* to the Spitfire's first flight or selection of its final design features and tooling up, for them.

• FACT: The British did indeed secure a Rolls-Royce-powered He 70A variant – it took many months for high-level government negotiations over the 'swop' of an He 70 and Rolls-Royce Kestrel type engines between Britain and Germany to result in a Rolls-Royce-engined He 70G. Ernst Heinkel had been keen to secure more power for his smooth new machine – alloy constructed smoothness being its novel criteria. The German Government changed in 1933 with the advent of Nazi rule, and engine technology was relevant after the enforced years of banned powered flight under the Versailles Treaty – Rolls-Royce's designs being preferred as an engineering benchmark for large capacity (V12) engines. The new German Government took months to discuss and finally agree the release of an He 70 in return for Rolls-Royce engine know-how in the form of four Kestrel engines. How many He 70s Britain was to receive is hard to establish. What is known is that after one He 70G had been agreed for Rolls-Royce, the deal collapsed. The Germans were also well advanced with the Daimler Benz and Jumo engines and they even had an aircraft, the Walter Blume-designed Arado AR 80 V1, that used a Rolls-Royce Kestrel engine and curved design cues.

• The Rolls-Royce Kestrel V-engined, Heinkel 70G1 (which followed on from Heinkel's 1935 model year F variant of the He 70) was originally registered as He 70A D-UBOF and then for import to the British register in March 1936 as G-ADZF. A British civil aviation certificate of airworthiness, its permit to fly, was issued on 6 April 1936 in London. This was after the He 70 'swop' had been finally agreed as a contract in late 1935 and the aircraft was purchased by Rolls-Royce for £13,000. The aircraft was prepared and re-engined not in Britain, but in early 1936 at Heinkel's factory in Germany and flew, piloted by a Captain Sheppard, to Britain on 26 March 1936 – three weeks *after* the Spitfire's first flight, where, via Croydon, the He 70 joined the new Rolls-Royce test section at Hucknall, Derby.[11]

• The Spitfire prototype's metal cutting and wing construction was near completion by late November 1935, the airframe was completed in mid-January 1936, and it first flew on 5 March 1936. In contrast, the Rolls-Royce Heinkel 70 was re-engined at Heinkel's Rostock works in Germany beginning in late January 1936 and worked on in February and March.[12] Therefore, any suggestion (and there have been many) that this specific Heinkel 70G was either in Britain, or studied in a wind tunnel or research facility *prior* to the selection, design, tooling and building of the first Spitfire, is destroyed by the dated records. Neither could any study of the Rolls-Royce He 70 in Germany in very early 1936 have seen the Spitfire's design changed, tested, and re-tooled in a few short days or weeks. Only latterly in the late 1930s, did Rolls-Royce use their He 70 with its unique nose profile as a wind tunnel test basis for radiator flow research, which came after the Spitfire and its Merlin engine development. The He 70's previous square nose profile 1932–1936, made its 'secrets' utterly irrelevant and redundant to Spitfire development. It was the Rolls-Royce-designed Kestrel He 70 that was the basis of later Rolls-Royce research findings – not the pre 1936 He 70 design!

• The Spitfire's own use of the ellipse was chosen in 1934 and its definitive ellipse shape was settled in December 1934/January 1935 – long *before* (nearly a year) the Rolls-Royce-powered He 70G was created, or seen in Britain. R.J. Mitchell did not get to inspect the Rolls-Royce He 70G in detail until 26 May 1936[13] – over two months after the Spitfire's first flight, although he had briefly seen the He 70 in April.

• It is therefore fundamentally impossible for the Spitfire in its design and prototype building process to have stolen design techniques from Rolls-Royce's He 70 G, as this Heinkel did not become reality until after the prototype Spitfire was almost physically complete.

Upon such collection of very pertinent points, it can be seen that the claims that Shenstone or Mitchell et al. 'copied' or were inspired by the He 70 are flawed to the core – whichever way round the allegation is spun – *with* or *without* the falsehoods of the 1934 Paris Air Show – He 70 'unveiled' and 'seen' theories. The facts presented herein, ought to set the record straight for the internet discussion era and for the historical record.

* * *

Shenstone's Personal Response to the He 70 Allegations

Aside from the true facts of design, time, place, and event, as described above, there are the words and records of the man himself. He was a quiet, shy man who was not a showman, a man with little interest in being a design celebrity, a man who was not a dilettante. A man who was twenty-seven years old when he suggested and shaped the Spitfire's ellipse – a wing he called 'our' wing, not 'my' wing.

From his own standpoint, Shenstone confirmed in several contexts, ranging from his own records to his interview with Dr Alfred Price, his view on the claims, making the often quoted statements:

> The ellipse was well known and had been seen before on other aircraft before Heinkel used it.
>
> Our wing was much thinner than that of Heinkel and had quite a different section. In any case it would have been asking for trouble to have copied a wing shape from an aircraft designed for an entirely different purpose.[14]

Shenstone's own notes and comments to others clearly show concern with the claims of 'copying' from the He 70. He said of the claims:

> This is quite untrue… the He 70's shape only faintly resembles that of the Spitfire.[15]

The Spitfire's modified ellipse was asymmetric in shape, was of a greatly differing planform and construction, and had a different aileron design to the He 70 (Shenstone having been published on aileron design and Mitchell being 'hot' on aileron design too). The Spitfire's ellipsoidal wing tips were also a very different radii to those of the He 70. The broad chord, gull-winged, thick section Heinkel wing was not designed to supply high performance turns or dog-fight aerobatics at high altitude.

Unless Shenstone is to be called a liar by his accusers, it must, in the face of this collation of factual evidence, be accepted that he did not copy the He 70 wing planform, and neither was it a new design that inspired him in terms of the ellipse.

Shenstone was in fact very clear about the He 70 – he utterly refuted the allegations of copying its elliptical shape, but he clearly and publicly admitted that the He 70's overall total body smoothness was much to be admired and that he used it as a singular aerodynamic criteria for the Spitfire's *overall* skin smoothness. This openness is not psychologically consistent with trying to hide something. It is not a paradoxical denial or admission, so his claims are not internally inconsistent. As Shenstone always wrote and said:

> The Heinkel 70 did have an influence on the Spitfire – but in a rather different way… I was impressed by the smoothness of its skin.[16]

So there it was – it was openly admitted that the Heinkel 70 *did* influence the Spitfire – but *not* in terms of the ellipse as the subsequent myth has claimed. Shenstone referred to the Heinkel's smooth skin – meaning the skin of the *whole* airframe – not just the wing nor specifically the wing design, let alone its planform. It is unfortunate that some observers seem to have misinterpreted Shenstone's comments about the Heinkel's smoothness, as being related to wing design – instead of the *overall* total form smoothness criteria that he framed.

Shenstone's further words on skin smoothness make his position even more clear:

> If the Germans could do it, then with a little more effort, so could we. Heinkel's layers of paint added greatly to the weight; we had to do the best we could without resorting to that.[17]

The caveat about paint and its weight, provides the reader with a further angle with which to judge Shenstone's views of the He 70 and the significance of them upon the Spitfire. He admired the Heinkel's smoothness – but not at *any* price and certainly *not* to be copied using such techniques. The issue of added airframe weight from all that paint and filler applied to the He 70, is also a significant detrimental design and production issue of the He 70, yet is not mentioned by those who claim the He70 was a new, incredible, revolution that inspired the Spitfire. For such claimants, it is an inconvenient truth, hidden from their expressed opinions.

So the He 70's was a smoothness that could never have been achieved on the Spitfire's alloy riveted stressed skin structure – not least as the He 70s smoothness was the result of hours of filling and painting to build up a layer so thick that rivets could not be seen. These materials would never have proved durable on a high-altitude, high-stress, fighter airframe, or been easy to maintain or repair, but the He 70's smoothness was to be admired and Shenstone said so to Mitchell, his men, to his family and publicly, even to Ernst Heinkel.

Shenstone's statements about the He 70's related smoothness led to more confused reporting – with claims that Mitchell wrote to Heinkel congratulating him on the He 70 wing – further supposed linkage say some. The reality is, as shown from Shenstone's own diaries, a different story:

> In 1933 I visited the Paris Air Show and saw there the Heinkel He 70. I had heard that its fuselage was all-metal, but when I saw it I could see no joints nor any sign of rivets. It looked like a plywood fuselage. Reports of technical things are so often wrong so I simply wrote to Heinkel, asking if it was metal, and congratulating him if it were. I over-did my congratulations a bit, to encourage a reply. I got it: However, to my surprise, Heinkel in his autobiography prints my letter, implying that it was from Mitchell. He says the letter was from a 'well known English designer'. I was not that. Anyhow, I was only 27.[18]

Shenstone has never made any secret of the fact that he used the Heinkel 70's overall finish as a total airframe smoothness criteria. This does not constitute copying a design feature – and especially not a wing planform. Shenstone did not hide his admiration for the Heinkel's predecessor, the little Bäumer Sausewind, but he quite correctly pointed out the huge differences between the Spitfire's wing and its task, compared with those of the Sausewind and the He 70.

Shenstone has been cited as having worked for Ernst Heinkel by some writers – perhaps linked with the Heinkel 70 wing 'cribbing' theory. This is an oft-repeated inaccuracy: Shenstone worked for Junkers and then (twice) with Lippisch. He may have met Heinkel, just as he met Willi Messerschmitt in 1938,[19] but he did *not* work for Heinkel, so had no deep knowledge or intrinsic linkage to, or of, the He 70.

Further Key Points

If the British had *really* wanted to crawl over the early He 70, why would they have waited to see the He 70 in its Rolls-Royce variant? The British could have studied the He 70 in 1933, or even when it visited Croydon Airport on 17 June 1934, a date by which it had been in service for over a year with Lufthansa, and had appeared at the 1933 Paris Air Show when it could also have been inspected, sketched and photographed in detail. A fact rarely mentioned is that the He 70 was a work in progress – it was often changing. From the A model onwards, it was modified with differing nose shapes, differing engine cowlings, changes to the fuselage and significant alterations to the cabin and canopy layout and to wing to fuselage panelling. Prior to the smooth, curved, Rolls-Royce-engined version's nose, so often cited, the He 70 was seen with several variations of a stepped and square nose profile.

It is also often claimed that the (false and erroneous) first sighting of the so-called newly unveiled He 70 by Shenstone in November 1934 at Paris, resulted in a set of drawings just days later in early December 1934 allied to a 16 November Air Ministry statement about the need for eight guns.

Given that November 1934 was not a first sighting or unveiling for the He 70, any argument built to support consequences from such claims becomes by default, void.

Of great note, the Supermarine Type 224's first flight in February 1934 of had led to a need to come up with the new design – the eventual Type 300 or Spitfire. Mitchell and his men undertook intense design work under Type 224 modification proposals in the summer of 1934. Hugh

Dowding assessed these defined Type 224 F.7 /30 modification proposals in the first days of November 1934, and issued written correspondence on 8 November 1934 – subsequent to his discussions with R.J. Mitchell on the matter. Shenstone spent many weeks in the early summer of 1934 touring America as part of a British fact-finding mission by Vickers-Armstrongs. He came back with the new, thin aerofoil details and was full of thin wing ideas and wing shape proposals. Mitchell, of course, had already considered the ellipse on his giant flying boat and used it on the tails of his racers. Shenstone had reinforced that view as far back as 1931.

Documents cited in 2008 by Alfred Faddy's son, David, and published in *Aeroplane Monthly* magazine[20] clearly reveal early attempts at a suggested heavily tapered elliptical wing for the modified design being drawn up by the Supermarine drawing office under Alfred Faddy, *before* the 1934 Paris Air Show – and two years *after* the He 70's real launch date. This drawing was in tune with Mitchell's meetings with the Air Ministry and coincident with an impending funding decision from Vickers, which constitute supporting strands of evidence of wing design development. Drawing 300000 No. 11 defines an early elliptical wing proposal, and pre-dates drawings cited as being made in early December – drawing 300000 No. 12 – the Spitfire's forwards distorted ellipse.

It is said that R.J. Mitchell had to be persuaded to adopt the ellipse by a number of people – Shenstone being but a single player. What of Clifton, Smith, Faddy, Fenner, Fear, Holmes, Davis, Payn, Mansbridge et al? Clearly this process did not just happen to occur, and Mitchell had already used elliptical tailplanes on his racing machines and done a lot of work on his large six-engined monoplane flying boat's elliptical wing in 1929–1931. So Mitchell knew all about the ellipse; it was nothing new to him or the Schneider Trophy teams – the Shorts-Bristow Crusader and its broad, pure ellipse, and the Piaggio Pegna's ellipse being entirely relevant.

As early as 1910, Hugo Junkers was testing a model wing of elliptical shape for flow characteristics. This wing, photos of which were in the Junkers research archives for anyone to see, show a wing planform very similar to subsequent ellipses. One might as well absurdly argue that if as some claim, Shenstone copied the Heinkel elliptical wing, then Heinkel (or rather the Günters) copied it from Junkers. Neither statement is accurate. And again, what of Zhukovskii and his elliptical airframe designs of 1910? What of Pegna's 1929 elegant ellipse? What of Lanchester? Where should the argument end?

Some say that the Spitfire wing was over-engineered and that a lighter, tapered wing would have had benefits, and done the job, Agnew[21] tell us that no other major designer employed the ellipse other than Hawker in the Tempest. This erroneous claim seems to be used to suggest that the ellipse was perhaps unworthy or of unproven nature…

So, what then of the other elliptically winged monoplane fighters circa 1936–1945?

What of the leading American fighter the Republic P-47 Thunderbolt and its elliptical wing, which served across a wide theatre of the war in large numbers? Its designers, Gregor and Kartvelli, were influential design leaders, as was Alexander Seversky – a proponent of the ellipse. What of Lockheed using an elliptical wing on its 1941 jet fighter design the L-133? Were these not 'major' designers?

The ellipse was also seen on the 1944 Hawker Fury at Sydney Camm's lead – Camm who consulted Shenstone during and after the war. What of the Dewoitine 513/520, or the American, Seversky P-36 of 1937? During the Second World War the Russians produced the Spitfire-esque, elliptically winged fighter, the Lavochkin La-7, and also the Yak 9.

Even Heinkel re-used the elliptical wing idea in his He 176/8 and He 280 jet fighter designs – notably a forwards distorted ellipse variant, aping the Spitfire's. Heinkel also sent a design engineer to Japan where an ellipsoid wing was seen on the Mitsubishi A5M as well as the Aichi VAL 22. Junkers also added elliptical tips to high flying versions of its Ju 88 bombers. Even Supermarine drew up further elliptically winged aircraft – the B.12/36 bomber, and two Spitfire derived single-engined light bombers (one with a gun turret and another a dive bomber to specification 0.37/ 34 from April 1936).

Any claim that the ellipse was not used by other major designers, in light of the above examples, can only be politely termed as incorrect and the reader can draw his or her, own conclusions as to such claims' origins or their agenda…

Of interest, the French Dewoitine 513/520 is not accused of having 'copied' or been influenced by the He 70's elliptical wing and tail – yet this aircraft flew its first flight weeks *before* the Spitfire's…The Dewoitine's ellipse, devoid of Shenstone's and Smith's advanced aerodynamic and structural science, suffered from instability and higher drag, and would take three years of re-design to take to the air as the Dewoitine 520.

Summary of He 70 Issues

In Conclusion of the examination of the erroneous claims about the He 70 somehow being an influence upon the Spitfire's design, there are the final defining facts about the He 70 and the Spitfire that are the rocks of the rebuttal to the claim.

Firstly, and critically, we should not forget that it was no less than Ernst Heinkel himself, as recorded by him in German, in his autobiography *Sturmisches Leben* (Turbulent Life), who states that when he visited Venice in 1927 to see that year's Schneider Trophy contest, he saw two British aircraft (the Supermarine S.4 and the Shorts Bristow Crusader) and that he was filled with the desire to build similarly beautiful aircraft, himself. He then went out and hired the designers that could deliver that style the – Günter Brothers.

So by his *own admission*, Ernst Heinkel's desire for curves, ellipses and smooth bodywork (the essential design elements of the two aircraft cited above) did not begin with the He 70. It *began* with Mitchell's S.4 and Bristow's Crusader in 1927. This must conclusively and definitively prove in Heinkel's own words, that the Spitfire's elliptical design cues did not originate with the He 70 as so many modern opinions have since claimed in such gross error.

The second fact of massive significance to the story, was the discovery, following a visit by the Air Ministry's Stewart Scott-Hall to Germany in the summer of 1935, where he was granted the first British, close inspection of the He 70, (as cited in Scott-Hall's subsequent Air Ministry report of 22 August 1935), that it became apparent the single most important issue of the He 70's total overall smoothness, was achieved by means that could never have been applied to a mass production fighter aircraft. The truth was that for the He 70, its smooth skin came from hours of filling and paint that added, between 1 lb/sq ft and 3 lb/sq ft of weight, in filler and paint to *every square foot* of the He 70's total skin area! This was a massive weight penalty of the greatest significance, with many hundreds of lbs or kgs in weight added.

Thirdly, and of critical importance to the verdict, is that to achieve its smoothness, the He 70's body skin was *not* attached to the main airframe, but only to the longitudinal stringers beneath it. This cheap but risky engineering solution reduced indentations, wrinkling and elastic buckling or 'panting' of the skin by avoiding attaching it fully to the aircraft's main chassis structure. But this 'trick' *greatly* reduced skin strength as well as total airframe strength, requiring thicker gauge chassis metal in the load bearing, front part of the airframe. Only through this trickery could the He 70 achieve its smooth skin. Mitchell was hardly likely to copy this technique.

The He 70's recently much-vaunted wing, also had to be redesigned soon after its launch due to wing drop at approach speeds with full flaps, imagine today's critics reaction if the Spitfire's ellipse had suffered that problem.

The above facts are *never* cited in the great He 70 'Spitfire - influence' or 'copying' claims of recent years. The lecturer and design writer Kenneth Agnew failed to mention these vital arbiters in his (academically published) criticism of the Spitfire's design and its designer where he suggested the Spitfire was built upon an unproven hunch as a deliberate epitaph!

It must now be clear that the Spitfire could never have 'copied' nor been inspired by the He 70, as it would never have worked if it had – just as Shenstone *always* said.

Shenstone is proved correct by the properly researched facts.

Even as late as 2012, in a lavish new Spitfire history book, *Spitfire Britain's Finest Hour* by Nigel Cawthorne, that author boldly claimed that the Rolls-Royce He 70 was in Britain at the time of the Spitfire's development and that the He 70 is believed, across a broad arena, to have been an inspiration for the Spitfire. Such gross errors must be addressed and corrected solely for the historical record.

Some Spitfire authors, it seems, are unable to grasp the reality and genius of Supermarine's work. The evidence herein offers future observers a corrective remedy.

Prior to the Second World War, the Spitfire's wing was the *first* modified, forward swept, uniquely plotted monoplane fighter-based ellipse-type wing that combined new thinking and two new ultra thin aerofoils – an invented, bespoke piece of aerodynamic and structural tailoring in comparison with textbook wings of any shape. From such original design genius, came the unique, iconography of the Spitfire's wing shape.

No one else had ever done these things. But R.J. Mitchell did, with the core help of fewer than a dozen men, one of whom was the Canadian Beverley Shenstone, the Spitfire's aerodynamicist and wing designer – the man who as R. J. Mitchell's son said, was 'significant' to the Spitfire.

12

Atlantic Commuter

Shenstone's diary clearly shows that there were long hours and that he and the team worked into the nights; sometimes a team member would come to his house on the estuary at Netley and stay over after working to the small hours. With a wife, and a young baby son, allied to an incredible work load, stress levels were at times high. Yet being by the sea and the broad river inlet, and being able to muck about in boats and wander the beaches and woods in an idyllic 1930s England clearly helped make the Spitfire days, happy ones. From his work and his personal diary and notes, it becomes clear that Shenstone was a workaholic. Maybe he and the Mitchell team were obsessed? If they were, it was with good cause, with correct reason and with the correct outcome.

After Mitchell's untimely death, there was still work to be done and, there was the story of Mitchell's bomber.

Shenstone's notes and lifelong friendship with Alexander Lippisch make the importance of this relationship very clear. If the observer is in any doubt as to the closeness of the relationship, he or she must look no further than the Supermarine four-engined bomber proposal to meet the Air Ministry specification B.12/36 of 1936. The B.12/36 featured a delta wing with elliptical tips. Beverly Shenstone was the chief aerodynamicist on the B.12/36 and utilized a Lippisch-type delta wing on the aircraft – a wing concept whose invention he had contributed too. Was this the world's first delta-winged bomber – prop powered, but still a delta wing and designed for production before 1939?

Junkers had tried an ungainly, fixed undercarriage, flying wing shape in 1929 on his G38, but only two were completed, but the sleek Mitchell / Shenstone delta winged Supermarine B.12/36 specification bomber pre-dated the jet powered delta wing craft and even pre-dated the advanced Messerschmitt swept-wing fighters of the last days of the war. It would be over a decade before Avro, with the Roy Chadwick-designed Vulcan to some degree reflecting the basics of Lippisch's delta wing research, made the flying triangle work. The American B-58 Hustler would soon do likewise, as would the French Mirage fighter. Saab would refine the idea with its double delta, Draken fighter. Concorde's wing would surely provide ultimate vindication for Lippisch's work – and Shenstone's contribution to its birth.

The B.12/36 could have been as revolutionary as the Spitfire. Its shape would have allowed huge fuel tankage and a large bomb bay, so its range and payload would have been phenomenal, although its shallow wing and fuselage depth may, in Shenstone's view, have prohibited the carriage of the very large bombs that the Lancaster and Stirling later delivered. Mitchell's bomber was designed to compete with a Vickers proposal for the Air Ministry bomber specification and Rex Pierson and George Edwards were both amazed by it.[1] Given that Supermarine got the prototype order and that Vickers did not, praise from the Weybridge offices was noteworthy. By the time of the prototype's destruction, the Avro Lancaster was already in planning, and the decision was taken for Supermarine to concentrate on building Spitfires.

The fact remains that in the Supermarine B.12/36 proposal, Mitchell and Shenstone had, for the second time, come up with a unique, ground-breaking aircraft – and it was a delta-winged heavy bomber. Only Mitchell's death and wartime fate interrupted its birth. For Shenstone it was a blow, because he had already envisaged that such a design could easily be converted into producing the world's first delta-winged, ultra-long range transport aircraft – a unique airliner that would have been far in advance of anything the Americans could have delivered.

Furthermore, it would only have taken minor steps to remove the leading edge pylon mounted propeller power sources and substitute them with jet power plants to have given Britain a large, long-range, delta-winged, jet airliner – in the 1940s. Without exaggeration, all this was within Supermarine's grasp; only war and fate precluded it. It could have been Mitchell's and Shenstone's greatest, other, national contribution.

Shenstone wrote:

Mitchell's answer to the B12/ 36 specification, was to make the fuselage as small as possible and put the bombs in the wings. Wing structure was a D-nose monospar as in the Spitfire, behind which almost all the bombs prescribed could be accommodated without drag. It was a very attractive machine. … We know how the types of and sizes of bombs changed rapidly during the war. The Supermarine bomber could not have competed, whereas that ghastly Stirling and the attractive Lancaster had body room for large bombs.[2]

Despite the issue of bomb size development, the thought of the world's first tailless delta-winged bomber coming from the same people who created the Spitfire was reality; it was built. In its destruction, Shenstone perhaps lost another stepping stone to becoming a major name, yet the possibility of the Supermarine B12/36 specification bomber morphing into an airline and military transport, is a tempting glimpse of a post-war aviation world that could have had a different history. The bomb bay issue may also have been solved by the B13/36 revised specification.

The delta wing (in glider and powered form) was a great advance, and had a place in the knowledge that lay behind the Spitfire's wing design. It also was a more obvious basis for the B12/36. Again, Shenstone had been with Lippisch in the vital 1930–31 years of delta experimentation – so he had a hand in the delta design itself; as such B12/36 was not 'cribbed' from anyone.

Less than two years after R.J. Mitchell died, Beverley Shenstone left Supermarine. However, his status now meant that he had a profile and the government was soon to find a use for Shenstone and his ever active brain. The offer that came from the Air Ministry stemmed from Shenstone having existing relationships with the people that ran it.

By 1938 Shenstone had worked with Stewart Scott-Hall for five years. Scott-Hall had been the Air Ministry's Resident Technical Officer based at Supermarine in Southampton and was closely involved with the development of the Spitfire before being transferred to the aircraft test facility at Martlesham. The Supermarine years had also introduced Shenstone to figures at the Royal Aeronautical Establishment (RAE) at Farnborough. There he had met men such as Alston, Morien Morgan, C.J. Stewart and many other engineers and scientists. The names of H.L. Cox and H. Roxbee Cox (later Lord Kings Norton) were also to become significant. Also convergent on the scene was former test pilot Major Oliver Stewart and his new British aviation publication, *Aeronautics*, which was to launch its first long-planned edition in August 1939. Shenstone contributed to this with his article 'Aircraft of Two Nations … A Comparative Analysis'. This was penned under his own name – rather than his pseudonym of 'Brian Worley'– a name derived from the name of Shenstone's first son and an anagram of the surname of an old friend.

Just before this happened, Shenstone, by now renting a flat in west London, had more of his 'luck'.

C.J. Stewart from the RAE was appointed Director of Civil Aviation Research and Production (DCRP) for the Air Ministry. Stewart asked Shenstone to join him, working as his Senior Scientific Officer (SSO) at £750 per annum – a small increase on his final salary at Supermarine. Their boss was Roderick Hill. Soon after taking up his new job, Shenstone bumped into Vickers-Armstrong's Chief Designer, Rex Pierson, whom he knew well and had travelled around America with in 1934.

> I ran into Rex Pierson in Berkeley St. In his straightforward manner he said: 'You were a bloody fool to leave Supermarine.' He didn't tell me why, and I was stupid enough not to ask.[3]

Even though war was imminent, the future of civil aviation, notably long-haul aviation with which to service the British Empire, was still a main area of focus for the Air Ministry. Shenstone was thrown into the discussions for the official specifications for transatlantic and, tropical route airliners – Specifications 14./38 and 15./38 – four-engined airliners. Issues of pressurization, engine choice, land or water-based designs, were paramount, and it was the Shorts company and the Fairey company that were selected to work on these vital aircraft at a time when the American DC-3 had signalled a warning to the world. How long would it be before the Americans designed a larger, four-engined, long-haul version? Yet the British, in 1938, were still focusing on luxury and space rather than payload and range – a historically critical error. In military terms, the old conceited, stick in the mud, attitudes still prevailed – 'a good kick up the rear' (to use RAF parlance) was needed.

By 1939, the Canadian William Maxwell Aitken, Lord Beaverbrook, entered the scene as the figure head of the revitalized Ministry of Aircraft Production, which was soon to focus upon the need to commission a range of military and civilian types of aircraft. Many Air Ministry people were streamed into this unit. Beaverbrook was to gain the public relations glory for shaking up the system and making things happen at a pace faster than the somewhat turgid progress that the competing factions of British aircraft industry had previously been used to. Behind the scenes, the power, the real unsung hero who delivered the required, well-aimed 'kick' to the posterior of government and aviation, was to be Air Chief Marshal Sir Wilfrid Freeman – who was to be Shenstone's new boss.

Without doubt, Beaverbrook got things done, but just below his elite level – his politically linked level – Wilfrid Freeman and his team, which included Shenstone and Edward Warren, were the people who got out there into the factories and into the nuances of design, to change things. The old, 'we have always done it this way' attitude had to be changed if Britain was to survive. Shenstone and others, notably J.V. Connolly, fostered this cultural change – less waste, more effort, more thinking and a streamlined production and procurement process. By the summer of 1940, a general acceleration of airframe operations procedures within the industry was happening. Under Wilfrid Freeman's inspired leadership, Britain became capable of saving itself.

Air Chief Marshal Sir Wilfrid Rhodes Freeman, GCB, DSO, MC, RAF was born on 18 July 1888 and died on 15 May 1953. A holder of what would now be called privilege, he was a product of Sandhurst and then a pilot in No. 2 Squadron of the Royal Flying Corps and saw service in the First World War. By 1926 he was Commandant of the Central Flying School. Freeman was asked in late 1935 to get on with rearming the RAF, and in doing so, he brought decisive thinking and aeronautical knowledge to the Air Ministry and its procurement procedure. Just after the start of the war, he was moved to become Deputy Chief of the Air Staff, yet he was greatly missed and was returned to the Ministry of Aircraft Production (MAP) to re-invigorate it. He drove the vital selection of the Mosquito and the Lancaster. Without Freeman, the Spitfire, Hurricane and other types may never have seen the light of day. In 1942, he also influenced the design and production of the Merlin-engined, North American P-51 Mustang – ensuring that the aircraft was in service in sufficient numbers to deal with the aerial crisis over Germany in 1944.

Freeman was the power house, the driving force and vision behind the decisions of the MAP. There were many battles to fight and the internecine world of quarrelling civil servants allied to military egos and not-so military egos, amid the tiers and layers of government, must have been a heavy burden. But Freeman was the genius whose work ensured not just Allied survival, but also supremacy. His life is celebrated in a superb biography by Anthony Furse.[4]

Shenstone brought with him to the MAP, an attitude based on international experience – in Canada, Germany, America, and from the free-thinking psychology of Mitchell's Supermarine team. As such, Shenstone was instrumental in identifying areas where vast improvements could be made. Such thinking was to find resonance with Air Chief Marshal Freeman, himself a man of international experience, vision and lateral thinking.

In the 1930s, Shenstone had observed how there was very little interaction between British aircraft designers and their respective companies – even when, as with Supermarine, they were part of the greater Vickers entity. A lack of interchange, a secrecy between companies, seemed to have become an established culture; it was a psychology of suspicion. There was much to do to ensure that British designers and British factories shared ideas, worked together and did not duplicate work and waste precious resources. Even at Vickers there were issues, as Shenstone noted:

> Rex Pierson, Weybridge's chief designer, was easy-going and easy to talk to, but even so there was no full interchange of experience between him and Mitchell. Barnes Wallis, also at Vickers, Weybridge, kept his cards even closer to his chest. Mitchell and his men had little use for Wallis's geodetic construction as it was very complex and not suited to stressed skin, the geodetic skeleton being the complete structure.... As we all know, the geodetic structure implied a fabric covering but this would not stand up for long to speed of over about 200mph. During the war Vickers had considerable difficulties with this problem and Wallis devised a clever woven metal covering which eased the problem to a certain extent.[5]

In late 1938, Shenstone travelled to Berne, Switzerland, to give a lecture at the *Internationalen Studiekommison Motorlosen Flug*. There he travelled to nearby Augsburg and met Willi Messerschmitt – courtesy of Handley Page's Gustav Lachmann. It was at this time that Shenstone spotted the still-secret Me110 twin-engined fighter-bomber. It made him realize just how important it was to get back and develop new British types. George Bulman was also on the trip – together the two men reported back on the sheer scale of German military and industrial preparation.

Upon his return, Shenstone was posted to Bristol in the west of England. There he worked closely with the Bristol company on their latest twin-engined light bomber aircraft types and more closely on the development of Bristol engines. He was based at Durdham Down, and more of Shenstone's good luck followed when one of the senior directors of the company, Mr Butler, part of the great combination that was the Fedden and Butler command of Bristol engines, offered Shenstone a rented room in his home. This put Shenstone right at the heart of the enterprise at the highest level. In Sir Roy Fedden, Shenstone found an interested listener, and a potential ally upon the subject of the all-wing configuration. Fedden would, as soon as 1944, present a lecture on the future of civil aircraft and predicted the mass development of all-wing civil airliners, and the use of active boundary layer control.[6] Once again, Shenstone was in the right place at the right time, with the right people; his surfeit of good luck, seems incredible.

After spending 1938 and 1939 working on both future design and production themes, Shenstone found himself streamed off to a new role under the head of research, H. Grinstead. In this new job, Shenstone travelled through the industry visiting airframe manufacturers in an effort to reduce the use of extrusions where they could be replaced by drawn or rolled alloy sections. The use and cost of alloy extrusions was a serious matter for the British. Demand for aluminium was above 30,000 tons per annum in 1939, let alone in the heavier demand of the later war years. Extrusions were large lumps or billets of metal forced under immense pressure through a shaped outlet or nozzle – producing perfectly shaped and formed components of one piece that were ideal for wing spars and chassis members. Freeman ordered that all supplies of extrusion presses, even ones from Germany, be snapped up in 1938–39. By 1940, a way had to be found to reduce extrusion consumption – Freeman made Shenstone one of the men in a small team whose remit was to focus on the extrusion problem.

Shenstone visited a company named 'Ebenstos' on 5 July 1940[7] who were working on advanced plastic extrusions – so advanced, that Freeman ordered the MAP to work closely with the company, N.E. Rowe and H. Grinstead becoming consultants to Ebenstos. Shenstone began to study and focus on the new plastic and composite technologies – advising Beaverbrook on the process after he took an interest in plastics and sent one of his own team, named Bickel (later an Air Canada Board member), to assist in the MAP's investigation into plastics.[8] These were the first tentative steps of composite construction.

Shenstone and the DCRP unit were evacuated to Harrogate in Yorkshire where Shenstone was to work under N.E. Rowe – another important name that would resonate across a future not yet cast. Also present in the DCRP offices with Shenstone at Harrogate was Bill Boddy – the famous motoring writer and racer who was the 'father' of *Motorsport* magazine. Harrogate, it seems, was an interesting collection of talents.

The period in Yorkshire was known as the 'Harrogate Programme' and Freeman himself was based in the Harrogate offices until he could engineer a return to London for the whole team. During this period, Shenstone was also closely involved with modifications to the design of the Westland Lysander, whose kinked and forward-angled wing aped the latest glider research and provided excellent short take-off and landing qualities. After surviving the winter of 1939–1940, which swathed Yorkshire in snow drifts of Canadian proportions, Shenstone was posted back to London just in time for the start of the Blitz. Shenstone's notes state that he and his colleague 'Jock' Gray had been billeted with a local family in Harrogate.

The next job was for Shenstone to persuade airframe manufacturers of the benefits of using plastic instead of metal.

Soon after joining the Directorate, Shenstone was appointed a member of the Structures Sub-Committee of the Aeronautical Research Committee at the Air Ministry. Although he had never specialized in structures, Shenstone's notes indicate that he had learned much at Junkers and under the tutelage of the Supermarine team.

While based in London, Shenstone inspected numerous crashed German aircraft – notably aspects of the structural design and engineering solutions. This included forensic measuring of alloy gauge thicknesses and extrusion techniques. Shenstone created a written and illustrated report that he sent to W. Farren, asking if it should be published. Farren (later to head the Farren Mission into Germany to secure advanced aeronautical designs and their designers) replied in the affirmative. Shenstone later discovered that his report had been published anonymously by the Ministry with no credit to its author.[9]

It was this time that reinforced to Shenstone his thoughts about the idea of publishing research data as data sheets that could be easily accessed across the industry. He had begun working on it in 1938–1939 and in Yorkshire, and through liaison with K. T. Spencer laid the foundations for the Royal Aeronautical Society Data Sheet series of publications. In May 1941, K.T. Spencer wrote to Shenstone saying:

> Roxbee Cox showed me yesterday proofs of the first half dozen or so Royal Aeronautical Society Stressed Skin Data Sheets, housed in their imposing jacket and they brought back the discussion you and I had when you were in labour with the big idea, walking over the Yorkshire Wolds. They look to me a magnificent end-result for your efforts…[10]

In later years, Dr Anthony J. Barrett CEng, FRAeS, the man who was the driving force of the Royal Aeronautical Society's Technical Department as it became the ESDU data reference base and shaped its efficiency and relevance in the modern era, credited Shenstone, R. Cox and H.L. Cox, as the people who created its foundations in the early days of the war. Barrett credited[11] Shenstone with the work of collating the latest information on engineering design – much of it then relating to stressed skin construction and being in German. The building of a reference point of data sheets covering all aspects of aircraft design and production would eventually become the ESDU data unit – a world class RAeS engineering resource of respected standing.

Shenstone's success in 1938–1940 saw him singled out – and there was also his knowledge of German design and manufacturing to consider, not to mention his aerodynamics expertise as seen on the Spitfire. These must be some of the factors why Shenstone was selected to be sent to America as part of the British Air Commission (BAC). Shenstone was the man who could advise on new aircraft designs for the Allies and consider how those machines would tackle German aircraft.

In late October 1940, Shenstone departed from Liverpool on the *Western Princess*, a small liner bound for New York, arriving there in the first week of November. The *Western Princess* was torpedoed and sunk on her return journey off the Irish coast. Shenstone was based in Washington DC with the British Air Commission under H.C.B. Thomas at 1985 Massachusetts Avenue. Thomas had been resident technical officer for the Air Ministry at Lockheed during the procurement of the Hudson, so knew his stuff. In 1941, Shenstone's main role was to ensure that any American aircraft for RAF purposes were tuned for RAF requirements as discovered in the previous two years of war. Soon, Shenstone would take an interest in the design (and later modifications) of the North American P-51 Mustang – although quite how much his knowledge of the boundary layer and radiator requirements, as learned on the Spitfire, contributed to the Mustang's design, is unclear.

From 7 to 12 August 1941, members of the British Air Commission in Washington DC, including Shenstone, met up with Sir Wilfrid Freeman on board HMS *Prince of Wales*, at Placentia Bay Newfoundland, where Roosevelt and Churchill met to discuss the details of Lease Lend and its procurement. The United States would enter the war within months.

In Washington DC, Shenstone had run into his old acquaintance, the world champion glider pilot Peter Riedel – a German whom he had met in 1930s Germany. Riedel had spent a lot of time in the United States, outscoring every glider pilot in the gliding championships, and had become somewhat Americanized. By 1941, he was the German Air Attaché in Washington DC. He was also allegedly running German aeronautical intelligence gathering projects – keeping a close eye on design developments at a time when America had not yet entered the war. It was a difficult situation for two old friends, as Shenstone recalled:

Peter Riedel was Air Attaché at the German Embassy and I wondered whether I might see him and whether I should recognise him or ignore him. I never saw him, but he saw me, as he told me after the war. Next day I was telephoned by an American reporter who wanted an interview which I refused. He wanted to know what I was doing and I merely said what was publicly known, that we were ensuring that what we bought was what we wanted. He did put a tiny bit in the paper, calling me co-designer of the Spitfire, a considerable exaggeration, but in spite of that it got about. I remember vividly when some time later in Washington I complained about this co-designer thing to George Bulman, the rightly famous Hawker test pilot. George was really down to earth and his reply was simply: 'Well, that's all you've got, isn't it?'

A year or more later, when the US was also at war, I happened to meet a journalist in Washington at lunch. He only knew I was with the British Air Commission. He told me the whole story about Riedel and it turned out that he was the man who had 'phoned on behalf of Riedel to discover why I was in the USA.[12]

Shenstone's phrase about the fact that the journalist 'only knew I was with the British Air Commission' offers us a hint that his other roles may have been less obvious. Riedel was soon recalled to Germany, and upon discovering the truth of what was going on, and the murder of the Jews in Germany, he defected whilst at the German Embassy in Stockholm. He escaped the Nazis, and via a circuitous boat trip to North Africa, managed to settle in America after the war.[13]

Shenstone met test pilot George Bulman several times in America and was full of praise for the manner in which Bulman, without any training, or the kind of specialist kit deemed essential by American pilots, notably oxygen, simply climbed aboard the P-38 Lightning and just flew it – expertly. Bulman's comments about Shenstone's role in the Spitfire design, where he replied 'That's all you have got…' in response to Shenstone's denials about media claims he was the Spitfire's co-designer, may also provide the reader with an external viewpoint of some significance. Bulman, it seems, had little problem with the concept of Shenstone having been a major influence on the shape of the Spitfire.

As 1942 dawned, Shenstone was posted to the top US research establishment Wright-Patterson airfield at Dayton, Ohio – or Wright Field, as it is better known. He was not the only British representative, as he noted:

> The boss of our little group was Group Captain Alec Ryde. Alternates for short periods were Group Captain Wincott and Group Captain Jimmy Adams. All the Americans called Alex 'Captain Ryde', an unconscious de-rating, so we decided to balance it by referring to him as 'The Group'. Wright Field became like a militarised Farnborough. Our joint secretary was Mary Brown, who later joined the USAF equivalent to the WAF and learned to fly. She addressed me simply by my last name and thought that my initials B.S. were vulgar.[14]

Shenstone commuted back to Washington DC on a weekly basis in order to report in person to the British Air Commission. He would fly by TWA and Pennsylvania Central Airlines from Dayton to Washington on Monday evening's and return by train on Tuesday evening. Visits to the West Coast were also undertaken, which helped give Shenstone a good understanding of the operations of US domestic airlines. He summarized these experiences in a letter report that he sent back to K.T. Spencer at the Air Ministry. Although Shenstone did not know it at the time, the report found its way to the 1st Brabazon Committee who were then considering post-war aviation needs. Latterly, Shenstone would be appointed to the 2nd Brabazon Committee.

Shenstone got to know several of the US airline heads, including Barney Vierling at Pennsylvania Central – soon to become Capitol Airlines, who later ordered the Viscount. Shenstone also studied the issues of wing icing and worked with NACA people on the subject. This led him to advise the Canadian aviation on the subject – via the assistance of his old friend Jack Dyment at Trans Canada Airlines.

Wright-Patterson air base was soon to expand, and the entry of America into war would see it become a key design and research centre – the 'Farnborough' of the US. Top experts and top secret activities were centred on the facility, and at the end of the war, it was the first staging post for the German aeronautics and rocket scientists and the technology they brought with them, who arrived under Operation *Paperclip*. Shenstone became a resident at Wright-Patterson in 1941 and as late as summer 1945 was on hand to bring his design knowledge and fluent, technical, German language skills, to bear.

Soon after the war, Wright-Patterson was to become the home of Project *Grudge*, which led in the early 1950s to Project *Bluebook* – a classic of the 'psy-ops' mass psychological operational technique run by the US Government to 'investigate', or rather, frame and control the exploding phenomena of the 'UFO'. The war years, notably over Germany, had revealed sightings of weird and wonderful craft by pilots on both sides, claims of fire balls, 'foo-fighters', flying triangles, and fast-moving swept winged devices, as well as the classic saucer and bell-shaped objects, had flooded in. Shenstone, a German speaker and technical analyst, was not only an aircraft designer, but also the only man in the Allied camp with such experience gained from working with the beginnings of such technology during his time in Germany, and had retained close contacts with German designers up until 1939. As such he was a top expert who could help assess such claims. During the war, in Britain and the USA, Shenstone was present at the highest level to assist in the assessment of advanced designs and sightings. After the war, when hundreds (not the few dozen so often suggested), of German scientists and designers (including Lippisch), had turned up at Wright-Patterson, there began the rash of 'UFO' sightings that have populated the phenomena ever since.

Many of these post-war sightings are reputed to have been the testing of seized, German advanced technology – notably delta wings, flying wings, discs, parabolas and boundary layer-controlled devices. Shenstone's knowledge of such technologies cannot have been useless, but this does not make him party to any grand 'UFO' theory. His name appears in one 'UFO' related book[15] where his knowledge of the boundary layer aerodynamics is cited in relation to the Avro flying disc experiments that took place amid the great migration of advanced British aeronautical design and production to Canada just after the Second World War – a migration that not only stalled, but one that saw one of its top experts, Shenstone, leave Avro and return to Britain to work for an airline in 1947 – which the book fails to mention…

Avro's Chief Engineer after 1947 was John C.M. Frost CEng, FCASI, MRAeS, who was also an expert in glider design, having worked for Slingsby Sailplanes, a period that included his designing the Hengist troop carrying glider. Frost then went on to de Havilland's and contributed to the Vampire and the swept wing DH.101 – the first swept wing jet after the works of Lippisch. Frost then led the design of the CF100 fighter, the first Canadian designed and built military aircraft. Frost also worked on Avro's flying disc and vertical take-off prototypes. He shared with Beverley Shenstone in later years an enthusiasm for human-powered flight.

It is clear that the Allies – from Moscow to Washington DC, via London – did indeed seize upon advanced German, Nazi-funded, technology and the Cold War was framed by such advances manifesting on both sides. It is therefore obvious that advanced technology stemming from the 1930s and 1940s science of the Germans, was real, existed and was used in the 1950s and 1960s aerospace race, but this does not a UFO or ET theory confirm. And for Shenstone, there is no evidence of anything other than diligent research and advanced thinking. The names of Lippisch, Schauberger, Von Braun, Miethe, Klein, Schriever, etc., are all mentioned in connection with rockets, flying saucers, flying wings, and a host of exaggerated and often (although not always) conspiracy-type theories, some of which involve Wright-Patterson airfield.

Whilst men like these did indeed pass through Wright-Patterson air force base circa 1945–1946, and did contribute to post-war supersonic design and space travel, there is scant evidence to support some of the wilder theories that now surround them. Just because the Germans had a rocket programme and a record of orbital flight research by Dr Sanger and others, does not mean that any research into flying discs, flying wings, anti-gravity, or Coanda effect flying discs, was anything other than a similar accident of history. 'Little green men' were of unlikely relevance but in the 1950s there was a fever pitch for such subjects. However, it is rational and valid to say that the mysteries of Hangar 18 at Wright-Patterson AFB, Dayton Ohio, did present a number of questions stemming from wartime events.

What *can* be said with certainty is that for reasons unknown, the advanced science emerged from one place, Germany, notably Silesia/Bohemia, and at a period of time in the 1920s and 1930s, when advanced aerodynamics reached a peak of research and expression that manifested in these specific circumstances. The fact that in Germany, Beverley Shenstone was briefly part of that heady, pre-Nazi era world, and remained a lifelong research partner and friend of Alexander Lippisch, does not create or confirm any part in some of the wilder stories now so fashionable. It cannot be denied however, that being part of scientific developments in 1930s, and being part of their assessment by the Allies up to 1947, could not have been anything other than exciting and stimulating for an aerodynamicist of Shenstone's abilities.

Canada or Britain?

Inside the British Air Commission function, Shenstone was also able to liaise with the Canadians – and he was, of course, still close to Professor John Parkin who was by now a luminary of the Canadian National Research Council (NRC). Of note, Shenstone's old mentor and now godfather to his son Brian, Professor John Parkin was influential in the fields of tailless aircraft design and was also studying composite aircraft construction – be that in wood or advanced plastics.

Whatever the materials, it was the production process that would need modernizing – moulding technology started at this time. By the summer of 1940, Shenstone was already aware of the 'Gordon Aerolite Spitfire' plans – the building of a composite, moulded Spitfire body in Britain by Aero Research Ltd, and the Canadians were by 1941 attempting to build a wooden, moulded Avro Anson via the Aircraft Research Corporation of Trenton, New Jersey. Shenstone had also investigated plastic extrusions at the British Ebenstos company in 1940 and had advised Beaverbook on the development of plastics. In Germany, a composite Bf109 was also rumoured.

Shenstone's work at Wright-Patterson continued, and via Wilfrid Freeman's driving force by 1942, the designs for the Mustang were known, and the idea to re-engine it with a Merlin engine in place of its Allison power plant, were soon to be born. The P-51D Mustang was also aerodynamically modified – with a thin fuselage and a developed boundary layer radiator design that utilized the 'Meredith effect' as found on the Spitfire's radiator. How much Shenstone contributed to these design features is hard to establish, but he was there as the design was formulated and it was his job to assess and input the design requirements.

It seems that the Canadians wanted their man back. Moves were made to align Shenstone to Canadian research liaison while he was still at Wright-Patterson under the British Air Commission umbrella. From May 1941, Shenstone joined various Canadian subcommittees in an adjunct capacity, for example he attended the Canadian Wooden Aircraft meeting in Ottawa. Shenstone could also call on the expertise of de Havilland and their wooden wonder, the Mosquito – a design that owed its existence to the support of Wilfrid Freeman, and Shenstone's old colleague J.V. Connolly had been associated with Freeman's liaisons with the de Havilland team.

Shenstone also joined another Canadian group run under Professor Parkin – the Subcommittee on De-Icing of Aircraft, which was formed in December 1941. Shenstone was the link between the Canadian, American and British strands and interests.[1] The principal outcomes were the creation of ducted hot air wing de-icing systems and glycol sprays – both far superior to the heavy grease known as 'Kill Frost' – previously applied to aircraft leading edges in the 1939s.

Flying wings or the all-wing, were also part of the deal. It was Shenstone who had fed Professor Parkin much that he had seen and learned on the theory in Germany circa 1929–1931. At the Wasserkuppe, in 1930, Shenstone had also met Robert Kronfeld, and Geoffrey T.R. Hill, who went on to create the experimental Pterodactyl range of tailless aircraft. Hill and Lippisch had also met and discussed their theories, with Shenstone as the translator. In an interesting coincidence, by 1942, Geoffrey Hill was in Canada working with Parkin in the NRC wind tunnel on flying wing, tailless research. But before the Canadians got their man back, Shenstone was to be posted back to London as Assistant Director, Research and Development of Air Transport. It was from this point, that Shenstone's career in civil aviation really took root. By now, Shenstone was a recognized design expert and in 1943 joined the 2nd Brabazon Committee. Yet the lure of his homeland remained, and his wife and children were safely ensconced on the western side of the Atlantic.

While still at Wright-Patterson in early 1943, Ralph Bell, the Director General of Aircraft Production and Munitions Supply in Canada, offered Shenstone a post as the head of an aircraft design team in Canada. On 5 March 1943 Bell cabled Archibald Rowlands, the Permanent Under-Secretary at the MAP, asking for Shenstone to be released. This was turned down, with the MAP/British Air Commission stating that it wanted to keep Shenstone.[2]

For some months, Shenstone remained with the Commission. He commuted back and forth across wartime Atlantic skies to America by military C-54s, and converted Lancasters. With his colleague Jock Gray, he began to assess the needs of civil airline routes, and the airliners to serve them after the war would finish. Shenstone was sure that the days of the grand flying boat were over; his wartime travels by C-54 – the precursor of the DC-4, DC-6 and DC-7 family of Douglas transports – had convinced him that high density cabins, in fast airliners would be the future. British flying boat proponents were appalled and with giant British flying boats still being planned for a post-war, 'Empire' future, Shenstone's reluctant decision that the day of the flying boat would soon be over was not a popular position for a member of the Brabazon Committee. Shenstone's old colleague, Joseph Smith at Supermarine, with whom he had worked so closely on the Spitfire, and now the Supermarine chief designer, was particularly upset and said so in some colourful language.[3]

Shenstone wrote:

> This flying boat report indicated that they were 'out' for commercial use. It was a red rag to many people and tended to demolish whatever little popularity I might have had. But I was right.[4]

Shenstone was indeed to be proved correct, the large flying boats were gone within a few years, and the Saunders Roe Princess was, sadly, stillborn. Shenstone was also appointed to the committee that was to define required ranges for future airliners – he served with Campbell Orde of BOAC and C.B. Collins of the Air Ministry. It was at this time that Shenstone became an enthusiast of the large, twin-engined aircraft concept. Thirty years later, he opined that the large twin-engined Airbus types had proved him correct, and that he felt there was: 'no limit to twins as far as safety is concerned.'[5]

In spite of all this interesting work, Shenstone was tempted back to Canada – the offer from Bell, and other offers, were the lure. Shenstone wrote to Wilfrid Freeman offering his reluctant resignation, firstly on 2 November 1943, and then again on 29 December 1943. Freeman refused to accept Shenstone's resignation and made his view very clear at their meeting to discuss the matter.[6] Shenstone takes up the story:

> On 10th January 1944, I received a letter with an illegible signature: 'I am directed to refer to your letters of 2nd November and 29th December 1943 and to inform you that after careful consideration, it has been agreed to accept your resignation to take effect from 31st March 1944 which will be your last day of duty'. So it was with some relief and some misgivings that I was spirited across the Dorval in a Lancastrian, an imitation commercial aircraft based on the Lancaster bomber.[7]

Freeman even wrote to Shenstone trying to retract his acceptance of Shenstone's resignation. If a man like Sir Wilfrid Freeman wanted to keep Shenstone, it must be considered that his talents were both significant and recognized. However, Shenstone did leave and Canada got its man back – but not without a twist in the tale.

Shenstone's time working for Ralph Bell was short. Before long, Shenstone was offered a senior role by the Canadian Government as a technical advisor to C.D. Howe – Minister of the Department of Reconstruction. This role put Shenstone high into Government status and allowed him to become involved with the Canadian aviation industry – specifically with the new North Star – a pressurized, re-engined, Rolls-Royce-powered version of the DC-4 being manufactured by Vickers Canada – Canadair. This also saw old Shenstone contacts J. Dyment and J. Bain in the frame, and allowed Shenstone to use his very close ties with Rolls-Royce. Another of Shenstone's group of friends, W. S. 'Bill' Bird, also joined the North Star development team – he had been a resident technical officer for the British Air Commission in America.

Shenstone was a key player in the leading of the design and development process of the Canadair North Star. This was a greatly modified version of the design based on the Douglas C-54/DC-4. Numerous meetings and research papers were produced about the DC-4M or North Star. Trans Canada Airlines (TCA) were concerned about operational issues specific to their use of the upcoming DC-4 and a modified version, re-engined with Rolls-Royce Merlins, the DC-4M, was first mooted in June 1944. Shenstone moved to Montreal to be on hand at the Canadair factory on 7 October 1944. The instruction to Canadair to proceed with the North Star, was issued on 28 July 1944 at a meeting attended by How, Symington (TCA Chairman), Hives of Rolls-Royce, Dorey, Bain (TCA) Franklin (Managing Director Canadair) and Shenstone – who subsequently noted:

> The Canadian Government wanted to ensure that the DC4M (NorthStar) airliner for T.C.A. fulfilled the British airworthiness requirements and decided to send Elsie McGill B.Sc. who had done such airworthiness work before, to U.K., to ensure that the requirements were being fulfilled. I was to go with her, as I knew the places and the people, mainly in the Air Registration Board. We flew across on May 1st 1945. I got back to Canada on July 4, leaving Elsie to complete the work. This trip strengthened my view that the flying boat was dead, or at best dying.[8]

The North Star was a success and became the backbone of the RCAF transport uplift, a British named version, the 'Argonaut' also saw sterling service with BOAC. Once past their prime, the BOAC machines were sold off to East African Airways and their tropical routes – where the Merlin engines were not happy and cooling proved an issue.[9]

The reason Shenstone decided that the flying boat was dead, lay in the time it took to get back from Britain from this trip. As his diary reveals, first he had to travel from London to Poole in Dorset. There, in the harbour and beset by high winds, it took many attempts to board the Boeing 314 Clipper flying boat from a motorboat. After a flight of nearly three hours, they landed at Foynes in Ireland – where in strong cross winds, the Boeing 314 dipped a wing tip into the water on alighting. This was a major incident with probable sinking only narrowly averted and the crew had to climb into the wing to balance the aircraft on its hull. Mooring took many attempts in the conditions. Finally, after delays, the Boeing took off for Botwood and then Baltimore – cruising at 145 knots. The total journey took over two days and according to his diary notes, Shenstone's only highlight was not his near-death experience but the serving of an Irish roast beef luncheon after take-off from Foynes, beef having being almost unavailable in wartime Britain.

In comparison with the high speed trips across the Atlantic, Shenstone had made in DC-4/C-54 type aircraft, the long frustrations of even a ride on a Boeing 314 Clipper were a clear signal: flying boats were outmoded. They were dead.

Soon after his return to North America, Shenstone also received an offer of employment from de Havilland Canada, but this did not come to fruition. However, there are anecdotes suggesting Shenstone advised on the design of the Canadian genesis of the de Havilland Chipmunk, and he had close connections with de Havilland, not least through Sir Wilfrid Freeman who had been the driving force behind the framing and production of the de Havilland Mosquito – even called by some, 'Freeman's Folly' so closely was he involved. In his notes Shenstone says he turned down an offer from de Havilland on the grounds that to accept would have been 'improper'. The context of this may well have been his close relationship with the firm – and Freeman's…

On 12 March 1945, Freeman wrote to Shenstone[10] in Canada and asked him if he would like to come back to England, to be chief technical advisor of a new post-war airline – what was to become British European Airways Corporation. On 23 March 1945, N.E. Rowe wrote to Shenstone pressing him to accept Freeman's offer.[11] Shenstone turned this offer down. Wartime Britain did not appeal. However, another interesting offer, to be taken even more seriously than Freeman's, this time evidenced by a series of dated letters starting in March 1945,[12] came from Rex Pierson at Vickers Armstrongs at Weybridge. The importance of this offer is critical in terms of the reader appreciating just how significant Shenstone's post-Spitfire status was, because Shenstone was offered a role that, in his own words, 'could have led' to him to becoming Chief Designer at Vickers' – and as an immediate deputy to Pierson, that was not an unreasonable claim. Of note, in early March, Vickers Managing Director, Major Hew Kilner, called on Shenstone in his office in Canada, and offered Shenstone a senior role at Vickers.[13]

Shenstone replied that he would consider the offer, but that he preferred to remain in Canada. On 30 March 1945, Hew Kilner cabled Shenstone. This was a formal job offer and the cable read: 'Would you be interested engagement Vickers-Armstrongs Weybridge working under Pierson but not under Wallis. Salary £2000 pounds?'[14]

Shenstone's notes reveal his thoughts about this offer:

> I was attracted by the stability such a job would offer and working with people I knew, but I did want to stay in Canada, and I thought it unfair to expose 2 young sons to the dislocations and limitations of immediate post-war England. I did not accept the offer. George Edwards got the job and he did it better than I could have done it, as I learned later when I did return to England.[15]

If Vickers-Armstrongs were prepared to offer Shenstone £2000 per annum (double his Air Ministry salary) in 1945, the reader can begin to grasp just how brilliant and how highly regarded Shenstone was by those that knew of him and his works. Ironically, Shenstone was later to return to England to take up another career – not as an aircraft designer, but as an airline technical director. He may have regretted not working for Rex Pierson – the man who told him in Berkeley Street Mayfair in 1938, that he was a 'bloody fool' for leaving Vickers Supermarine. However, in further irony, Shenstone was destined to work very closely with Vickers in the coming years.

The fact of Vickers-Armstrongs pursuing Shenstone for a very senior design role, perhaps even the senior role at Vickers, has never been revealed before and as an offer, irrespective of Shenstone's personal opinion or recorded views, can only serve to illustrate to the reader the unknown significance of the man. Shenstone is, of course, rightly full of praise for the man who became chief designer, that brilliant icon of British aeronautics, Sir George Edwards.

While in Canada, Shenstone also returned to his love of gliding, becoming a founding figure of the Soaring Association of Canada. He also secured the location, seizing and transport of a series of war-prize gliders from deep within Germany in the late spring of 1945 and had them delivered to the home of Canadian gliding for study and use.[16] This included two Baby Grunau types and an elegant Musger Mu 13d. This episode was to take on interesting proportions that would directly benefit the development of gliding in Canada.

In 1944, the lead figure of the Soaring Association of Canada (SAC) was a Dr Don MacClement.

He became aware that in late 1944 and early 1945, American forces were searching Europe for advanced German aircraft designs. Through a series of contacts, the chance of securing surplus or 'war prize' gliders for Canada was mooted. MacClement, like Professor Parkin, and Shenstone, was very interested in tailless design and specifically, that of the Horten brothers. Shenstone (then Chairman of the Technical Committee of the Soaring of Association of Canada), was well placed to further the idea, and he was recruited to make it reality while he was in London in 1945.

There, Shenstone managed to organize a member of the Canadian Army to search for gliders – notably Horten all-wing gliders, in Germany. The search was too late – the Hortens and their gliders had been captured by the Americans, who had at least stopped the British burning any more gliders than they had already! However, Shenstone's man had got hold of a Mu 13d glider and three Grunau Babies – for 'research purposes'. At this time, Shenstone's brother Douglas was in Europe, and so was his old gliding friend, the world-class champion pilot, Philip Wills – who was also scouring Germany for advanced aircraft. The records of the Soaring Association of Canada and the record of the Wills family both confirm that Shenstone organized the Canadian Navy to collect the gliders. Christopher Wills, son of Phillip Wills, and President of the Vintage Glider Club and past world class champion glider pilot, recalled the story to the author: 'The Mu 13 had come from Denmark, it been seized by the Germans and taken back to Germany. There, it and the Grunau Babies were later seized by the Allies. There was the sight of a Canadian Navy destroyer sailing down the River Elbe with four gliders strapped to its deck!'[17] This took place several months after the end of the war.

The person who organized this was Beverley Shenstone, who it seems, had the clout to arrange for warships to collect gliders! Shenstone's other noteworthy, extramural wartime/post-war Canadian activities included:

- Member Associate Committee on Aeronautics National Research Council Ottawa, 1944–48

- Member Aerodynamics Subcommittee, National Research Council. Ottawa, 1944–48

- Chairman Technical Committee, Soaring Association Canada, 1944

- President, Soaring Association Canada, 1946-47

- Canadian delegate to Airworthiness Division PICAO (Forerunner to the ICAO), 1946
- Consultant to the Avro Lancastrian project to civilianize ex-Lancaster bombers
- Influence on DHC Chipmunk design suggested but unreferenced to date.

Shenstone was, in fact, a founding figure in the Soaring Association of Canada with a lead role in revitalizing gliding in post-war Canada, working with A.N. Le Cheminant and J. Simpson. He was also a Committee member of the Canadian Aeronautical Institute (CAI) – now retitled Canadian Aeronautics and Space Institute (CASI). He also made contributions to the 'Ottawa' man-powered flight project of the CAI.

An offer from Provisional International Civil Aviation Organization (PICAO) to become their chief of airworthiness in Montreal had to be turned down – as again, C.D. Howe was reluctant to let Shenstone go. Shenstone was also unhappy with how his work for Howe was framed by how he was being treated by Franklin at Canadair. Shenstone says he was 'messed about'[18] by Franklin. Shenstone's records show that on 31 March 1945 and 19 February 1946, he had discussions with the Minister – C.D. Howe – regarding his position. Shenstone wrote in private:

> Somehow, I had not really fitted into the Canadian aviation picture, having nothing creative to do: I was working for him, the Minister, I was making reports for T.C.A., for the Department of Transport and the National Research Council.[19]

The offer from PICAO was significant and given that organization's later ICAO status, may well have been a tempting prize. The situation resolved itself, when in March 1946, yet another major aviation company offered Shenstone a job. This time it was Avro (A.V. Roe) Canada who wanted to pay Shenstone $13,000 Canadian per annum, as a Director, to stay in Canada. He accepted! Shenstone set to work on a number of projects, one of which was a straight-winged, jet airliner of advanced design – the C102 with two Rolls-Royce engines in each wing. It was a contemporary of the Comet – the two aircraft first flew within days of each other. Sadly, engine development issues caused a critical delay and the entire project faltered. The C102 was still, however, the first jet airliner to be built and to fly on the North American continent. It was a Canadian triumph and but for bad luck could have marked a major milestone in Canadian commercial aviation.

One of Shenstone's new colleagues at Avro Canada was Waclaw

Czerwinski, the Polish émigré designer. Shenstone says there were so many Poles at Avro that one area of the drawing office was called 'Polish Corridor'. Shenstone also worked with W.Z. Stepniewski and IATA's Stan Kryczkowski. But it was Czerwinski who was to get closest to Shenstone – the pair were both gliding enthusiasts and together soon hatched plans to design and build a glider. In fact, two designs emerged from their collaboration.

Before these took to the air, yet another Atlantic commuting trip was heading Shenstone's way.

The Spitfire meanwhile was about to claim a peacetime record. Few people know that between 29 April and 5 May 1947, a privately purchased war surplus ex-RAF Spitfire PR MkXI flew across the Atlantic Ocean in one go. Piloted by James (Jaime) Storey an Argentine, ex-RAF photographic unit pilot, the specially polished and prepared Spitfire flew from Bournemouth via Gibraltar, on to Dakar in Senegal, and then over the South Atlantic in one flight to Natal, Brazil. It flew onwards to Rio de Janeiro, Montevideo and Buenos Aires, Argentina to take up a civil registration. The Spitfire was fitted with a 170-gallon under belly tank and two 20-gallon tanks mounted on the wing roots, giving a total of over 300 gallons in total with a duration of 10 hours. Fuel was provided by the Shell company, and an over-ocean escort was provided by an Avro York of Don Bennett's, British South American Airways. The non-stop over-ocean sector of the flight was the longest-ever single flight by a Spitfire. The Spitfire's wings had taken it over the Atlantic Ocean in a flight over well over eight hours. No other single-engine Second World War fighter had achieved such a feat.

14

British European Airways

Make do and Mend

In London, after the trials and tribulations of the war years, the newly formed British European Airways Corporation (BEAC) – better known as BEA – was an airline tasked with providing both a national, state, service and functioning as a company. The balancing act between state carrier and apparent commercial airline, just as at BOAC, cannot have been easy to command.

At the war's end, BEA's fleet was a mix and match job lot of diverse types ranging from the DC-3, the Vickers Viking (a Wellington bomber derivative), to the small de Havilland types. Yet the airline still had the remit of providing daily European services, carrying mail, and serving Britain's own diverse domestic route network – covering everything from flights to the Channel Islands, Liverpool Speke, Edinburgh and the far outer islands of Scotland to name just a few. The route network and the aircraft types it needed to service them were diverse and challenging. Maintenance facilities were scattered widely and the impending move to London's newly designated airport on Hounslow Heath was to be a trip through a sea of mud populated by islands of wooden huts.

Into this somewhat concerning flux walked Beverley Shenstone – heading back from Canada where proper food, central heating, winterized competence, and space, were the norm. He and his wife must have had a bit of shock with rationed food and petrol and a make do and mend mentality, amid the rain and mud of a tired, post-war nation. It was not quite like living close to the Solent at Netley in Hampshire in the heady Spitfire days of the 1930s…

In Canada, the course of events for Beverley had begun to become a little unclear. By 1947 his position at Avro Canada was concerning him; work was beginning to dry up – he was not busy enough. Noting Walter Deisher's empty desk and his own lack of work, Shenstone asked Deisher what he expected him to be doing. There was no constructive response. In typically forthright manner, Shenstone's reply was that he reckoned it was time for him to go.

Given that the British and Canadian-based Avro concern was soon to be working on the delta-winged Vulcan, and the boundary layer specific, Coanda effect Avro flying disc, it could be assumed that Shenstone – a man with expert knowledge in these fields – ought really to have been involved at the leading edge of such developments. Yet, for reasons we may never know, he chose to return to his airline transport passion. How closely was he involved with Vulcan design and the emerging Avro 'Silverbug' flying disc (to become the 'Avro Car' in the early 1950s), we do not know, but perhaps not closely enough might be the answer.

Writing of his feelings about the years 1944 to the end of 1947 when he returned to his native land, Shenstone clearly had no illusions:

> I learned that these four years in Canada showed me that the only work worth doing is work involving clear-cut responsibilities which should show results. Titles such as Advisor to or Assistant to should be spurned unless one fears responsibility.[1]

Commenting on the failure of the post-war Canadian aircraft industry, Shenstone notes that the costs of development and production had become so high that it was unlikely that Canada could, without help from other countries, have remained a leader of development and production. He also wonders whether the Canadian industry should have been nationalized at an early date. From a personal standpoint, Shenstone took the decision to return to the cradle of aircraft design – Great Britain. Upon leaving Canada, he wrote:

> In spite of this, I do not think I wasted my time I my own country. I learned a lot and luckily had opportunities in my future to use what I had learned.[2]

Having failed to secure employment offer from Gordon McGregor at Trans Canada Airlines, there were no vacancies in the technical department, Shenstone put out feelers for his next move. He recorded that:

> I failed to get work in Canada, but (I) was sensible enough to N.E. Rowe who had just joined British European Airways as Research Director. The next thing I had was a note from BEA's Managing Director, J.V. Wood, whom I had met on business during the war, when he was with BOAC.
>
> He asked me to meet him in Montreal, as he was coming across very soon. So we met and he invited me to come to London to be interviewed by some BEA Board members. He sent me an air ticket. Apart from meeting Gerard (Pops) d' Erlanger the Chairman, I met several other Board members, one of whom was A.H. Measures, a real old-timer in civil aviation, who was acting Chief Engineer. The Technical Director, Philip Wills the famous glider pilot having recently resigned.[3]

The Board of BEA offered Shenstone the role as Chief Engineer at a salary of £2500 a year – and kindly paid for the shipping of his family, household effects and two sailing dinghies to Britain.

Canada finally relinquished its grip on Shenstone, and he ended up at BEA – where Freeman and Rowe had offered him a berth, as early as March 1945.

The Shenstone family eventually found a house on the river Thames at Wraysbury, Bell Weir House, in the grounds of a mansion at Bell Weir Park. The new house was literally on the river bank with its own steps down to the river. This house next to the weir and lock allowed Bev to indulge in his favourite pastime of mucking about in small boats, with instant access to the water. Bev's youngest son, Blair, recalled how his mother brought an entire fitted kitchen over from Canada with her, including items unheard of in Britain such as a double oven, a huge fridge and a collection of modern household appliances. The three boys, Brian, Derek, and Blair, also had proper Arctic-style Canadian 'parka' coats with fur collars and cuffs. Thus fully winterized, they stood out from local children not fortunate enough to be so well protected against the harsh British winters of the era.

At this time, BEA was based at Northolt Airport, which was half an hour's drive north of Wraysbury. But BEA was soon to leave Northolt as it took up its new home at London Heathrow Airport – on Hounslow Heath – the infamous highwayman Dick Turpin's old hunting ground and parallel to the ancient road from London to Bath. Nearby was a public house where aviators gathered, the seventeenth century *Peggy Bedford*, which in true modern British style was tragically demolished in the 1990s.

At Northolt there were very few facilities in the Edwardian-era buildings. The maintenance buildings were damp and draughty and had doors opening to the elements on all sides. Shenstone's notes tell us all this and that in his view the special facilities for airframe maintenance were poor and badly lit. Phillip Wills had had to operate with such limited resources and put up with interventions from civil servants. Shenstone was luckier, the immediate construction of a 40,000sq ft overhaul workshop helped, but within just over a year, BEA moved to London Heathrow and began to assert itself within its partially State-controlled function.

When Shenstone arrived at BEA with its ex-wartime aircraft of what he terms a 'lash-up' fleet, the airline's average engine overhaul rate was between 400 and 500 hours. Through the fortunate coincidence of hard work, better facilities and more spares, the overhaul rate was soon at 1000 hours. The fleet numbered nearly 100 aircraft including the DC-3, Viking, Scottish Aviation Pioneer and the ancient de Havilland Rapide. Ultimately, it would include the Ambassador, Viscount, Vanguard, Herald, Argosy, Comet, Trident and a range of helicopters – one of the largest civil airline fleets of helicopters ever seen. This domestic network of helicopters carried mail and passengers, including the operation of shuttle service between regional airports and the main BEA hubs.

Managed in the 1950s by Peter Hearne, a former Saunders-Roe aerodynamics student and engineer, the BEA helicopter fleet had its origins in an experimental unit founded in 1947 with three Sikorsky S-51s and two Bell 47s. By 1952, scheduled services ran across East Anglia and from Wrexham to Liverpool and Cardiff. In 1954, BEA began a scheduled helicopter service between Southampton, London Heathrow and Northolt using Bristol 171 helicopters. In 1955, a link from Birmingham to Heathrow was started. In the 1960s, BEA founded a separate BEA Helicopters Ltd, which operated a vital service between Penzance and the Scilly Isles. Offshore oil flights to the emerging North Sea oil industry also started in the mid-1960s. The BEA helicopter division was the largest and longest-lasting airline helicopter service.

Peter Hearne went on to a very successful airline and corporate career, ultimately heading GEC Marconi's aviation division, being a President of the RAeS and Vice President of the British Gliding Association. He says of working for Beverley Shenstone at BEA:[4]

BEA played a major part in the development of the Viscount and the combination of Masefield, Shenstone, Wilkinson and others pushed for the seven hundred and eight hundred series. It was in fact the combination of Vickers activity and BEA who made the Viscount what it was and Shenstone deserves a lot of credit for this.

Peter Hearne confirms that Shenstone tended to be:

Fairly quiet at meetings, listened to what people had to say and then made a decision on the matter. The fact that BEA's engineering, apart from the Trident, went as well as it did, is an indication of the value of his decisions.

Intriguingly, in relation to his chief engineer's past, Hearne adds:

I think he had a fair idea of the importance of his role in the Spitfire design but the point is that the majority of the Spitfire team were under thirty years old. Beverley spoke of his Spitfire work in relatively closed conversations but he couched it in terms of team effort.

In a submission to Parliament in a Supplementary Memorandum (AS29A) by the British Gliding Association in 1999, relating to the stewardship of

British gliding affairs by aeronautical professionals and previous
Presidents of the RAeS being associated with gliding, Peter Hearne
described Beverley Shenstone as having 'been the individual mainly
responsible for the aerodynamic design of the Spitfire'. For a man of
Hearne's status to state such, provides the reader with further evidence
of just how revered Shenstone was within the closed world of his arena.

* * *

Of an early trip on a BEA Viking, Shenstone, the airline's new chief
engineer, noted:

> When going aboard a Viking aeroplane, the steward asked me to take a
> forward seat during take-off. I asked why I had to sit further forward. The
> unexpected answer was: 'You can move forward or aft, as long as you
> move!'[5]

One day at BEA, after walking through the engineering hangar with his
Chairman, Beverley recorded:

> One day Sholto (Lord Douglas of Kirtleside) turned up to have a look at this
> hangar, which at the time was being used to do work on the Airspeed
> Ambassador. Sholto marched in, only to find nobody there. He walked up
> to a row of inside doors and without hesitation opened one and found the
> staff having coffee. Afterwards, I asked Sholto how he picked the right door.
> 'Experience. My boy.' was the answer.[6]

It is clear from his own words that Beverley felt at home at BEA and had
found his niche.

> How lovely England was in those days! Hardly any traffic, lots of bicycles
> and no real hardship. Still some rationing, but few cars. We bought a house
> on the Thames.
>   I inherited Philip Wills' secretary Margaret Hines (Davey) and his ghastly
> old Humber allocated car. Margaret Davey left BEA because her husband's
> job was changed. Then for a short time, my secretary was Mrs Ruth Riley.
> For the rest of my working life I was blessed with having Miss Joyce
> Meldrum for secretary: Dependable, critical, helpful, up-to-date on goings
> on. A source of good advice, and at times 'both ears to the ground'.[7]

Beverley's team at BEA included the highly experienced doyen of flying
boat operation and airframe maintenance expert Hugh Gordon as Chief
Maintenance Engineer. The Chief Performance and Development
Engineer was R.C. Morgan and Ivor Gregory was Chief Inspector.
    It was time of great potential, as Shenstone's hopeful, yet self-aware,
words indicate:

Here was a new airline, barely two years old and full of possibilities and I was there. Why? Here I had real responsibilities.... I was not advising anyone, but doing a clear-cut job, but with some shaggy edges. What I had to do was take and accept the responsibilities and make the right decisions most of the time. One cannot always be right, but I have never gone as far down as the American saying: 'The successful man is one who is right fifty-one per cent of the time.' If one feels that he must always be right, it is dangerous because if you believe in the impossible, you slip beyond facts into fancy which in airline work lie next door to danger.[8]

BEA was a young upstart compared with the apparently newly formed British Overseas Airways Corporation (BOAC), which, in reality, was a re-invention of Imperial Airways and British Airways (a name later re-used for today's British Airways – itself a reverse-engineered amalgamation of BEA and BOAC). BOAC was also staffed with highly experienced wartime combat pilots and navigators. BEA attracted some of them, and also included a number of former Air Transport Auxiliary ATA members – or 'Ancient and Terrified Aviators' as a saying at the time went. The ATA had, in fact, been formed by d'Erlanger – who ended up at both BEA and BOAC – as Shenstone himself did. Champion glider Phillip Wills had also been key to the air transport operation and also took a role in the film *Air Ferry*, which depicted the unit's wartime work.

BEA, in Beverley Shenstone's view, was still on a swift learning curve:

We had nothing like the expertise of BOAC.[9]

In these early BEA days, the airline had three separate maintenance bases: one at Northolt close to London, another in Manchester and the third at Renfrew. Shenstone, with the agreement of Hugh Gordon, set about rationalizing the facilities. Shenstone's original plan had included closing the Scottish base at Renfrew. He ran up against BEA Board member Sir Patrick Dollan who fought a successful campaign to keep the Scottish facility open. In a new young airline based in a country that was then the cradle of aircraft design with many design houses and half a dozen major manufacturing names, BEA would not be short of suitable aircraft. With a dressed up fleet of high flight hours, DC-3s named the Pioneer Class and bedecked in BEA's bright red and silver house colours, supported by equally hard-worked Vickers Vikings, the airline was soon an important part of the post-war national psyche.

Aircraft submissions came in the form of the Armstrong Whitworth Apollo and the Miles M60 Marathon, which stemmed directly from a Brabazon Committee recommendation for a high wing feeder airliner of approximately fifteen to twenty seats, such a specification clearly being an intended to replace the national de Havilland Rapide fleet.

The Apollo was rejected, but under government direction BEA took seven out of an order for thirty Marathons, which were intended for use on the Highlands and Islands division. The all-metal Marathon was the world's first airliner to meet all the new International Civil Aviation Organization (ICAO) design requirements. It had the makings of a winning formula, but it was small. Despite the arrival of the first Marathon in full BEA livery at its base in February 1952, the airline never put the aircraft into mainline service – deciding that it was far too small. The effects on the Miles company were not fortuitous: the government had forced BEA to take an aircraft designed for a Brabazon Committee specification that was now years out of date. BEA held firm and never flew the Marathon in BEA service, yet it went on to fly with RAF, various colonial airlines in Africa, an even in Burma and Japan.

However, E.A. Hagg's beautiful Airspeed Ambassador was soon to join the BEA fleet as the Elizabethean Class. This was an elegant high-winged aircraft with a pretty, finned tailplane and spacious cabin. It had an air of class and when seen slipping from a cloud into sunlight, provided a symbol of 1950s elegance. It was, however, powered by reciprocating engines and vibrated along at only 250 knots. Ordered in 1948, it was delayed into service until 1952. Twenty-one Ambassadors were built, and BEA was their only mainline operator – although latterly BKS ran four, Dan-Air flew three and Shell and Rolls-Royce ran private examples as company craft. An outfit named Overseas Aviation ran four.

The BEA Ambassador featured in the Munich air disaster of 1958 – at which the then under-researched science of runway contamination, rather than the aircraft, was the significant factor. The accident led such problems to be studied. By late 1960, the Ambassador had been eclipsed by the Viscount fleet and BEA was selling Ambassadors off at the sum of £69,500 each, in refurbished condition.

Shenstone thought the Ambassador was a good aircraft, saying:

> Hagg was a real artist, a brilliant designer and a perfectionist whom I had met when I was ADRDAT (before going to Canada). Apart from being rather delayed coming into service, a very dramatic instance of interest took place when the Ambassador prototype took off as a twin-engined airliner and landed as a glider. The attempt at landing was so hard that both engines and propellers, broke away. The lightened vehicle then took off and landed a couple of hundred yards later with no damage.[10]

BEA was perhaps 'advised' to take the Ambassador, and this occurred at the same time that Vickers was betting everything on the Viscount and its new turbine engines – for BEA! A great deal of debate took place and for a time relationships became strained between the players.

The Ambassador and the forthcoming Vickers Viscount would, however, go a long way to providing BEA with regular, reliable services, ones with passenger appeal, that would earn money. Shenstone wrote:

> D'Erlanger was keen to make BEA pay and be independent. For that he was ousted. Nowadays the way out is in the opposite direction. At the final dinner with d'Erlanger, the Board were thinking of resigning, but Pops (d'Erlanger) persuaded them not to do so. The new chairman's name was announced. Lord Douglas of Kirtleside turned out to be the ideal chairman and during his many years with us, was appreciated by all and he made BEA pay![11]

It was d' Erlanger who brought in Peter Masefield – a former aviation writer and expert turned wartime civil servant. Shenstone had known Masefield before the war when he was on the staff of *Aeroplane* magazine. They pair had also encountered each other during wartime work – as far afield as Canada. Shenstone was a friend of Masefield and clearly admired him greatly. Of their BEA days together, Shenstone wrote:

> There is no doubt that he is brilliant, but in BEA he tended to do the barking himself instead of letting us, the dogs, do it.[12]

One of Beverley Shenstone's first campaigns at BEA was to reduce operating costs without reducing the quality or safety of engineering and maintenance standards. He did this by creating a rolling programme of planned replacement of parts on BEA's aircraft. This meant increasing efficiency by dispensing with the tradition of checking a part or a structure only at an elapsed time schedule, and instead assessing the part of item based on its working life and hours flown. In other words, a constant yet flexible maintenance regime replaced a schedule set in stone.

By modifying and improving parts, extensions to their useful life and a curtailing of the time needed to inspect them on the ground could be created. This also increased the number of hours airframes could work on a daily basis – thus saving money. Furthermore, instead of taking an aircraft out of the air to inspect it for its certificate of airworthiness, these inspections were done on a rolling basis across a number of planned periods whilst the aircraft continued in service. Such a regime was closely monitored by the regulating authorities in the UK.

The plan was to create an effective form of statistical maintenance control. By analysing defects and failures, similar events in the future, could be side stepped by changing procedures and replacement schedules. It was an incredibly simple idea, and it saved BEA a great deal of money once the initial start-up and change costs had been absorbed. It was a long-term plan that was typical of Shenstone's forensic thinking.

Shenstone, with Hugh Gordon (he of the Imperial Airways, Short's C Class flying boat expertise), also brought to BEA a salary incentive mechanism known as the premium bonus scheme for the engineering workers. Shenstone had done piecework at Massey-Harris factory in Canada and in Germany at Junkers in 1930 had witnessed what he thought was a bad incentive scheme. Shenstone and Gordon designed a scheme so popular that one group of workers who did not have it went out on strike until they got it, and SAS (Scandinavian Airlines System) copied the BEA scheme for their own engineering department.

By 1950, after a trial period in one workshop, the BEA engineering department workers and their seventeen unions asked for the scheme to be rolled out across the maintenance teams. Man-hours to do jobs were drastically reduced.

BEA lacked a proper maintenance facility at its new London Airport base, and Shenstone was adamant that a proper, warm, winterized building on a scale to match Canadian facilities should be built. Few know that the massive pre-stressed concrete hangar that erupted onto the face of the new airport was very much Beverley Shenstone's brainchild. It cost £2.5 million to build – a massive sum in the 1950s – but paid for itself time after time through allowing BEA's maintenance workers the best work conditions. The total floor area was over 200,000 sq ft. By 1960, BEA had spent £10 million on 65 acres of engineering base employing 4000 people. In the normal world of corporate hierarchy, anyone running such a facility would rank as a captain of industry, yet Shenstone, Morgan, Wilkinson and BEA just got on with it. By 1962, BEA engineering had reduced its cost level by 13 per cent.

In this great building, everything BEA needed to maintain, repair, and service its diverse fleet was in one place – even if it was centrally heated and the British workers, being unused to central heating, kept opening the windows in the middle of winter – much to their Canadian boss's ire!

As the 1950s progressed, with a new Queen on the throne, BEA was operating with two bases, over 60 outstations, and an engineering staff of 850 and operations line staff of 1750. Every new aircraft type required the re-education of those who were to maintain it, and the older aircraft in the fleet such as the DC-3s and Vickers Vikings were racking up flying hours and flight cycles in the order of 40,000 hours for the DC-3s and

10,000 hours for the Vikings. The Vikings, although dependable, required intensive maintenance and modification by the manufacturer.

Shenstone's BEA figures for 1954 show that the airline's engineering requirements to keep its fleet safely up to date in airworthiness terms and in the daily utilization, would cost £3,700,000. Approximately one-third of that sum would be spent on work done outside BEA by engine, airframe, and overhaul contractors and outstations. In 1954, the engineering wing of BEA accounted for 25 per cent of the airline's total expenditure.

According to Shenstone, flying, maintaining and modifying in service airliners was far more complex in operational terms than just making the aircraft in the first place. Of note, Shenstone was convinced that actual operating experience gave airline engineers an insight into airliner use and development that no manufacturer should ignore. He did not see the relationship as one where the aircraft designer and manufacturer prescribed what airlines should use as if they were a patient following doctors' orders. Instead, according to Shenstone, the two should work together: such thinking was not universal at the time...

By 1959, the Shenstone engineering team at BEA included R.C. Morgan as Chief Project and Development Engineer, with Beverley leading K.G. Wilkinson as Assistant Chief Engineer, with J.G. MacLean as Engineering Training Manager. I. Grant-Murray was Chief Inspector, I.J. Gregory was Chief Maintenance Engineer and J. Cuming was Purchasing Manager. Other leading names in the department included those of C.A. Jupe and W. Mann as lead Inspectors, S.A. Sharp as Maintenance Control Superintendent and E.R. Major, J. McGuire and R.K. Farquharson as Section Managers. H.G. Rossiter, W.B. Shaw, R.H. Whitby and A.S. Clark were Development Managers. F.J. Fellows and B.H. Russell were Assistant Purchasing Managers. Under these men and their teams of staff, BEA Engineering achieved the outstanding results of reliability that were the hallmark of its heyday.[13]

A measure of Shenstone's success in improving BEA's engineering standards and efficiency as the airline grew and as it gained all the modern facilities that it and its first chief engineer Philip Wills had been denied, can be assessed from an episode in the summer of 1951.

TAA (Trans Australia Airlines) had arranged some deserved publicity for themselves through an article in the aviation press (*Flight*, 17 August 1951) that drew attention to the airline's very high daily utilization rates for its fleet of aircraft, which included new Convairs. These figures were the envy of many, and Beverley Shenstone wanted to have his say, characteristically in print, rather than in person.

Shenstone's response was to demonstrate that BEA could also achieve similar figures despite suffering the handicap of having its aircraft spend much more time on the ground during flight turn-arounds on its much shorter sector stages. TAA' s figures, however good, reflected its long route sectors with consequent less time on the ground, and its more benign operating environment.

In a response entitled 'Keeping Them Flying' (*Flight*, 21 September 1951), B.S. Shenstone – as the author was titled – explained that BEA's average stage sector length was 223 miles and that the en route stops were not quick transit stops, but full stops in varying countries with differing practices with longer delays for loading, customs and paperwork that are not common in Australian operations. Despite these adverse factors, BEA's figures were shown to be comparable in many ways with the TAA operation in its much easier operating environment with newer aircraft. For BEA, achieving annual aircraft utilization figures of around 2000 hours per year, across its mainline prop fleet was the aim.

One thing was very clear, Shenstone was very proud of what he and BEA had achieved in one of the most hostile short-haul environments in the airline world – across a fleet that in the early days, was in the form of the DC-3, ageing and even with the 1945 Viking, based on wartime designs. The Ambassador and the Viscount had yet to come fully into service.

As the 1950s opened up and the post-war effects eased, there were many external influences – such as design trends, market forces and world events, all of which would affect airliner design and airline operations.

As the future unfolded, BEA had to adapt. But first came a huge success – one engineered between the old friends at BEA and Vickers-Armstrongs Ltd. Between them, they put the VC2, or Vickers Viceroy (soon to become the Viscount), on the global map.

15

Viscount, Vanguard and Trident

The specification for a new, short to medium haul British airliner had been drawn up in the early 1940s by the second Brabazon Committee – upon which Beverley Shenstone had served – before he turned up at BEA, itself the de facto launch customer for this very aircraft.

The idea was to replace the DC-3 and create a new type of airliner that would also eclipse the Viking and any upcoming foreign competitor, which were likely to be American. As befitted the age, a row over power plant type took place – should a tried and trusted reciprocating power drive a prop, or one of the newfangled, part-jet turbine propeller jobs? As Vickers chief designer Rex Pierson considered his choices, N.E. Rowe – another Shenstone contact of old – along with Phillip Wills, directed the Brabazon Committee towards a jet turbine engine driving a propeller – the prop turbine – as the new power plant of choice for short range airliners.

Whatever the dictates of the Committee, the fact was that by 1945, Vickers-Armstrongs under Pierson and then under George Edwards (later Sir George) went their own way and created their own interpretation of the rules – they were not prescribed to by the Brabazon Committee specification, but perhaps guided to meet its suggestions. Vickers were the people who took the Viking/DC-3 replacement idea and expanded it to create a pressurized, four-engined, high quality airliner with many new features notably in the power plant. It is clear that the Vickers proposal was designed to move the game ahead, and it did so most convincingly. Vickers, with the Pierson/Edwards team, achieved this through their outstanding talents.

The main issue concerned the engines. Edwards and Vickers, supported by the BEA camp, held out against the then current perceived wisdom that favoured reciprocating piston engines, to ensure that the Viscount was powered into a long-term future by the smooth, economical and efficient jet-prop turbine-engined that several engine companies were developing.

After winning that battle, they had to choose between the various versions of the jet prop turbine that British engine makers soon churned out. The Rolls-Royce Dart was Vickers' choice.

Unlike other engines on offer, including rival prop turbines, the Dart was build around known parameters; it did not come with features so advanced that they might be fragile. The Dart was robust with a centrifugal compressor (rather than axial flow) and had rugged turbine blades. It took a long time to get it right and the competition was fierce – forcing Vickers into a difficult position.

Faced with delays and uncertainty, and Government pressure, BEA ordered the twin-engined, high-winged conventionally powered Airspeed Ambassador as a stop-gap measure – perhaps not fully appreciating that the PR effects of such a decision would be a blow to Vickers. However, the Ambassador was not a prop jet nor capable of redefining the genre, whereas the VC2, or Viscount as it became known, most certainly was.

The Viscount achieved a perfect balance between costs and performance. It exceeded the runway length and take-off performance parameters of its operators requirements, cruised without subsequent penalty, yet eclipsed their existing equipment, and provided an airframe that however carefully tuned in terms of its wing design, engine economy and seat per mile costs, delivered a level of comfort and safety that was new.

Edwards and his team forensically tuned every aspect of the design – notably the up-swept tail and horizontal stabilizer that preserved the handling qualities and reduced fatigue effects on the spar and skins from the engine and wing slipstream flows. High lift, double-slotted flaps lowered landing speeds in comparison with other new designs and every passenger had a large window that could act as an escape hatch. The spectre of hull fatigue (which was soon to manifest in the Comet disasters) was avoided by careful design and through using elliptical shapes for all apertures – thus avoiding square corners or tight radii where stress and cracks could build up.

The jet-prop Viscount was smooth, safe, strong, handled beautifully and also had the inbuilt capability to be developed and stretched into a bigger version. The cabin also brought new standards to airline seating and service. It was, however, built around a single main wing spar, which resulted in some resistance from the American market. There were no issues with the single spar – providing that it was inspected and replaced as per design schedule. BEA were soon to become experts at this 'filleting' of Viscounts that needed scheduled spar maintenance work.

Peter Masefield did not join BEA until late 1948, but had been well connected enough with Vickers to know that the Viscount was going to be special. By supporting the Viscount and its engine choice against obvious competing engines in the market place, the Napier Naiad and the Armstrong Siddeley Mamba, BEA sent out a signal at a time when the Viscount projected needed all the support it could get.

The early Viscount 630 model was small, with fewer than fifty seats. But with more power to come from the Dart engine and a longer fuselage easily possible, the BEA-influenced Viscount 700 series with over fifty seats suddenly became the commercial tool that the BEA Board could take a risk on; some of the Board (now under W. Sholto-Douglas – Lord Kirtleside) had been concerned about the costs of being a launch customer for a new type of airliner. Shenstone, ever the pragmatist, had not wanted to be party to the creation of a short-term wonder – a sort of blue riband aircraft, but neither did he want to miss the chance of having an advanced airliner built to his own airline's needs.

He noted that the seat mile costs had to be improved – notably against the fifty-seater twin-engined prop types of the era, and by adding seating capacity in a longer body, BEA pushed Vickers to stretch the Viscount into the subsequent Viscount 700 and later 800 series.

The BEA engineering department under Beverley Shenstone, K.G. Wilkinson, and R.C. Morgan worked closely with the Edwards team to achieve the balance of stretch and size without invoking major structural costs that would reduce any seat mile cost gains otherwise secured. Small localized reinforcement and some tuning of the rate of roll on the 800 series wing were the only real issues that stretching the airframe revealed. The Vickers flight test team achieving sound solutions to the larger Viscount's issues.

'We helped them sell it,' said Shenstone of the Viscount 700/800 series that went on sale in 1950.[1]

The Canadian link also continued with TCA's Gordon McGregor (a long-time friend of all concerned) introducing the Viscount to North America – where it soon achieved large sales as the definitive airline tool of choice.

Within months the 700 series would reinforce that view: the faster and longer 800 series would become the ultimate Viscount. By 1958, BEA was operating over eighty Viscounts as the backbone of its fleet. Many other airlines the world over, soon did likewise – after more prompting from Canada's McGregor who helped Vickers break into the American market. Yet perhaps, even greater than that achievement, was the sight of Viscounts in the liveries of Lufthansa, KLM, Alitalia, Air France and a spectrum of other national carriers populating the skies of Europe and the airport ramps of the world. The Viscount sold 424 airframes in total, across 42 airlines in over 30 countries.

BEA and TCA/Air Canada had a notable hand in the success of the aircraft.

The BEA engineering department had been part of something special. What happened next was confusing, messy and expensive – at the hands of many.

* * *

Trident Troubles

Beverley Shenstone spent 1947–1964 as chief engineer at BEA. In 1960, he was also the first airline chief engineer in the world, to be elected to an airline Board. That tenure was a long time by the airline industry standard and it allowed him to carve a niche for himself, and for the airline. It also put him in a perhaps unique position when it came to new equipment.

Having so successfully helped his old friends at Vickers (Vickers had offered him the chance to become one of their leading designers in 1944) to develop the Viscount into an airliner not just for BEA, but also for the world market, there came the need to consider a new short to medium-range jet liner for BEA's core routes. The prop versus jet argument was raging across the industry and many differing opinions existed. Where did the future lie?

In the meantime, BEA needed aircraft and the delayed Vanguard, an excellently engineered Vickers turbine-powered product designed for BEA under Shenstone's close guidance, so perhaps even in the correct operational context, in a sense designed by BEA, came late to the 1950s prop-jet market and fell into the mess of the jet versus prop debate. BEA ordered twenty Vanguards. The order was placed with Vickers in October 1957 at a cost of around £1 million per aircraft – a large sum and equal to the cost of a Caravelle. Gordon McGregor's Trans Canada Airlines TCA (soon to become Air Canada) ordered twenty winterized Vanguards at a total cost of £23 million.

Although delayed into service due to a compressor problem in its Rolls-

Royce Tyne engines, the Vanguard worked well on BEA's diverse route network. But in Beverley Shenstone's own private words:

> We thought it would be another Viscount, but its growing pains and a year's delay plus the promise of jets spoiled it and the only other buyer was Air Canada. We should have waited for the jets rather than ignoring them at the time.[2]

Despite this, there was much Shenstone philosophy in the Vanguard, which was arrived at with close co-operation and agreement with Vickers. As with the Viscount, Edwards and Shenstone, and their respective teams at Vickers and BEA, had produced a great aircraft, yet one designed for and by its owning airline.

The Comet disasters, the intense maintenance requirements of the big reciprocating engine powered airliners such as the DC-7, Boeing Stratocruiser, and Lockheed Constellation, allied to the delays in the exquisite Bristol Britannia, all combined to create a state of confusion for airline planners. Many ignored the rush to jets. Some, such as Australia's Queensland and Northern Territory Air Service (QANTAS), with its unique range and performance demands, grasped the jet concept early on and took clear, decisive, fleet equipment decisions and never looked back.

The pace of development was clearly demonstrated by the French Caravelle twin jet taking to the air in 1956. The French, were pioneering a new market with their rear-engined (but not T-tailed) Caravelle – an aircraft with almost glider-like wing aspect ratio, a Comet nose section and two British Rolls-Royce Avon engines. It was in many ways, the perfect short to medium-haul airframe for its time. The British ignored the French orders for the French Caravelle – at their peril, as its worldwide sales soon proved. *Today,* the reader may wonder why BEA did not simply order Caravelles, but at *that* time, the thought of buying a French aircraft was, of course, an anathema to the British – despite the rather curious almost simultaneous contradiction of BOAC's penchant for the Boeing boardroom and its forthcoming 707... And the belief was that regional short-haul jets had little future.

But could BEA see that the Caravelle would soon lure away its customers with the appeal of jet power? The Caravelle had been just another beautiful French prototype to be bought by Air France alone – hadn't it? Did the British from their somewhat conceited ivory tower of 1955, really accept or predict that the Caravelle would become the European, and American export success that it later became?

For the visionary Shenstone however, it was the Caravelle's rear-mounted engines – and consequent high lift coefficient 'clean' wing that was the key to the future. He could also converse with Vickers expert, Dr Dietrich Küchemann, who was like, Lippisch, Multhopp and Voigt, all by then in America, versed in the ways of swept wings. Dr Doetsch was also on hand at Vickers to lend crucial wing design experience.

The clean, swept wing, was first suggested in 1930s Germany – as had been the all-wing or nurflügel, the Lippisch delta wing shape, and in the Messerschmitt rocket plane. Shenstone knew this – he and he alone of his contemporaries was there at the beginning of it all. Shenstone knew that such a wing, unencumbered by engine cowlings and pylons, with its uninterrupted slats and flaps, was very aerodynamically efficient and much more stable in handling effects; it would be ideal for an airliner. The idea of rear engines gave a quieter cabin, much better engine-out asymmetric power thrust lines and reduced foreign object ingestion with far less fan blade damage than a wing pylon mounted engine. Fire risk was also considerably reduced.

The down side of the T-tail, and it was a not inconsiderable down side, was the effect on the stalling characteristics (the deep stall). At high climb angles, the high set tail dips into the stalled main wing wake and loses so much efficiency that the aircraft then loses its ability to pitch its nose down to regain airflow and flying speed over the main wing. Thus the aircraft becomes 'locked in' and is irrecoverable. Numerous tweaks such as a larger, higher fin with bigger and more powerful elevators can reduce the problem – as can altering the centre of gravity and the fitting of the stick-pusher devices on pilots control columns which ram the stick forwards for a nose down pitch as sensors indicate the onset of the stall.

However, with suitable training, protection and use of high-lift devices the T-tail deep stall issue is not one that has limited its use or its continuing fashion. The rear engine design also needs a stiffer main wing spar (due to a lack of bending relief normally supplied by wing mounted engine pylons), and a stronger, heavier tail.

By 1958, the developed Caravelle, despite a massive increase in its list price (at £1 million per airframe) was winning orders across Europe (which it continued to do for years) and was soon to sell in the vital American arena. These orders spurred BEA into initially ordering ten of the economically less viable, *four*-engined Comet as a jet competitor on European routes. BEA had little choice, there was no off-the-shelf, British Caravelle competitor. Beverley Shenstone recorded:

> Comet was bought to get us to the front line again. We considered it a stop gap... BEA kept using it on the surprisingly popular long runs such as London–Beirut or London–Cyprus.[3]

The threat of long-range intercontinental jets stopping off en route in Europe and picking up local passengers from BEA's slower propliners never really materialized. But the short-haul speed problem remained and the prop-jet Vanguard failed to meet that need. The lack of a British-built Caravelle competitor with short-haul performance set Shenstone thinking. So BEA, under Shenstone's technical lead, knew that it had to make plans for a short-range (1000–1200 miles) jet liner. In 1957, BEA issued a call for submissions to meet a seventy to eighty-seat, jet-powered, 1000-mile ranged, intra-European jet requirement. The lure, of course, was that the winning airframe supplier could have a jet equivalent of the Viscount on its hands – a potential domestic and export success.

On 23 January 1959 in *Flight* magazine, BEA's Shenstone postulated that the market may need two types of jetliner – a fast 1200 miles 80–120-seat airliner for mainline routes and a smaller 50-seat regional twin jet for sectors of 300–500 miles.

Years later, both these thoughts came to pass, notably the regional jet market that the BAC 1-11 pioneered with its European and North American airline sales. Nothing, however, came of the Hamburger Flugzeugbau HFB 314 – a proposal for a German-designed, state-funded T-tailed rear-engined jet that could have provided stiff competition to the British and French types of the era.

The point is though, that the British had, in the form of the Vickers (later BAC) design studio, a raft of airliner projects ready to roll. The genius of George Edwards and his design team under the likes of Ernest Marshall, Hugh Hemsley, Basil Stephenson, et al., saw to that. The Hunting Company-derived BAC 1-11 twin jet also proved the point – only the age-old issue of engine development held it back.

Before all that came to pass, the eclipse of the propliner and the rush to regional as well as long-haul jets in the late 1950s caused a change of emphasis within the airline business, and as BEA's chief engineer, Shenstone was at the core. In 1956, he had been pushing for a tri-jet with up to 1200 miles range, to be complemented on shorter regional routes, by the Vanguard prop fleet; a jet and a prop fleet mix also offering passengers two fares options as well. Yet by 1959, it was clear that the Vanguard would have to be replaced by a fleet of small, short-range regional jets that might even be suitable for BEA's Channel Islands and Scottish Divisions routes.

At Vickers, the key development was that it had turned the twin-engined Vanguard jet derivative – the Vanjet – into a three, and then finally a four-engined jet (which itself became the superb VC10), which stepped into the breach created by the government when it killed off Vickers' advanced V1000/VC7 airliner close to its first flight. That decision was a disaster that, as stated by George Edwards, effectively handed over the future world market for large jet airliners to the Americans. It was loss of historical proportions. At one stage the Canadians, in the form of Trans Canada Airlines and Gordon McGregor, tried to save the V1000/ VC7 with an order – even flying to London to lobby the Government. But the Canadians were ignored.

There was also backing for a de Havilland Type 118, four-engined jet that rivalled the V1000/VC7 yet which only existed on paper – as opposed to the V1000's reality of being 80 per cent complete.

Another regional jet proposal was the Bristol 200, penned under chief designer Archibald Russell. It was to have Orpheus engines, and by 1957, events had led to a suggested Rolls-Royce RB 121 power plant. The aircraft was powerful, rear engined and T tailed – so it had a clean wing and good runway potential. With approximately 80 seats and an obvious capacity for fuselage stretch to 100 or 130 seats, it looked like the aircraft BEA needed. It also looked like an aircraft with export potential – a vital point for a foreign currency starved country like Britain, still so massively in debt from the war. Avro (A.V. Roe) also responded to BEA's call for proposals. The Avro 740 aircraft was of similar design – with a wing of between 30–35 degrees sweep and rear engined – but with a novel V-shaped tail surface combination.

BEA seriously considered the Bristol 200 as their front-runner. But at the same time, BEA was taking the decision to ask de Havilland for a special version of the Comet – a clipped wing, short range variant, even if it did have four fuel-guzzling engines that were inconveniently buried in the wing roots close to the cabin. To the BEA Board, the accountants, and to Shenstone, the attraction of sharing many components and services between the BEA Comets and any potential short jet, were obvious. Shenstone also had close links with de Havilland's at Hatfield – notably via its Canadian offshoot with which he had had involvement in the war. BEA and Shenstone were fans of de Havilland and admired the handling qualities of their aircraft and all that they had learned from the Comet disasters.

Enter the de Havilland DH.121 proposal in response to BEA's call for a short-haul jetliner.

BEA needed to leapfrog the Caravelle's passenger appeal and runway performance and add speed – which meant adding power. This factor, framed by Beverley Shenstone, was the genesis of the BEA tri-jet formula across the submissions from the British manufacturers, and de Havilland could throw in its research into a swept, high speed wing. Therefore the proposed de Havilland 121 was a 615mph/990kmh jet with a 35-degree wing sweep at ¼ chord. It was rear engined and had a low-set tail plane (this slowly moved up the fin to the mid-fin, and then the T-tail configuration as the design progressed). The early submissions were Avon powered, which was underpowered, and required a 6000ft runway. Later submissions had larger Medway 141 engines with 30 per cent more thrust per engine than the Avons, giving a 5000ft runway capability. Sadly, the Medway engine and the inherent airframe development it would have allowed, was curtailed.

It was a time of great activity for BEA and for Beverley Shenstone. Here was the chance to influence aircraft design without being part of the single interest mentality of a manufacturer's drawing office. And Shenstone was in a strong enough position to influence the design process based on his knowledge, which was, in the view of many, in excess of that one might normally associate with an airline's engineering manager.

On 9 April 1959, *New Scientist* magazine published a double page feature on Beverley Shenstone, and was fulsome in its praise of this remarkable and influential man, yet it also stated:

> Most striking of all Shenstone's acts of design guidance is to be found in the tail of the new jet liner due for delivery in 1964 (the DH.121-Trident). When that specification was being worked out, he was convinced that the jet engines should be placed, not in the wing or under the wing, but at the tail. He opened his discussions with Vickers. Soon he was negotiating with Avro, Bristol, and de Havilland. They were all opposed to tail engines at the start. He produced his arguments in greater detail, but there were still doubts in the minds of the manufacturers. He returned to this battle with still more evidence of the advantages and in the end they were as enthusiastic as he was. The DH.121 will have tail engines. So will the Vickers VC10 for the British Overseas Airways Corporation. Both companies might have arrived at the same decision without Shenstone's missionary work, but there can be little doubt that he pushed the one into an immediate tail-engine design and that he started the other thinking.[4]

Shenstone was clear to anyone who asked; BEA was a huge opportunity for him. He could be involved in design, engineering and maintenance, and management. The job had more scope and, as Shenstone said: 'Was more interesting than designing one thing.'

Did Shenstone's belief in the rear-engined formula mean that Shenstone was the father of the rear-engined jet airliner? Given that Vickers put a jet in the back of a Wellington in 1943 (and then abandoned rear-engined configurations until the Vanjet studies), and that the rear-engined Caravelle was shown in model form in late 1953, the answer has to be, no.

However, can we credit Shenstone as the defining influence behind the rear-engined (and T-tailed) British tri-jet, and of influencing the VC10 and de facto the 727 (de Havilland having naively shown the DH.121 at an early stage of its design – in a move not reciprocated by Boeing when the 727 emerged)? If *New Scientist* is to be believed, the answer could well be, yes.

We can also add that the rear-engined T-tail formula, supported by Beverley Shenstone, has lived on through various small jets such as the Fokker, Canadair Bombardier, Embraer types – and remains the default design for fast, high lift, rocket-ship business jets that can get in and out of difficult airfields. It has, however, faded as a configuration for the four-engined airliner. When in 1958, BEA chose de Havilland and their DH.121 tri-jet, for BEA's £30 million tri-jet order, the other bidders were, as described in Shenstone's Mitchell Lecture speech: 'Not only disappointed, but furious.'[5] There were questions raised about de Havilland's ability to deliver – all of which became inconsequential after Duncan Sandys' 1957 White Paper that amalgamated the British airline industry and saw the de Havilland 121 become the Air Company 'Airco' 121 and latterly the Hawker Siddeley Trident, with the manufacturing work spread about for reasons that were not always related to technical themes.

As for BEA, well were they not simply doing what they had done with Vickers over the Viscount – adding airline and market place experience to a great idea to turn it into a better aircraft with wider appeal? The fly in that ointment came in 1959 when a dip in international airline passenger numbers caused the BEA Board to panic and downsize the new tri-jet – perhaps without considering what would happen after the downturn reversed. The aircraft would not enter service for several years – would the downturn last that long? No one seems to have asked.

Instead of the Shenstone-led specification that was the original DH.121, BEA's Board opted for immediate revision of the type – with smaller engines and a smaller cabin for the new jet, which became the Trident 1 specification. The range, power and appeal of the aircraft beyond BEA's immediate requirements, were curtailed, which was hardly BEA's problem. What BEA was concerned about was *its* aircraft amid a downturn in ticket sales. But we do have to wonder why de Havilland's Board acquiesced so easily and, in doing so, threw away many potential export orders for the new tri-jet formula? The answer is that they had no choice. And the Trident 1 – the emasculated DH.121, was Kirtleside's and his Board's aeroplane, by order.

Interviewed by the author about the changes to the BOAC-specified VC10, Brian Trubshaw echoed Vickers' Sir George Edwards saying: 'BOAC got what they asked for.'[6] Interviewed by the author about the BEA changes to its demands for the DH.121, de Havilland's John Cunningham said: 'BEA got what they asked for and then the changes they asked for. What happened was a shame as the industry suffered.'[7] What was clear, was that de Havilland's team, led by Aubrey Burke and Chief Designer T.C. Wilkins running the DH.121 project, were caught between the proverbial rock and hard place.

What was even more ironic was that as BEA was downsizing the DH.121 Trident proposal, it was using four-engined Comets on key European routes. It should not be forgotten that at this time BEA and BOAC were unique in having their aircraft designed for them – rather as Pan Am and TWA had once also enjoyed. BEA and BOAC had expectations from their suppliers and, in turn, their suppliers saw nothing odd in remaining within such narrow commercial or marketing boundaries. The world, however, was about to change. Having cast the altered Trident 1 solely for a revised BEA perception based on a late 1950s scenario, the aircraft that was then delivered a few years later was limited by its performance and had to be later stretched – *back* towards its originally suggested size. A booster engine was also added in the tail fin to improve the take-off performance of the Trident 3b but crucially, this was in terms of payload, not runway length requirement.

Shenstone was amid all this, and it is clear that he performed his job title and stuck to pursuing the BEA remit. His employer was BEA. Yet the ground was shifting under him and BEA. Shenstone also had the overseas experience and vision to know that his role could expand far beyond the BEA need: the BEA Vickers success with developing the Viscount had proved that. A further debate then started about the by-now smaller-engined Trident 1 and its take-off abilities. Had BEA not hamstrung the aircraft and handed the world market for a short to medium-haul tri-jet to Boeing and its own forthcoming 727 tri-jet? This is a claim still made today and is not all it seems, although it is clear that even if the original DH.121 might not have matched the 727's wing performance, it would still have had a much wider appeal than the Trident 1 that eventually appeared.

On the surface of it in terms of take-off and climb performance, the 727 *was* ahead of the revised, downsized Trident 1. But as Shenstone so ably pointed out:

> (a) The Trident was designed for BEA and BEA's route network – which in the main featured long runways at major European airports, and that (b) the Boeing 727 was designed for a US route network with more difficult runway requirements – which (c) by the time the aircraft arrived, had actually been made longer and easier. So (d) the 727 was over-engineered for its role and had higher operating costs than the downsized Trident.[8]

The 727's seat per mile costs were alleged to have been up to 20 per cent higher – 5 cents per seat mile higher, according to BEA…. The observer may quite correctly wonder how those BEA figures rated with the fuel-guzzling Spey engines of the Trident in all its versions, notably as the Trident 3b with the fourth take-off booster engine, to compete alongside the revised 727-200 Advanced model?

Perhaps the key point is that BEA had no need of a short runway, high-altitude high-performance airliner. Few of its runways posed such severe operational problems as the American fields – notably those that were 'hot and/or high'. It is often suggested that the original specification DH.121 may have been able to meet the American Airlines standard 4000ft take-off run requirement if it had had the RB 141 Medway engine. However, those that criticize BEA for downgrading the DH.121/Trident and taking away its sales potential, need to be reminded that they conveniently often miss the point that, even with its originally planned larger Medway engines, and greater range with a longer cabin, the first DH.121 was not designed to be a 'hot and high', big slatted and triple slot flapped, parasol winged, rocket ship – in the manner of the 727-100, where Mr Sutter at Boeing created an entirely different, unique and brilliant beast…

Support for fitting the Trident with the Smiths/Ferranti triplex automatic landing system as a standard features also came from Trans Canada's Jack Dyment – and old friend of Beverley Shenstone. Making a guaranteed landing in conditions that would otherwise see a costly diversion, was, according Dyment, a massive advantage for an airline. According to Shenstone, Lord Kirtleside was the biggest backer of Autoland at BEA Board level. The Trident's Autoland work paved the way for Category 3 A/B operations down to 70 metres visibility across the industry.

The reality was though, that despite some Trident export success, the de Havilland machine struggled through several re-inventions and only sold 117 airframes, including sales to Cyprus, Pakistan, Kuwait, and

China. The 727, which was far more adaptable, had a high-lift wing, and more power, sold worldwide in huge numbers – 1831 examples being sold.

Economy and seat per mile costs had played a major role within BEA's tri-jet design brief – something that precluded aerial 'hot-rod' performance when it was not needed. Yet, the production Trident was sleek and fast, cruising at 615mph and had a high-speed biased aerofoil section that could get to Mach 0.90 in service – it handled at high speed like a true de Havilland dream. Lower down the speed range, at take-off, its performance was limited by the aerofoil's weaker low speed characteristics. There were two attempts at getting the leading edge high lift gear to be more efficient – hence the Trident 1's droop leading edge and the Trident 2's revised, lightweight leading edge slat equipped design.

It is true to say, however, that the wind tunnel and wing work needed to make the Trident competitive – including a span increase, Kuchemann tips and a completely revised leading edge system as found in the Trident 1E and Trident 2 – cost time and money and did not create the answer. Neither did the massive fuselage stretch of the Trident 3b and its fourth RB162 booster engine regain the Trident's ground. Beverley Shenstone, in a style typical of his quiet reticence, said little at the time on the Trident debacle. Maybe he could have said more? However, as a newly elected BEA Board member, he was hardly in a position to publicly declaim the downsizing of the Trident.

Ex-BEA helicopter division manager, Peter Hearne, interviewed by the author, recalls:

> Shenstone was definitely unhappy about the Board decision to downsize the Trident. As a Board director, he could not frame or pursue his views on the matter at the time: if he had done so it would have meant abandoning any plans he might have, for the rest of BEA's development, so he was constrained on what he could say publicly on the matter.[9]

Of note, Shenstone privately wrote of the downscaling of the original DH.121 (whose rear-engined tri-jet configuration was very much his own belief):

> Comet 4 was bought to get us to the front line again. We considered it a stop-gap and hoped to return them to de Havilland when our own special Trident appeared. This involved BEA's short-sightedness once again. The Trident requirements showed a short-haul 1000 miles aircraft with fewer seats than the Vanguard and was considered to be a hot-shot or Blue Riband first Class sort of thing. I was furious about Trident 1 at the time and said

that no growing airline ever buys a front-line aircraft with fewer seats than the old one…. Putting your money on a new smaller aircraft, is just asking for it.[10]

He could say little publicly at the time, but his diaries confirm that he was 'Furious about Trident 1.' He also discusses in his notes, the merits of a downsized VC10 or Vanjet, as proposed by George Edwards at Vickers – suggesting that this aircraft may have been the preferred answer as it could have been built in various versions, perhaps as either a DC-9 style twin jet or a longer range tri-jet.

Through such previously unpublished words, the difficulties of the Trident design changes amid the upper echelons of the operation of BEA, are for the first time aired. The Trident suffered as a result of British self-centred reaction to a temporary down turn in passenger numbers. In mitigation it was an airline and a Board that had become used to having its aircraft personally designed to its narrow specifications without the need to consider other contexts. Hindsight was not applicable at the time.

So ended the BEA DH.121/Trident design debacle. It produced an incredibly swift, quality aircraft yet one born of market trends, customer needs and political imperatives that changed during its birthing pains and which left it, and BEA, open to criticism, amid the machinations of government.

Within these arenas, in the aftermath of the Trident story, lay the legacy of the big, twin engined air-bus standard airliner – now known as the 'Airbus' type and related to the twin jet 'big twin' formula – and of course the brand name known as 'Airbus Industrie'. The small twin jet story also grew from these debates, and the British Aircraft Corporation (BAC) as the amalgamated collection of companies was now termed, gave birth to the BAC 1-11 twin jet. The French Caravelle team went on to create the supersonic 'Super Caravelle', which became Concorde and saw the men at Vickers who had built the VC10, Viscount etc., join forces with their rivals to create the Concorde. Meanwhile, the French were also creating a large twin-engined Caravelle successor in the form of their original Airbus A300 type proposal. And at exactly the same time, the British airliner manufacturing firms were also creating their own version from the Trident experience and BEA's continuing need and support for a high-capacity short-range aircraft.

Two very similar aircraft were being developed at the same time, yet on separate tracks. Amid all this, the growth of the European Community with all its subconscious implications for politics, finance, and shared developments, was building to a peak.

By 1965, Vickers had suggested a reverse-translated VC10 – a VC11 – which was, in effect, a re-hash of the Vanjet that had given birth to the VC10 in the first place. Yet it came to nothing – in the end it was Vickers themselves who sacrificed the VC11 in the hope of pursuing the twin-engined air-bus type concept.

In the meantime, the Hunting company had been absorbed into BAC and its own small regional twin jet design, the HC 107, soon became the BAC 107 and then as the BAC 1-11 made its mark alongside the Trident in the UK fleet at BEA. It was also to give birth to the charter jet operations so epitomized by Freddie Laker. The 1-11, or 'One-Eleven' as BEA soon branded it, was a small twin jet with great hopes. Yet its sales potential was trapped by the failure to develop the Spey engine.

BEA would still need a new air-bus type aircraft and in August 1965 its chairman, Anthony Milward, stated that by 1970 the airline would require a fleet of at least thirty air-bus type airframes. In 1966, shortly after Beverley Shenstone had left BEA, the airline was rumoured to even be considering purchasing Boeing 727s. It was such an irony – to consider the Trident's tri-jet rival, after all that had passed seemed incredible. But the Government refused to sanction the expenditure.

However, the air-bus type requirement resulted in two design developments for a British air-bus or from then onwards, the airbus designated airliner.

The first project saw Hawker Siddeley create a big twin jet by taking a Trident 3 fuselage and mating it to a new high-lift, moderately swept, super critical wing with big fan engines mounted under the wings and a conventional tail. This aircraft was called the HS.134 and was announced in 1966. Its design was led by Phillip Smith with Derek Brown as chief project engineer. It was a remarkable aircraft of great foresight. Although it was never made, its concept re-appeared in 1979 when Boeing announced its own big twin – the 757 – which looked like an exact copy of the HS.134. In a poignant and ironic commentary on the British airline industry and its sufferings under political interference and its effect on airline management, we should perhaps note that the 1980s launch customer for the Boeing 757 that so closely aped the HS.134 of 1966, was none other than the European division of British Airways – or put more obviously, none other than what had been BEA itself...

The HS.134 was the first definitive 'big twin', air-bus type proposal. BEA and Shenstone looked carefully at it, but there was political problem – one that not even Shenstone could overcome. This was that, at exactly the same time, the British Government was signing up to the European, tri-partite collaborative airliner project that was the beginning of the Airbus A300 story. BEA was also looking at George Edwards' other British air-bus-type proposal – that being the BAC 2-11 and then its consequent wide-bodied, 3-11 derivative.

The 2-11 (and derivative 3-11)[11] was a wide-bodied, twin jet with the forthcoming Rolls-Royce RB 211 fan engine. It retained the T-tail and rear engine configuration that had proved so popular. In effect, it was a natural follow-through of the short-haul jet theme that the Trident and 1-11 had exemplified. Of note, the 3-11 was the first wide-bodied twin jet proposal (the rival HS.134 retained the narrow body, single aisle concept). The 3-11 had grown from a single-aisle narrow-body 1-11 proposal – the 2-11. As such, the 2-11 and the derived 3-11, were visionary predecessors of what became the large wide-bodied, big twin concept in the 1980s to the present day – the Airbus itself.

Shenstone and BEA had also seriously considered the benefits of the HS.134 – the first big twin. But as Shenstone knew so well, by then operating in the gathering storm of government and political machinations, the British Government was not going to support the HS.134 as well as the proposed 2-11/3-11 British air-bus programme as well as the European Airbus A300. The costs of the developed BEA Trident 3b also lurked in the background: Shenstone (who by late 1964 had announced impending his departure from BEA for a directorship at BOAC) was clear.

Just as with the V1000/VC7, the VC10, the Valiant bomber, and the TSR2, the ill-informed, badly thought out and short-term manoeuvrings of politicians then erupted into the face of the British aviation industry when in 1968, the Government pulled out of the specific European Airbus project that it had supported at the cost of home-grown ideas, on economic grounds (yet at the same time, was still funding Concorde).

The then Labour Government had curtailed British military aircraft development in 1965/66, and ordered a vast arsenal of American military aircraft, off the shelf.

These were dangerous political times and Shenstone had to be careful. Despite Labour's machinations, and unhelpful comments about BAC from Roy Jenkins, at least Tony Benn, whatever his ideological differences with Edwards and the British airline community, agreed that the preservation of a British aviation manufacturing base, was a good idea! For BAC and BEA however, the giant, wide-bodied 3-11 would have been a direct competitor to the A300/A310 and Boeing 767 aircraft and with its clean, high-lift wing and T-tail might have secured greater sales in demanding operating environments. The single-aisle HS.134 would surely have precluded the Boeing 757 and the Airbus A320/1 and MD Super 80 machines by two decades and left them still-born in a market place perhaps dominated by one aircraft – the HS.134.

The British, Wilson-led government, had by late 1967 abandoned the Edwards 2-11 (and 3-11 plan) in order to support the Airbus A300, only then to walk away from the A300 itself in 1968. Soon after, that it appeared that the government was offering a chance to resurrect Britain's own air-bus concepts – including the 3-11! Yet by 1970 and the arrival of a new pro-Europe Conservative Government under Edward Heath, that chink of light was gone; Britain climbed back on board the European unity social science experiment and its now revised and smaller Airbus conglomerate with its A300 B airframe supported by political will, not to mention financial subsidy…

At Vickers, the 3-11 (or 'Three- Eleven') as it was now branded, went the way of the V1000/VC7 – its death framed yet another politically forced abandonment of a massive market opportunity that could have supported and sustained Britain's design and manufacturing base for years. The loss of the 3-11 (as with the V1000), was historically significant. The confusion, the mess, was of staggering proportions and the blame lay mostly with politicians of varying political hues.

The contradictions, the waste and the sheer frustration of this period in British Government and its effects upon civil and military aircraft design and airline operation are clear for all to see. Just as with so many other great British designs, they illustrate the failures in political leadership, and the effects of such upon the British manufacturing industry whose management were left to deal with the consequences of decisions that were not their own. Through such decisions, the British once again handed the entire world market for an airliner type to foreign competitors.

Beverley Shenstone witnessed all this, and his sharp words about the effects of political machinations of the mid-1960s, are echoed by many who were also forced to stand and watch government and certain others attempt to emasculate British aviation. As his time at BEA, after over fifteen years with the airline, came to an end, Shenstone reflected in private:

> What I find exasperating is amateurism at high levels, particularly high political levels, such as Permanent Secretaries and Ministers, who don't know the difference between power and thrust, and to whom international safety requirements are complete mystery. It is not normally their fault that they have a high level of ignorance, but it becomes dangerous when they have power as well. This political weakness of assuming that specialised

knowledge is not necessary, or is instantaneously achievable causes enormous difficulties, if not dangers, to the operator and to the government.[12]

Many observers of the civil and military aviation world will agree with those sentiments.

16

Airliners, Gliders, and Man-Powered Flight

The security of the BEA years (1947–1964), although at times stressful, left Beverley Shenstone with the platform from which he could carve his new niche as a that rare thing, a combination of being both a kingpin within his industry and of a commentator upon the workings of his industry. The culmination was perhaps his elevation to the Board of British Overseas Airways Corporation for just over two years until his retirement. Photographs of Shenstone boarding BOAC blue riband jet airliners, show a man with a smile on his face. Jetting off across the world as a BOAC ambassador in the first class cabin of a VC10 was a privilege reserved for the lucky few in the 1960s. Shenstone clearly enjoyed it, so too did his sons, and second wife, Doris.

In the years 1946–1969, his output was prolific. Despite his reputation for taciturn reticence, there were times when it is clear he had wished he had kept his mouth shut.

In his 1950s engineering world, with no PR adviser or spin doctor to hand, Shenstone was very much his own boss, and had become used to being widely quoted in the aeronautical press. He was regularly quoted, and often invited to submit articles to leading publications such as *Flight*, whose archives are littered with news items and major feature articles written by Shenstone on airliner design, engineering issues, maintenance and opinions of matters such as small jets and supersonics.

It was just before Christmas 1953, when Shenstone woke up one morning to find his name splashed across the national newspapers, where he was being pilloried by union leaders and captains of industry alike. Even his friends at *Flight* published a full-page item headed rather ominously by the title 'Mr Shenstone's Comments'.[1]

What Shenstone had done, in the closed world of a trade and professional lecture at the Institution of Production Engineers conference in Southampton, was to criticize the standard of workmanship of some aspects of the British aviation industry. In the media-feeding frenzy, his remarks were reinterpreted to be an attack on all British aviation, and some famous names demanded retribution. Shenstone's position as BEA's chief engineer tended to add to the mess. Letters to *The Times* resulted – even one from Sir Geoffrey de Havilland. The Society of British Aircraft Constructors complained to the head of BEA, Peter Masefeld, about his employee. BEA had also just taken delivery of its new Vickers Viscounts; surely Shenstone could not be criticizing them?

Shop stewards and industrialists alike all jumped on the bandwagon to beat up Shenstone!

The problem was, that there were aspects of British quality control that *were* questionable and stuck in pre-historic practices, and Shenstone's views were (naively) intended to discuss his observations within the closed world of his colleagues. But the world and the media were changing. In the end, Shenstone survived, and even *Flight* magazine endorsed the actual context of his views, but it was a tough time.

Another area of controversy for Shenstone occurred in the early 1960s when the great SST (supersonic transport) project bandwagon took off and grand claims of exceeding twice or thrice the sound barrier within five years were bandied about as airlines considered the potential of supersonic transport and the Concorde project itself. Shenstone made numerous comments in the aviation press where he refused to leap aboard the marketing and PR bandwagon. On 31 March 1964, in a debate at the RAeS between himself and Dr A.E. Russell of BAC, Shenstone framed the 'Difficulties and Advantages of the Supersonic Civil Transport'. He was not popular when he disagreed with the suggested date for Concorde's entry into service – he said, at the lecture, that it would take ten years not five, to design and flight test the aircraft. He latterly commented on the difficulties of supersonic fuselage skin temperatures and how to avoid overheating or 'frying' the passengers. There were shouts of protest, but Concorde entered airline service close to the very date ten years later, that Shenstone, not its supporters, had suggested. So he had been correct – again. Just as Shenstone had also been correct about speed. The SST proponents had decided on Mach 3 as the speed they were aiming for, yet Shenstone, not least in the pages of *New Scientist*, on 15 September 1960, reckoned that Mach 1.5 to Mach 2 was the speed to go for – as Concorde latterly achieved.

He also called the SST Concorde 'The largest, most expensive and most dubious project ever undertaken in the development of civil aircraft.' He was deeply sceptical of a project created by and financed by governments *for* airlines – as opposed to, *by* airlines for themselves at their own behest and specification. At a lecture on the future of supersonic flight that Shenstone gave to the International Press Institute on 6 September 1963, after making comments about the cost and purchasing mechanisms of the Concorde, Shenstone was asked if he thought it wrong to build Concorde. Shenstone's reply was typical of the man. He said: 'I am very glad that Concorde is under way and I shall be glad to fly in it, but not in five years'.[2] *Flight International* reported on this debate on 3 October 1963, with the headline of 'Shenstone on Supersonics'.

In the 1950s and 1960s, BEA and Shenstone's expertise were called upon by a number of emerging new airlines who wanted help setting up their engineering, safety and operations departments. Such airlines included JAT of Yugoslavia and, notably, the re-born Lufthansa, which in late 1954 sent its top management team to see BEA and the German-speaking Shenstone, on a consultancy basis prior to recommencing post war operations.

The summer of 1964 also saw Shenstone present the prestigious R.J. Mitchell Memorial Lecture – the subject being, air transport development. Throughout the 1960s, Shenstone's views were widely sought. He became something of a guru, or perhaps a druidic or sage-like figure; he was experienced, wise, and calm, with knowledge that stemmed from gliders and man-powered pedal pushing machines, to advanced jetliner design. He was appointed President of the Royal Aeronautical Society in 1962/63 and oversaw the return of the Lawrence Hargrave historic papers relating to early flight to Australia after a long period of controversial debate surrounding the documents of the English-born, but Australian resident, aeronautical pioneer. Shenstone was also present for the award of the Society's Bronze medal to Walter Horten at Farnborough in 1964. Shenstone enjoyed his last role as a Board member of BOAC as technical director, working alongside his old colleague Charles Abell from 1964 to 1966 – the wonderful years of blue and gold livery adorning Rolls-Royce Conway-powered Vickers BAC VC10s and Super VC10s and similarly hued and powered Boeing 707 intercontinental jets.

* * *

Gliders

Shenstone made numerous contributions to the establishment of gliding and soaring in Canada, not least through his work for the Soaring Association of Canada on numerous technical and management projects, but also notably to create two Canadian gliders.

In 1946 Shenstone linked up with his old university at Toronto, in a project that would result in a glider latterly to be named after the head of aeronautical engineering at Toronto University – Professor T.R. Loudon.

With Waclaw Czerwinski, the Canadian-based Polish glider expert, and Shenstone working together, the aim of the project was to assist students in gaining practical airframe skills. Shenstone created the glider in a 'Glider Specification C1'. The students were to be co-designers under the lead of Professor Bernard Etkin, later to be Dean of the university's Institute of Aeropace Studies (UTIAS). The glider was the University of Toronto Glider 1 and from 1947 to 1950 was designed and constructed – eventually flying in 1950 and painted up in varsity blue with a smart white stripe. The Loudon flew from 1952 to 1956 and made some long crosscountry flights, but it was destroyed in a storm at Oshawa in the summer of 1956.[3]

The second Shenstone glider was the Harbinger of 1948 genesis, which was a two-seat glider design that was intended to offer performance not far off that of German single-seat gliders and allow excellent training characteristics. The Harbinger was designed as an entry to a British Gliding Association competition announced in 1947. Again, as with the Loudon, it was conceived by Beverley Shenstone and his friend Waclaw Czerwinski, with assistance from R.D. Hiscox. Shenstone concentrated on the Harbinger's structure, whilst Czerwinski shaped its lines, although the pair did feed off each other to create a total package.

The Harbinger had light wings with load-bearing struts allowing a thinner spar. Special attention was paid to wing-fuselage turbulence reduction. Czerwinski was an expert Polish sailplane designer and Shenstone's work spoke for itself. In the Harbinger they created a modern, high-performance two-seat glider with excellent visibility courtesy of the swept forward wing planform – a favourite Shenstone tool. Harbinger failed to win the design competition that created it; a side-by side, rather than tandem-seated design was chosen – in tune with then current fashion. For a variety of reasons, notably a protracted development period and some balance issues, the Harbinger failed to find a production niche. In its Mk I and Mk II variants – the Mk II had a longer nose to cure a centre of gravity issue, only two airframes were built – one of them completed in England after many years of gestation, and the other flew in its native Canada after a similarly delayed build where Jack Ames and Henry Dow worked on the glider until a Mr Albie Pow of Ontario, did additional work. In 1957 the Harbinger 1 was purchased by the Canadian gliding luminaries A. Le Cheminant and R. Noonan and eventually they made it fly. The British Harbinger now rests at Bicester gliding club.[4]

According to some highly qualified observers, Shenstone is also reputed to have influenced the design of other gliders – notably from the stable of Elliots of Newbury and their EON range – some of which reflected late 1930s German design.

The next Shenstone-influenced Canadian aircraft was the BKB-1, a flying wing-type glider designed by Canadian resident and Canadair employee Stefan Brochocki – who had been inspired by the amazing shapes of the Horten flying wings. In Canada in 1953, where he was a glider pilot, Brochocki set about creating a new glider design for club use. It was a flying wing with shades of Fauvel and Horten, yet also of its own style. He was supported by Shenstone who invited him to prepare a paper on the design of this new flying wing glider for the eighth Organisation Scientifique et Technique du Vol à Voile (OSTIV) conference in 1960. Shenstone presented the design paper on Brochocki's behalf. In 1959, Shenstone had arranged for the BKB-1 to be included in published reference works on sailplanes. Brochocki was assisted by Fred Bodek, also a Canadair employee, who helped with the design of the controls. In later years, controversy surrounded the BK1B when a designer named Kasper who flew the BK1B in a series of stunt demonstrations at airshows in America, allegedly laid claim to the craft and a subsequent derivative design. But it is surely to Stefan Brochocki, with whom Shenstone allied himself in the BK1B's early days, that credit clearly lies for its design.[5]

Over in Britain, by 1966, Sigma[6] was a high-performance glider designed from 1966–1969 with the intention of winning the 1970 world gliding championships. Under the direction of Rear Admiral Nicholas Goodhart (who went on to build a man-powered aircraft) Sigma had a 21m alloy wing of great stiffness and an advanced Wortmann type, variable wing area and camber flap system, which added 35 per cent to the lifting area to allow it to thermal and circle very efficiently on cross-country flights without sacrificing its ultimate, glide speed efficiency. The glider project was created by G.E. Burton, H.C.N. Goodhart, F.G. Irving. B.S. Shenstone, W.N. Slater, C.O. Vernon, L. Welch, and K.G. Wilkinson. J.L Sellars would join also the team. After a fire at the Slingsby glider factory in 1968, where it was being built, Sigma's progress stalled, but although it missed the 1970 world championships, it flew at Cranfield in 1977. With a protracted development, Sigma was eventually sold off as a working project to a Mr D. Marsden – a Canadian glider pilot.

* * *

Man-Powered Flight

Shenstone first became fascinated by the possibilities of man-powered flight in 1939 when he came across a series of articles in the German magazine *Flugsport*. These included details of man-powered flight in 1936 – but one that had been towed into the air. After the war, he wrote an article in *Aeronautics* on the subject – yet there was no response. In 1954, Shenstone entered a science competition organized by *Research* magazine and wrote an article entitled, 'Could a Man Fly'? This was published in the *Sunday Times* on 27 February 1955, where Shenstone framed the subject of achieving man-powered flight for a lay audience.

From the response to this article, a new professional impetus was created for the designing and building of man or human-powered aircraft. At this time most British and overseas research was into high-speed aerodynamics, but Shenstone wanted the benefits of low-speed aerodynamics, and the 'green' credentials of man-powered flight to be communicated. He located some of the early 1930s pioneers of man-powered flight, notably Haessler, Villinger and Bossi. With their input and after a growing British interest, Shenstone's restarting of the man-powered movement gained momentum. In 1959*New Scientist* magazine entitled an article about Shenstone as *Missionary of Muscle Powered Flight*.

For Shenstone, across several decades and numerous articles, it is clear that one of his major personal passions was to become the question of whether man could sustain himself in flight. The problems were not just of aerodynamics, but also of structures. He wrote numerous papers and gave lectures, notably in September 1955 when he presented his ideas to the Canadian Aeronautical Institute (CAI), now the Canadian Aeronautics and Space Institute (CASI) framed by his paper 'The Problem of the Very Light-weight, Highly-efficient Aeroplane'. Shenstone also wrote an article asking if man-powered flight had been achieved in 1936. Stirring up debate was one way of creating more interest in the subject. In 1957, Shenstone was then instrumental in setting up the Cranfield Man-Powered Aircraft Committee with H.B. Irving as Chairman, and J.R. Brown, R. Graham, T. Jones, A. Newell, T.R. Nonweiler, and B.S. Shenstone as original members.

By 1957 they had suggested a man-powered study to the RAeS in Hamilton Place, and in late 1959 this group formed the Man-Powered Aircraft Group Committee of the RAeS whose leading aeronautical figures included: H.B. Irving, G.M. Lilley, J. Naylor, T. Nonweiler, J.

Wimpenny and D.R. Wilkie. Official sanction and formal status now existed. In November, the Kremer Prize for achieving man-powered flight was announced. The sponsor was, Henry Kremer, a former de Havilland engineer and now a rich industrialist at the head of a major British company. Shenstone's appointment as President of the RAeS within the next three years can only have helped. A number or men, including de Havilland designers, also set up the Hatfield Group to pursue man-powered flight – Wimpenny and Haggas being well known names as well aerodynamicist Brian Kerry. A Southampton University man-powered flight group, and others including the Bristol-Weybridge Group, the Southend Group and the Woodford Group also competed for the Kremer research funding and prize. By 1979, after early works by the leader of human-powered flight studies in the USA, August Raspet, the American, another Shenstone acquaintance of old, Paul MacCready, had flown his man-powered *Gossamer Condor* to win the first Kremer Prize and also flown across the Channel in the *Gossamer Albatross*.

There is surely little doubt that the man behind the revitalized professional and public profile of man-powered flight was Beverley Shenstone.

* * *

Widely quoted, Beverley Shenstone was without doubt, one of the key players, if not *the* leading figure in airline thinking and engineering development of the 1950s and 1960s. Without Shenstone, we would not have the airline engineering structure as we know it today. Upon his death, Sir Peter Masefield wrote his obituary while others such as K.G. Wilkinson, managing director at British Airways, said that Shenstone had made a 'unique contribution to air transport'[7] It is fair to say that Shenstone's airline work made him one of the men who laid the foundations of the post-war civil air transport industry. His record reads like a citation of astonishing achievement. And yet the public, in the main, have never heard of him – neither have many of aviation's 'experts'.

Shenstone it seems, was an enigma. He was a major figure in aviation, yet being quiet, shy, and disinterested in self promotion or PR, he did not seek celebrity status for himself or for his work. In interviewing those who knew and worked with him, and through knowing his sons, it is clear that Shenstone was a professional of the highest standards. He also had commercial ability and was able to manage people – rare for a 'boffin'. There is a cliché often used about people of position not tolerating fools easily. But surely, professionals at the height of their powers would not expect a fool to be amongst their colleagues? Shenstone had little time for fools, but he was not loud, bombastic or arrogant. Instead, he was indeed the quiet Canadian, the man who said little, thought a great deal and then drew a resolute line in the sand. You knew what was what, and you knew where you stood with Shenstone the Canadian. Could he be tough and stubborn? Definitely, but very quietly. Was he a workaholic? It looks like it. He must also have been obsessed with his subject. Yet he was also a man of humour and outdoor activity, reserved in some ways, outgoing in others – beyond the workplace. Shenstone also encouraged people – especially students – notably those interested in early aviation, gliding and man-powered flight. Members of the various man-powered flight groups and student teams, have also commented on Shenstone's visits to them and his encouragement, technical advice, and time given freely: Shenstone it seems, was a true aviation enthusiast.

Flight magazine wrote of Shenstone: '*Flight* knows and respects Mr Shenstone as a modest and capable engineer and one who does not seek newspaper publicity'.[8]

Quietly, without fanfare, Shenstone invested time and money as donations to the furthering of tomorrow's research. It was Shenstone who drove the re-birth of the man-powered flight movement and the Kremer Prize. He was also a father and husband, and a man who loved to potter about on inshore and inland waterways. Beverley Shenstone was in some ways, a quintessential, dome headed boffin, yet unusually, one with commercial abilities, management skills, and a dry wit. He had friends in high places and friends in normal life. That symbol of British excellence, Sir Peter Masefield, said of Shenstone: 'My old friend. I did of course know him very well indeed.'[9] Of Shenstone's achievements, Masefield wrote that Shenstone was 'one of the quiet, competent, behind-the-scenes men who had a major influence on the progress of British air transport over almost a generation'.[10] Masefield also credited Shenstone with not only being an engineer whose skills ranged from man -powered flight and gliding to supersonics, but also as a 'penetrating writer' on the subjects.

Shenstone gave lectures, wrote papers, attended functions and offered advice at the highest level – upon request; he was one of the few who attended the August 1941 meeting between Roosevelt and Churchill, and he met the aviation-minded Duke of Edinburgh on a number of occasions. Beverley Shenstone, the Canadian of English and Scots extraction, may well have wanted to be remembered for the broader aspects of his works – particularly his place in the building of BEA and of Britain and Canada's airline operations, and his role in the development of Canadian aeronautical influence. Yet quietly, above all, there lay his contribution to the Spitfire – a contribution even less well known than his airline industry work and, one that he rarely talked about.

Without R. J. Mitchell, and his men, such as Beverley Shenstone, and their Spitfire, what would have happened?

Shenstone played a significant role in the Spitfire, as so too did others. At Supermarine, Shenstone was a young man in a young team, but he did spend seven years with the company – and six under R.J. Mitchell. Quiet Shenstone may well have been, but he was also a man amid a team of men who, in the most proper of senses, spent a lot of time together, men who worked intimately within their creation, the Spitfire, the aircraft that changed the fate of mankind.

These men and their labours, their Spitfire, had a massive effect and a defining influence upon the history of not just the twentieth century, but also upon the course of future history. These men threw off convention, they challenged perceived wisdom and they reached out to innovate; free thinking outwitted industrial might. History should surely be detailed with the names and deeds not just of those men who flew the Spitfire, but also with those of the men who created it. Beverley Shenstone was one of those men; he was also the man who shaped the Spitfire's wing – possibly the most important part of the aircraft and its performance. The story of how he achieved that feat has, after seventy-five years, now been revealed. The international nature of his story, must surely serve to illustrate that no individual designer and no single nation has a monopoly on clever design. Flight, in its design and its act, across all sky and all space, was, and remains, our future.

Epilogue: Tail Piece

Upon his retirement, Shenstone build himself a wooden boat – not a glamorous yacht, but a 28ft motor cruiser, which he named *Paasivesi*, Finnish for rocky waters. He designed it and commissioned its building on the Thames. The interior was a masterpiece of wooden construction and design ingenuity that he designed and built himself. He and his second wife, Doris, spent many happy summers cruising the inland waterways of Europe. The boat navigated French canals, German rivers, and Dutch waterways. In the harsh northern European winters, it was annually laid up in the country of its summer's boating, to await its Master's return from his home in Cyprus. Shenstone also travelled the world; his opinion was still in demand as an aeronautical consultant, and in his later years, he was close to the realization of the dream of man-powered flight.

Prior to Beverley's decline in health, he brought his motor boat home across the Channel and back to the River Thames. In 1979, just weeks before *Gossamer Albatross* achieved a man-powered flight across the English Channel to realize a dream, the old sage Shenstone sailed off into the sunset. He died on 9 November 1979, leaving a straight wake and but a ruffle in the air, yet he had sowed the waters and the winds with many deep thoughts. He had been part of the all-wing, tailless design story, worked on the development of the delta wing; he had advocated boundary layer control; he had been a major force in gliding and man-powered flight; he had promoted the T-tail rear-engined jet and also was an early believer in the twin-engined long range airliner concept now so fashionable. There were also his thoughts on sails, hulls, and hydrofoils. In 1972 he travelled to Lake Constance to meet up with his old friend Alexander Lippisch. There, they observed the first tests of Lippisch's water-skimming flying boat prototype and its combination of hydrofoil and flying hull, fifty years after it was first conceived and even longer after Giovanni Pegna's Piaggio Schneider racer of a hydrofoil aircraft may have inspired their thinking.

Shenstone also authored an impressive collection of papers and a legacy to the development of the airline networks that we now all take for granted, yet which just sixty years ago, were in their infancy. Shenstone made a contribution to science, and to wartime intelligence gathering, and to the war effort – not just through the Spitfire, but also through his work for the Air Ministry and its departments. Under Sir Wilfrid Freeman, and at the Wright-Patterson facility, Shenstone touched several aspects of secrets, science and advanced design. He also influenced Canadian aviation through his works – started off by the early patronage of Professor John Parkin and Air Vice Marshal Ernest Stedman.

In his loyalty to Britain and to Canada, Shenstone straddled two worlds, and contributed to both nations. As an American once said, 'If Shenstone had been an American, they would have named an airport after him!' Shenstone would have hated that, but perhaps in the light of events, myths, and untold deeds, this telling of his story, may set the record straight and signal his contribution to a wider audience, as well as revealing a new aspect to the Spitfire's story. Shenstone was undoubtedly brilliant, perhaps, some would say a genius, or a polymath of wide ability. He would have hated such words, and cringed at such descriptions – or any publicity. But his record *is* unusual, significant and historically important. Even more unusual was the way he gathered information, modified certain theories and then added his own design thoughts. It was the combination of such elements that so significantly contributed to the aerodynamics of the Spitfire and its unique blend of thin aerofoils, modified ellipse, lift and drag control, and boundary layer surface detailing that made it unique. All these were based on an alchemy of mathematics, theories, sculpting, modelling and mental visualization that stemmed from Shenstone's mind, then not thirty years old.

Shenstone's life began and ended around boats, yet beyond perhaps even his contribution to the Spitfire and to the airlines of the world, he left a cipher, a thought from the past for a future now defined. The following words, written in 1940 by Beverley Shenstone, are a fitting way to end his story, because, finally today, tailless flying wings – the all-wing aircraft concept – are an in-service military reality and more are being planned for both military and civil production. Indeed, the future of civil airliners has been agreed to be in the form of the all-wing, tailless aircraft. Boeing have released sketches of their planned and decided future – the 'blended wing' concept. It has its roots in the learning of the past, yet has been eclipsed for so long by conventional thinking. A past whose aeronautical thoughts and whose secrets Beverley Shenstone was part of.

Along the way, Dunne, Hill, Junkers, Lippisch, the Horten brothers, Northrop, and others, have attempted the tailless revolution, only to be defeated by the perceptions of the 'then' as opposed to the realization of the 'now'. Beverley Shenstone was a tireless advocate of tailless thinking; as such he promoted tailless design, and with R.J. Mitchell, crucially reduced the size of the Spitfire's tail as far as he dared. He knew it would reduce drag and add speed, because as he wrote a long time ago:

> Ideally, one day there will be no tails at all…. The tail, an anachronistic swollen thumb getting in the way and a constant reminder of our present primitive methods of balance, will drop off one day.

B.S. Shenstone 1940

Notes

Introduction
1. Shenstone as pseudonym Brian Worley. 'Fighter Fundamentals', *Aeronautics*, Vol. 2, No. 2, March 1940.
2. Shenstone diary notes.
3. Price, Alfred, *The Spitfire Story*, Jane's,1981.
4. Shenstone diary notes, 1940.

Prologue
1. Shenstone, p.177.
2. Ibid.

Chapter 1
1. Shenstone, p.2.
2. Shenstone, p.5.
3. Shenstone, p.6.
4. Shenstone, p.21.
5. Shenstone, p.17.
6. Shenstone, p.26.

Chapter 2
1. Shenstone, p.63.
2. Shenstone, p.59.
3. Shenstone, diary notes, 1929.
4. Shenstone, diary notes, 1929.
5. Shenstone, p.64.
6. Shenstone, p.66.
7. Shenstone, p.66.
8. Shenstone, diary notes, 1929.

Chapter 3
1. Shenstone, p.67.
2. Shenstone, p.69.
3. Shenstone, diary notes, 1929.
4. Shenstone, p.71.
5. Shenstone, p.72.

6. Shenstone, p.73.
7. Shenstone, p.77.
8. Shenstone, p.81.
9. Shenstone, p.82.
10. Shenstone, diary notes, 1930.
11. Shenstone, pp.90–99.
12. Shenstone, p.96.
13. Shenstone, p.98.
14. Shenstone, pp.100–101.
15. Shenstone, p.104.
16. Shenstone, p.113.
17. Shenstone, diary notes, 1931; 9 July 1931 *Toronto Evening Telegram*; *Toronto Mail*
18. Shenstone – correspondence with J.H. Parkin.
19. Shenstone, p.110 and J.H. Parkin, 'Aeronautical Research in Canada 1917–1957', pp.266–7, 568–75, 16–30, NRC Canada, 1983.
20. Lippisch, A., *Delta Wing. History and Development*. Iowa State University Press/Ames 1981.
21. Shenstone, B.S., *Flight*, 13 March 1931, p.238.

Chapter 4
1. Shenstone, p.112.
2. Shenstone, p.114.
3. Shenstone, p.114.
4. Shenstone, p.115.
5. Shenstone, p.115.
6. Shenstone, private notes, 10 June 1931.
7. Shenstone, p.117.
8. Shenstone, p.118.
9. Shenstone, p.119.
10. Shenstone, pp.119–121.
11. Shenstone, p.125.
12. Shenstone, p.125.
13. Shenstone, p.128.
14. Munro, William, *Marine Aircraft Design*, Pitman, London 1933.
15. Shenstone, p.126.
16. Shenstone, p.115.
17. Shenstone, p.127.
18. Shenstone, p.128.
19. Shenstone, diary notes, 2 January 1934.
20. Shenstone, p.134.

Chapter 5

1. Vensel, J.R. and Phillips, W.H., 'Stalling Characteristics Supermarine Spitfire VA', NACA, September 1942 to Prof J.H. Parkin, NRC Canada, via Shenstone.
2. Farren, W.S., Research, *Flight*, p.506, 11 May 1944.
3. *Flight*, 7 March 1942.
4. Ackroyd, J.A.D. and Lamont,P.J., 'A comparison of turning radii for four Battle of Britain fighter aircraft', *The Aeronautical Journal*, February 2000, pp.53–58.
5. Mason, F.K., *The Hawker Hurricane 1 Profile 111*. Profile Publications, Windsor, 1967.
6. Deighton, L., *Fighter*. Jonathan Cape, London, 1977.
7. Green, W., *Warplanes of the Third Reich*, MacDonald, London, 1970.
8. Hoerner, S.F., *Fluid Dynamic Drag*, Hoerner, Brick Town, 1958.
9. Green, W., *Augsberg Eagle, The story of the Messerschmitt 109*, MacDonald, London 1971.
10. Hoerner, S.F., *Fluid dynamic Drag*, Hoerner, Bricktown, 1958.
11.   Ibid.
12. Carson, Colonel, 'Best of Breed', *Airpower*, Vol. 4, July 1976.
13. Hoerner, S.F., *Fluid dynamic Drag*, Hoerner, Bricktown, 1958.
14. Nowarra, H.J., *The Messerschmitt 109 A Famous German Fighter*, Harleyford, 1963.
15. Shenstone, diary notes.
16. Ackroyd, J.A.D. and Lamont, P.J., 'A comparison of turning radii for four Battle of Britain fighter aircraft', *The Aeronautical Journal*, February 2000, pp. 53–58.
17. Shenstone, p.130.
18. Farren, W.S., Research, *Flight*, p.506, 11 May 1944.
19. Shenstone, pp.129–130.
20. Faddy, D., *Aeroplane*, pp.54–58, July 2008.
21. Shenstone diary notes.
22. Morgan, E.B. and Shacklady, E., *Spitfire the History*. Key Books, 2001.
23. Faddy, D., *Aeroplane*, pp.54–58, July 2008.
24. Mitchell, G., *R.J. Mitchell Schooldays to Spitfire*, p.140, Tempus 2006; The History Press 2009.
25. Clifton, A., *Wonderful Years*, cited by Gordon Mitchell, in *Schooldays to Spitfire*.
26. *Toronto Globe and Mail*, 2 April 1941.
27. *Toronto Star*, 2 April 1941.
28. *Toronto Times*, 12 April 1941.

29. Price, Alfred, personal correspondence with author.
30. Shenstone, diary notes, An Aeroplane Grows, 1940.
31. Shenstone, pp.129–130.
32. Shenstone, p.111, cited by Price, Alfred, *The Spitfire Story*, Jane's 1981/Haynes 2010.
33. Norwarra, H.J., He 1-11 *A Documentary History*, Jane's /Motorbuch-Verlag Stuttgart 1979.
34. Shenstone, p.128.
35. Shenstone, p.131.
36. Shenstone, p.137.

Chapter 6
1. Wills, Christopher, President Vintage Glider Club, personal interview ref Zanonia.
2. *Vintage Glider Club* magazine No. 127 Summer 2009, and numerous *VGC* News articles, by/via C. Wills.
3. Shenstone diary notes, 1929.
4. Shenstone – correspondence with J.H. Parkin, as per diary notes, Parkin memoirs pp.266–7, 568–75, 16–30.
5. Hooker, S.G., 'Two dimensional flow of compressible liquids past elliptical cylinders', *Reports & Memoranda*, Aeronautical Research Council (ARC), No. 1684.

Chapter 7
1. Faddy, D., *Aeroplane*, pp.54–58, July 2008.
2. Shenstone, diary notes, 1934.
3. Lippisch, A., *Delta Wing. History and Development*, Iowa State University Press/Ames. 1981.
4. Henshaw, A., *My Experiences with the Spitfire at Supermarine and Castle Bromwich 1939 to 1936*, Cited by Gordon Mitchell in *Schooldays to Spitfire*, Tempus 2006, and noted in *Sigh for Merlin* by Alex Henshaw, Hamlyn.
5. Muttray, H., 'Die Aerodynamische Zuzammenfugung von Tragflugel und Rumpf' (The Aerodynamic Aspects of Wing-Fuselage Fillets), *Luftfahrtforschung*, 5 October 1934.
6. Shenstone, B.S., 'A Method of Determining the Twist required on a Tapered Wing in order to attain any desired lateral stability at high angles of attack', *The Aeronautical Journal*. RAeS, 1932.

Chapter 8
1. Shenstone, pp.114–140.
2. Shenstone, p.129.

3. Shenstone diary and letters to J.D. Scott, 29 January 1960, cited by McKinstry and at Vickers Archive 377.

4. Ibid.

5. Note, R.H. Verney, 4 May 1935, National Archives AIR 2/2824.

6. Shenstone diary, 1934, American notes.

7. Shenstone diary notes, 1934.

8. Faddy, D., *Aeroplane*, pp.54–58, July 2008.

9. Worley, B.(pseudonym of B.S. Shenstone) 'Fighter Fundamentals', *Aeronautics*, Vol. 2, No. 2, March 1940. Also published in *Aeronautical Sidelights*, C. Arthur Pearson, London, 1941.

10. Ibid.

11. Green, W., *Augsberg Eagle, The story of the Messerschmitt 109*, MacDonald, London, 1971.

12. Vensel, J.R. and Phillips, W. H., 'Stalling Characteristics Supermarine Spitfire V A', NACA, September 1942 to Prof J.H. Parkin, NRC Canada, via Shenstone.

13. Mason, F.K., *The Hawker Hurricane 1 Profile 111*, Profile Publications, Windsor, 1965.

14. Ackroyd, J.A.D. and Lamont, P.J., 'A comparison of turning radii for four Battle of Britain fighter aircraft', pp.53–58. *The Aeronautical Journal*, February 2000.

15. Worley, B. (pseudonym of B.S. Shenstone) 'Fighter Fundamentals', *Aeronautics*, Vol. 2 No. 2, March 1940, 20.

16. Deighton, L., *Fighter*, Jonathan Cape, London, 1977.

17. Worley, B.(pseudonym of B.S. Shenstone) *Fighter Fundamentals, Aeronautical Sidelights*, C. Arthur Pearson, London, 1941.

18. Ibid.

19. Shenstone, B.S. and Howland, R.C., 'The Inverse Method for Tapered and Twisted Wings', *The Philosophical Magazine*, Vol 22, July 1936.

20. Shenstone, p.130.

21. Shenstone, p.131.

22. Shenstone, diary notes.

23. Lachmann, G.V., 'Seitsschrift für Flugtechnik und Motorluftschiffahrt', (Stalling of Tapered Wings), 15 June 1921, *Flight*, pp.10–13.

24. Shenstone, B.S., 'The Lotz Method', *Journal of Royal Aeronautical Society*, May 1934.

25. Shenstone, B.S., 'Sucking off the Boundary Layer original efforts for boundary layer control', *Aeronautical Engineering*, 27 January 1937.

26. Shenstone, Blair. P. H. interview with author.

27. Muttray, H., 'Die Aerodynamische Zuzammenfugung von Tragflugel und Rumpf' (The Aerodynamic Aspects of Wing-Fuselage Fillets), *Luftfahrtforschung*, 5 October 1934.
28. Hoerner, S.F., *Fluid Dynamic Drag*, Hoerner, Brick Town, 1958.
29. Shenstone, diary notes.
30. Shenstone, diary notes, confirmed by Price, A., *The Spitfire Story*, Jane's 1986, Haynes 2009.
31. Shenstone, diary notes, p.139, America, 1934.

Chapter 9
1. Georgii, W., personal letter to B.S. Shenstone, 15 February 1939.
2. Shenstone, diary notes, 1934.
3. Lippisch, A., Vol. 12, No. 3, *Luftfahartforschung*, 17 June 1935.
4. Shenstone, B.S. and Scott-Hall, S., 'Glider Development in Germany', *The Aeroplane*, October 1935. Reprinted as NACA Technical Memorandum No. 780.
5. Worley, B. (pseudonym of B.S. Shenstone) *Fighter Fundamentals*, *Aeronautical Sidelights*, C. Arthur Pearson, London 1941.
6. Shenstone, p.138.
7. Lippisch, A., 'Making Airflow Visible', RAeS Lecture paper, *Flight*, 22 December 1938.
8. Shenstone, diary notes, 1934.
9. Wills, Christopher, personal interview with author.
10. Shenstone, diary notes, 1934.
11. Shenstone, B.S. and Scott-Hall, S., 'Glider Development in Germany', *The Aeroplane*, October 1935. Reprinted as NACA Technical Memorandum No. 780.

Chapter 10
1. Shenstone, p. 144.
2. Ibid.
3. Shenstone, diary notes.
4. Shenstone, diary notes, Spitfire notes.
5. Ibid.
6. Shenstone, p.121.
7. Shenstone, p.116.
8. Shenstone, diary notes, Spitfire notes.
9. Ibid.
10. Ibid.
11. Ibid.

Chapter 11
1. Shenstone, p.132.
2. Rolls-Royce archives.
3. Taylor Archibald Gibson Archive.
4. Norwarra, H., *He 1-11 A Documentary History*, Jane's 1979/Motorbuch-Verlag Stuttgart.
5. Agnew, K., 'The Spitfire Legend or History? An argument for a New Research Culture in Design', *Journal of Design History*, Vol. 6, No. 2 (1993), pp.121–130.
6. *From Bouncing Bombs to Concorde. Biography of Sir George Edwards OM, Robert Gardner*, Sutton Publishing, 2006.
7. Shenstone, diary notes, 1933.
8. 'Drag Characteristics of He 70 Flugt Motorluft', December 1933.
9. Green, W. and Swanborough, G., 'Heinkel 70 G', *Air International*, pp.25–33, January 1991.
10. *Flight*, 23 June 1934.
11. Rolls-Royce archives.
12. Taylor Archibald Gibson Archive.
13. *Flight*, 2 April 1936.
14. Shenstone, diary notes, also cited by Alfred Price in *The Spitfire Story*, Jane's, 1981.
15. Shenstone, diary notes.
16. Ibid.
17. Ibid.
18. Ibid.
19. Shenstone, notes, as reported in *The Aeroplane*, 12 January 1940.
20. Faddy, D., *Aeroplane*, pp.54–58, July 2008.
21. Agnew, K., 'The Spitfire Legend or History? An argument for a New Research Culture in Design', *Journal of Design History*, Vol. 6, No. 2 (1993), pp.121–130.

Chapter 12
1. *From Bouncing Bombs to Concorde. Biography of Sir George Edwards OM, Robert Gardner*, Sutton Publishing, 2006.
2. Shenstone, pp.143–144.
3. Shenstone, p.134.
4. Furse, A., *Wilfrid Freeman: The Genius Behind Allied Survival and Air Supremacy 1939–1949*, Spellmount, 1999.
5. Shenstone, p.145.
6. Fedden, R., Cantor Lecture, 9 April 1944.

7. Shenstone diary and cited by Morgan and Shacklady in *The Spitfire Story*, Key Publishing, 2000.
8. Shenstone, diary notes, 1940.
9. Ibid.
10. Spencer, K.T., private letter to Shenstone.
11. Barrett, Dr. Anthony J., Interviewed in *Aerospace*, RAeS ESDU, June–July 1975, pp.34–35. www.ihsedu.com
12. Shenstone, diary notes.
13. Shenstone, diary notes; Peter Riedel; also author's interview with Martin Simons.
14. Shenstone, diary notes, 1943.
15. Vesco, R., *Intercept But Don't Shoot*, Grove Press, English Trns., 1971.

Chapter 13

1. Shenstone, p.170.
2. Shenstone, p.168.
3. Shenstone, p.175.
4. Shenstone, p.176.
5. Shenstone diary notes, 1965.
6. Shenstone, letters, record of correspondence 5 March 1943 to 20 May 1946.
7. Shenstone, p.173.
8. Shenstone, diary notes.
9. Davis, Peter, *East African an Airline History*, Runnymede Malthouse Publishing, 1993.
10. Shenstone, letters, record of correspondence 5 March 1943 to 20 May 1946.
11. Ibid. Letters
12. Ibid. Letters
13. Shenstone, p.169.
14. Ibid. Letters
15. Ibid. Letters
16. Bungey, L., 'The War Prize Gliders. Hitler's Contribution to Canadian Gliding', p.6, *Free Flight* SAC.4. 1989, Soaring Association of Canada archive.
17. Wills, Christopher, interview with the author.
18. Shenstone, p.181.
19. Ibid.

Chapter 14

1. Shenstone, p.177.
2. Shenstone, p.180.
3. Shenstone, p.184.
4. Hearne, P., private interview with the author.
5. Shenstone, p.184.
6. Shenstone, p.186.
7. Shenstone, p.179.
8. Shenstone, p.180.
9. Shenstone, p.181.
10. Shenstone p.187.
11. Shenstone, p.176.
12. Shenstone, p.181.
13. Shenstone, diary notes (BEA).

Chapter 15

1. Shenstone, p.181.
2. Shenstone, p.187.
3. Shenstone, p.186.
4. Anon., 'Missionary of Muscle Powered Flight', pp.797–798, *The New Scientist*, 9 April 1959.
5. Shenstone, B.S., R.J. Mitchell Memorial Lecture RAeS, July 1964.
6. Trubshaw, B., private interview with the author.
7. Cunningham, J., private interview with the author.
8. Shenstone, BEA / BOAC notes, 1965.
9. Hearne, P., private interview with the author.
10. Shenstonen BEA/BOAC notes, 1976.
11. Wood, D., *Project Cancelled*, Jane's, 1975.
12. Shenstone, BEA / BOAC notes, 1976.

Chapter 16

1. *Flight*, January 1954.
2. Shenstone, diary notes.
3. Shenstone, Loudon glider diary notes and *Aero Digest*, Vol. 56, pp.46–48, 5 May 1948.
4. Shenstone, Harbinger glider diary notes, 'The Harbinger', Scale Soaring UK, www.scalesoaring.co.uk
5. Shenstone notes, and Brochocki.
6. Goodhart, N.C., 'Sigma – Design of a Super-glider', p.475, *Flight International*, 27March 1969. Interview with the author.
7. Wilkinson, K.G., *Flight International*, p.2016, 15 December 1979.

8. *Flight*, January 1954.
9. Masefield, P., Private correspondence, November 1979, RAeS archive.
10. Masefield, P., Obituary to B.S. Shenstone, *Aerospace*, January 1980.

Appendix

B.S. Shenstone: Published Articles, Papers, Letters and Lectures – 1931–1979

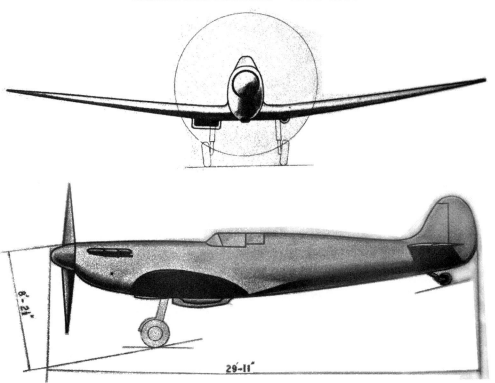

Student Editor: *Toike Oike*. A Canadian engineering students' publication, 1928.

'Certain Aspects of the Stability of a Flying Boat'. Thesis Submission University of Toronto, 1928.

'Hello Montreal!' *University of Toronto Magazine*, Toronto, March 1929.

Choice of Foreign Languages, Letter, *University of Toronto Monthly Magazine*, Toronto, 1930.

'A Study of the Inter-relation of Weight and Drag'. RAeS: 1930.

Junkers Junior Construction: Letter. *Flight*, 13 March 1931.

'Gliding as Sport and Science', Lecture before Engineering Society of University College Southampton, 25 November 1931.

'A Method of Determining the Twist required on a Tapered Wing in order to attain any desired lateral stability at high angles of attack', *The Aeronautical Journal*, RAeS, 1932.

'Wing Design', in *Marine Aircraft Design* by William Munro, Pitman, London, October 1932.

'The Lotz Method', *Journal of the Royal Aeronautical Society*, May 1934.

'Glider Development in Germany: B.S. Shenstone and S. Scott-Hall'. *The Aeroplane /Aircraft Engineering*, October 1935. Reprinted as NACA Technical Memorandum No: 780.

'The Inverse Method for Tapered and Twisted Wings: Howland R.C.K. Shenstone B.S.', *The Philosophical Magazine*, Vol. XXII, July 1936.

'The Good of Gliding', *The Aeroplane*, 8 January 1936.

'Stressed Skin Construction i nGermany', *Aeronautical Engineering*, April 1936.

'Wasting Money', Letter to the Editor, *The Aeroplane*, ref Aeronautical Research Committee, 20 October 1937.

'Sucking off the Boundary Layer original efforts for boundary layer control', *Aeronautical Engineering*, 27 January 1937.

'Some Sailplane Design and Information from German Sources', *Aeronautical Journal*, 1938.

Lecture Paper: Berne. Internationalen Studienkommission fuer den Motorlosen Flug ISTUS, 1938.

Lecture Paper: Porstmouth RAeS Recent Progress in German Aircraft, 12 January 1939.

'The 1938 Paris Aero Salon', *Aircraft Engineering*, January 1939.

'New Heinkel Aeroplanes', *Aircraft Engineering*, January 1939.

'Development During the Last Few Years', *Air Annual*, January 1939.

'Visualised Aerodynamics', Lecture RAeS Southampton, 7 March 1939.

'The Inside of Aeroplane Design', The Henlow Lecture, June 1939.

'Fins Inset From the Tips', *Aircraft Engineering*, September 1939.

'Planes Explained', B.S. Shenstone and Roger Tennant, pamphlet, 1942.

'The D.F.S. Reiher', Parts 1 & 2, *Soaring* (Canada), Vol. 9, No. 7–8, July 1945. Vol. 9 No. 9, September1945.

'Gliding in Canada', *Soaring* (Canada), Vol. 11, Nos 1–2, 1946/1947.

'Can Many Fly?' *Aeronautics*, Vol. 18, No. 3, February 1948.

'Two-Seat Sailpanes', *AeroDigest*, 5 May 1948.

'Aluminium Sailplanes', *Aeroplane*, 18 June 1948/2 July 1948.

'Keeping Them Flying. British and Australian Commercial Aircraft Utilization Compared: Some BEA Results', *Flight*, 21 September 1951.

'Two Seat Sailplanes', paper to OSTIV II, Madrid 1952.

'What would you do? An Airline Executive Ponders Aloud', *Aerplane*, 12 December 1952.

'Aerodynamics', *Research*, June 1954.

'Engineering Aspects of Airliner Operation', RAeS lecture, *Flight*, 16 April 1954.

'Man Powered Flight Technical Report', *The Aeroplane*, August 1954.

'An Experiment in Teaching Design', Shenstone and Czerwinski, *The Engineering Journal*, January 1955.

'More Sweep', *Aircraft Engineering*, July 1955.

'Why Airlines are Hard to Please: British Commonwealth Lecture', *Flight*, 1955.

'Could a Man Fly?' *The Sunday Times*, 27 February 1955.

'The Problem of the very light weight highly efficient aeroplane'. Low Speed Aerodynamics Research Association, London 12 November 1955. Reprinted in *Canadian Aeronautical Journal*, Vol. X, No. X: March 1956.

'Man Powered Flight', Stringfellow memorial lecture, *The Aeronautical Journal*, 1958.

'Standard Class Evaluation'. Shenstone and Zacher: Paper to OSTIV III Warsaw, 1958.

'Man Powered Aircraft Prototypes', *The Aeroplane*, October 1959.

'Flying the Hard Way', RAeS lecture, November 1959.

'The Sir Henry Royce Memorial Lecture. Power for an Airline', lecture paper, *The Aeronautical Journal*, November 1959.

'Supersonics Air Transports: An Airline Talks Back: Lecture National Aeronautic Meeting New York', 7 April 1960. Published in *Aircraft Engineering and Aerospace Technology*, Vol. 32, 9.

'A New Tail-less Sailplane', Brochocki, S.K, with Shenstone, B.S., conference paper submitted to OSTIV, June 1960.

'Man powered flight achieved in 1936?' *The Aeroplane*, 19 August 1960.

'Engineering Aspects in Man Powered Flight', *The Aeronautical Journal*, 1960.

'Obituary August Raspet', OSTIV, 1960.

'A guide for sailplane designers', OSTIV, 1960.

'Symposium on Airline Engineering', *The Aeronautical Journal*,1963.

Shenstone, B.S. and Wilkinson, Kenneth G., *The World's Sailplanes (Die Segelflugzeuge der Welt), (Les Planeurs du Monde) Vol II*, Zurich: Organisation Scientifique et Technique Internationale du Vol à Voile (OSTIV) and der Schweizer Aero-Revue/Aéro-Revue Suisse, 1963.

Organisation Scientifique et Technique Internationale du Vol à Voile (OSTIV), (series of articles) OSTIV-PUBLICATIONS I-XVIII (1950–1985).

Cijan, J. and Shenstone, B.S., 'Development and Progress of Standard Class sailplanes'. Paper: OSTIV VII, Argentina 1963.

'Small Competition Sailplanes'. Paper: OSTIV VII, 1963.

R.J. Mitchell Memorial Lecture: 'Air Transport Development: Parts One and Two', *Flight*, July 1964.

'Man powered Flight-State of the Art', *The Journal of the Cambridge University Engineering Society*, Vol. 35, 1965.

'Difficulties and Advantages of Supersonic Air Transport', *The Aeronautical Journal*, 1965.

'Man Powered Aircraft'. Paper: OSTIV VIII, England, 1965.

'The Influence of Aviation and Astronautics on Human Affairs': The Handley Page Memorial Lecture. *Journal of the Royal Aeronautical Society*, Vol. 69, 657, 1965.

'Hindsight is Always One Hundred Percent', *The Aeronautical Journal*, 1966.

The W. Rupert Turnbull Lecture 1966.

'Unconventional Flight', *The Aeronautical Journal*, August 1968.

'Transport Flying-Boats: Life and Death,' *Journal of the Royal Aeronautical Society*, Vol. 73, 1039, 1969.

'Gliding in Canada', *The Canadian Aviation Historical Society*, Vol. 4, No. 4, 1976.

B.S. Shenstone as Brian Worley

'Contraprops', *Aeronautics*, Vol. 1, No. 1, 1939.

'Taking it Lying Down', *Aeronautics*, Vol. 1, No. 2, 1939.

'Aircraft of Two Nations: A Comparative Analysis', *Aeronautics*, Vol. 1, No. 1, 1939.

'All Wing or No Wing', As B. Worley, Aeronautics Vol 1, No 2. December 1939.

'Why Fly High', *Aeronautics*, August 1940 No 6.

'Design for Take Off', *Aeronautics*, September 1940.

'Terminal Velociy Dives', *Aeronautics*, October 1940.

'Towed Troop Carriers', *Aeronautics*, November 1940.

'The Physiology of Flight', *Aeronautics*, Vol. 2, No. 1, 1940.

'Fighter Fundamentals', *Aeronautics*, Vol. 2, No, 2, 1940.

'How Big a Bomber?' *Aeronautics*, Vol. 2, No. 3, 1940.

'Hydrofoils', *Aeronautics*, Vol. 2, No. 4, 1940.

'Smooth Wings', *Aeronautics*, Vol. 2, No. 6, 1940.

Aeronautical Sidelights, C. Arthur Pearson, 1941.

Reference Sources

The private papers, diaries, research notes, articles (as in the appendix) and unpublished autobiographical notes of Beverley S. Shenstone.
Private Shenstone family documents and records.
Interviews with Shenstone family members.
Royal Aeronautical Society Archives.
National Aerospace Library.

Books

Baxter, Raymond, *Tales of My Time,*. Grubb Street, 2006.

Cole, Lance, *Vickers VC10*, Crowood, 2000.

Furse, Anthony, *Wilfrid Freeman: The Genius Behind Allied Survival and Air Supremacy 1939–1949*, Spellmount, 1999.

Gardner, Robert, *From Bouncing Bombs to Concorde. Biography of Sir George Edwards OM*, Sutton Publishing, 2006.

Glancey, Jonathan, *Spitfire the Biography*, Atlantic Books, 2007.

Lippisch, Alexander, translated by Gertrude Lippisch, *Delta Wing. History and Development*, Iowa State University Press/Ames, 1981.

Masefield, Sir Peter and Gunston, William, *Flight Path*, Airlife Publishing, 2002.

McGregor, Gordon, *The Adolescence of an Airline*, Air Canada, 1980.

Myhra, David, *Secret Designs of the Third Reich*, Schiffer, 2002.

Parkin, J.H., *Aeronautical Research in Canada 1917–1957: Memoirs of J.H. Parkin Volume 1&2*, Ottawa: National Research Council of Canada, 1983.

Parkin, J.H., 'Canadian Aviation and the University of Toronto', *Canadian Aviation*, 1:2, 1928.

Parkin, J.H., 'Wallace Rupert Turnbull 1870–1954: Canadian Pioneer of Scientific Aviation', *Canadian Aeronautical Journal*, 2:1, 1956.

Parkin, J.H., 'Aeronautical Research in Canada: The Organization of the Aeronautical Laboratories under the National Research Council and Some of the Special Problems under Investigation', *Aircraft Engineering and Aerospace Technology*, Vol. 21, 1949.

Parkin, J.H., *Aeronautical Research in Canada, 1917–1957: Memoirs of J.H.*

Parkin in Two Volumes, Ottawa, National Research Council Canada, 1983.

Price, Dr Alfred, *The Spitfire Story*, Jane's, 1976/Haynes, 2010.

Trubshaw, Brian and Edmonds, Susan, *Test Pilot*, Sutton Publishing, 1999.

Wood, Derek, *Project Cancelled*, Jane's, 1975.

Worley, Brian (B.S. Shenstone), *Aeronautical Sidelights*, William Pearson, London, 1941.

Periodicals
The Aeroplane
Aeroplane Monthly

Paper, archives and museum archives
Brooklands Museum archives
The Flight International/ Flight Global archives
The RAES archives
J.V. Conolly archives
Solent Sky Museum archives
National Records Office.
Engineering and Physical Sciences Research Council archives

Interviews with the author:
Douglas Bader
John Cunningham
Peter Hearne
Geoffrey Knight
Gordon Mitchell
Blair Shenstone
Brian Shenstone
Saxon Shenstone
Brian Trubshaw
Christopher Wills
Justin Wills

Index